"Sexual confusion is on   ps
into the midst of this   eo-
logical insight as it is relevant to the   sies
of our day. We are in debt to Denny Burk for his careful thinking,
practical application, and biblical conviction—all of which are on full
display in this important new book."
  R. Albert Mohler Jr., President and Joseph Emerson Brown
  Professor of Christian Theology, The Southern Baptist
  Theological Seminary

"Questions are swirling about as to the nature of human sexuality.
Denny Burk reminds us that the answers to our questions are found
in Scripture. He demonstrates conclusively that human sexuality is
designed to bring glory to God. God's glory is the purpose and heart-
beat of our lives, and that includes our life as sexual beings. Burk's
study is exegetically faithful, culturally aware, and filled with practical wisdom."
  Thomas R. Schreiner, James Buchanan Harrison Professor of
  New Testament Interpretation, The Southern Baptist Theological
  Seminary

"It is ironic that the most private and intimate activity that takes place
in human life—sexual intercourse—has become the most pressing
public political issue of our day. This makes it imperative that Christians think clearly about this matter. In this book, Dr. Burk offers a
thoughtful, clear, and candid analysis of the issues. In doing so he has
produced a volume which will be of great usefulness to pastors and
people alike in thinking through the myriad ethical issues the church,
families, and individual Christians now face."
  Carl R. Trueman, Paul Woolley Professor of Church History,
  Westminster Theological Seminary

"Denny Burk is a Christian leader who is not afraid to take on the
sexual revolution with the sword of the Spirit. His prophetic witness
will help equip you to embrace what seems freakish in today's porno-
topia: the joy of sex, rightly ordered toward the glory of God."
  Russell D. Moore, President, Ethics and Religious Liberty
  Commission; author, *Tempted and Tried*

"This is a readable, enjoyable, practical, encouraging, wholesome, balanced, wise, refreshing, and deeply biblical approach to the ethics of human sexuality. This book is deeply needed in today's confused society. I highly recommend it!"

Wayne Grudem, Research Professor of Theology and Biblical Studies, Phoenix Seminary

"Denny Burk has produced an elegant, comprehensive, and highly instructive book on human sexuality, as understood biblically, ethically, and theologically. Every pastor and seminary professor could benefit much from reading and interacting with the lucid discussions he offers, and all Christians will find here enormous help in thinking through the meaning of sexuality from a solid biblical perspective. This book will serve the church for decades to come in providing its sane and wise guidance."

Bruce A. Ware, Professor of Christian Theology, The Southern Baptist Theological Seminary

"This is a welcomed addition to a subject humans can never think about or talk about enough! It is biblically and theologically faithful, but it is also quite practical. All the 'hot button' issues are addressed fairly and comprehensively. Pastor-theologians will especially appreciate this fine treatment of an issue the Bible clearly addresses and our culture has hopelessly confused."

Daniel L. Akin, President, Southeastern Baptist Theological Seminary

"We live in a culture saturated in sexual immorality. The church can only properly address this culture when our ministry is drawn from the deep well of sound doctrine. Denny Burk draws water from this well and serves it up for Christians to drink. His book is richly biblical and profoundly relevant, and so serves as a reliable guide to the challenging questions of sexual ethics facing us today. If you want to understand these complexities and help others to do the same, then this book is for you."

Heath Lambert, Executive Director, Association of Certified Biblical Counselors; Senior Pastor, First Baptist Church Jacksonville, Florida

"In a day of twisted thinking on marriage, gender, and sex, Dr. Burk gives us scripturally grounded, biblically solid, scholarly, practical insights into the intimate moments of life that should bring glory to God and the fulfillment of his beautiful plan."

Mac Brunson, Senior Pastor, Valleydale Church, Birmingham, Alabama

"Responding to the song of the Sirens, our culture steers to dash itself to death on the rocks of sexual sin. In this book, Denny Burk shows the way to the mast of biblical truth and urges us to lash ourselves to it. Read this book. Stop your ears. Turn from deadly sirens to the Lord Christ. Live."

James M. Hamilton Jr., Professor of Biblical Theology, The Southern Baptist Theological Seminary; author, *God's Glory in Salvation through Judgment*

"Dr. Burk has made a groundbreaking contribution to the modern debate on sexuality. He presents the biblical view of sex and demolishes current attempts to misrepresent the same. His application of biblical truth to contemporary cultural issues in sexuality is crystal clear. Whether a Christian pastor or believer, this volume will be your go-to book for help in engaging the changing sexual landscape."

Jerry Vines, Pastor Emeritus, First Baptist Church, Jacksonville, Florida; two-time President, Southern Baptist Convention

"Denny Burk is one of evangelicalism's brightest young minds, and he brings that mind to bear in *What Is the Meaning of Sex?* This book is a thorough, biblical, and judicious engagement of all things sexual. Burk biblically rebuts the sexual spirit of the age and equips the reader to confront the pressing cultural and ethical issues associated therewith. I wish every student in my seminary would read this."

Jason K. Allen, President, Midwestern Baptist Theological Seminary and College

"Clear writing, thoughtful arguments, wise positions, courageous countercultural stand. I learned some things I didn't know and honed what I did. Denny is a skilled Bible interpreter and shrewd critic of politics and culture."

Andy Naselli, Assistant Professor of New Testament and Biblical Theology, Bethlehem College and Seminary

"Denny Burk is a true sexual revolutionary—not a revolutionary defined by 1960s standards, of course, but a revolutionary against the spirit of today's sexual zeitgeist, which is marked by sexual confusion and brokenness. Denny calls us away from an Eisenhower-era sexual Puritanism and toward a view of biblical sexual ethics—patterned after the gospel—that connects us to Jesus's cross and resurrection. Anyone familiar with Denny's blogging will know his seamless arguments and elegant prose, a treat this book amplifies. And as he does in his blogging, Denny tackles today's toughest issues with biblical grit."

Andrew T. Walker, Director of Policy Studies, Ethics and Religious Liberty Commission

WHAT IS THE MEANING OF SEX?

DENNY BURK

WHEATON, ILLINOIS

What Is the Meaning of Sex?
Copyright © 2013 by Denny Burk
Published by Crossway
        1300 Crescent Street
        Wheaton, Illinois 60187

All rights reserved. No part of this publication may be reproduced, stored in a retrieval system, or transmitted in any form by any means, electronic, mechanical, photocopy, recording, or otherwise, without the prior permission of the publisher, except as provided for by USA copyright law. Crossway® is a registered trademark in the United States of America.

Cover design: Brandon Hill

Cover image: iStock and Veer

First printing 2013

Printed in the United States of America

Unless otherwise indicated, Scripture quotations are from *The New American Standard Bible*®. Copyright © The Lockman Foundation 1960, 1962, 1963, 1968, 1971, 1972, 1973, 1975, 1977, 1995. Used by permission.

Scripture quotations marked AT are the author's translation.

Scripture quotations marked ESV are from the ESV® Bible (The Holy Bible, English Standard Version®), copyright © 2001 by Crossway, a publishing ministry of Good News Publishers. 2011 Text Edition. Used by permission. All rights reserved.

Scripture quotations marked HCSB have been taken from *The Holman Christian Standard Bible*®. Copyright © 1999, 2000, 2002, 2003 by Holman Bible Publishers. Used by permission.

Scripture quotations marked KJV are from the *King James Version* of the Bible.

Scripture quotations marked NAB are taken from the *New American Bible, revised edition* © 2010, 1991, 1986, 1970 Confraternity of Christian Doctrine, Washington, D.C. and are used by permission of the copyright owner. All Rights Reserved. No part of the New American Bible may be reproduced in any form without permission in writing from the copyright owner.

Scripture quotations marked NET are from *The NET Bible*® copyright © 2003 by Biblical Studies Press, L.L.C. www.netbible.com. All rights reserved. Quoted by permission.

Scripture references marked NIV are taken from The Holy Bible, New International Version®, NIV®. Copyright © 1973, 1978, 1984, 2011 by Biblica, Inc.™ Used by permission. All rights reserved worldwide.

Scripture quotations marked NJB are from *The New Jerusalem Bible*, copyright 1985 © by Darton, Longman & Todd, Ltd. and Doubleday, a division of Random House, Inc. Used by Permission.

Scripture quotations marked NKJV are from *The New King James Version*. Copyright © 1982, Thomas Nelson, Inc. Used by permission.

Scripture quotations marked NLT are from *The Holy Bible, New Living Translation*, copyright © 1996, 2004. Used by permission of Tyndale House Publishers, Inc., Wheaton, Ill., 60189. All rights reserved.

Scripture quotations marked NRSV are from *The New Revised Standard Version*. Copyright © 1989 by the Division of Christian Education of the National Council of the Churches of Christ in the U.S.A. Published by Thomas Nelson, Inc. Used by permission of the National Council of the Churches of Christ in the U.S.A.

Scripture quotations marked RSV are from *The Revised Standard Version*. Copyright ©1946, 1952, 1971, 1973 by the Division of Christian Education of the National Council of the Churches of Christ in the U.S.A..

All emphases in Scripture quotations have been added by the author.

Trade paperback ISBN: 978-1-4335-3609-0
PDF ISBN: 978-1-4335-3610-6
Mobipocket ISBN: 978-1-4335-3611-3
ePub ISBN: 978-1-4335-3612-0

Library of Congress Cataloging-in-Publication Data
Burk, Denny.
    What is the meaning of sex? / Denny Burk.
        pages cm
    Includes bibliographical references and index.
    ISBN 978-1-4335-3609-0 (tp)
    1. Sex—Religious aspects—Christianity. 2. Marriage—
Religious aspects—Christianity. I. Title.
BT708.B88235   2013
241'.664—dc23   2013019477

Crossway is a publishing ministry of Good News Publishers.

For Susan,
You are still lovelier to me
Than anyone could ever be.

PROSPERO: *Then as my gift and thine own acquisition*
Worthily purchas'd, take my daughter. But
If thou dost break her virgin-knot before
All sanctimonious ceremonies may
With full and holy rite be minist'red,
No sweet aspersion shall the heavens let fall
To make this contract grow; but barren hate,
Sour-ey'd disdain, and discord shall bestrew
The union of your bed with weeds so loathly
That you shall hate it both. Therefore take heed,
As Hymen's lamps shall light you.

FERDINAND: *As I hope*
For quiet days, fair issue, and long life,
With such love as 'tis now, the murkiest den,
The most opportune place, the strong'st suggestion
Our worser genius can, shall never melt
Mine honor into lust, to take away
The edge of that day's celebration,
When I shall think or Phoebus' steeds are founder'd
Or Night kept chain'd below.

—William Shakespeare, *The Tempest,*

Act 4, Scene 1

Contents

Preface

I was ten years old when my dad first explained to me the birds and the bees. Like most kids my age, I was fairly shocked to receive the news. "That's where babies come from? That's where I came from? That means that you and mom . . ." I can only imagine what the look on my face must have been as the realization fell upon me like a bag of cold spaghetti. I am thankful that my dad did not laugh. Instead, we sat and talked while he answered all my questions. And I had a lot. My dad was a public high school science teacher of many years. He made a living explaining such things to naive adolescents. So I guess he was probably more prepared for such a conversation than most parents. Nevertheless, for all the technical precision, what prepared him most for our conversation was his Christianity. From the beginning, I learned from him that sex was a gift from God to be enjoyed exclusively within the covenant of marriage. It was my first lesson in sexual ethics, and it was an abiding one.

My earliest and most enduring lessons about marriage came from both my mother and my father. Perhaps above all else, I learned from them that it is a covenant made before God that is not to be broken. I have been married long enough to know that difficulties and trials sometimes strain marriages in ways one would never expect. Marriage is hard because life is hard. There was a reason that the apostle Paul said that those who marry would have much trouble in this life, "and I am trying to spare you" (1 Cor. 7:28). As I have gotten older, I have come to understand the great gift my parents gave me in their loving one another for a lifetime.

If there were times when they felt like they were hanging on by a very thin thread, I never knew it. Divorce was not a part of their vocabulary. So I grew up in the security of that love, and I am ever grateful to them for what they have given me. They say some things are better caught than taught. I caught the permanence of marriage from my mom and my dad. In many ways, this book is a continuation of that lesson.

This is a book about sex. It is also a book about marriage. But more fundamentally it is a book about the glory of God. For indeed God created the gift of sex to be enjoyed within the covenant of marriage so that he might magnify his covenant love for his people. God intends marriage and the joys of conjugal life to be a living parable about another marriage—Jesus's union with his church (Eph. 5:32). Marriage is to be an icon of Christ's self-sacrificial love for his bride and his bride's humble submission to him. It is to be a living and breathing depiction of the gospel. Thus when we ask the question, "What is the meaning of sex?" we are asking a question about purpose. The short answer is this: sex exists for the glory of God. Consequently, all sexual morality must be measured by its ability to achieve that purpose.

This book is an attempt to show from the Bible what the meaning of sex is and thereby how we ought to order our sexual lives under God. Having said that, it will be useful to set forth some parameters about what this book is and what it is not.

First, this book is a primer. It is not intended to be a comprehensive treatment of the subject matter. The original conception of this book was that it would be a relatively short work introducing a range of topics related to the Bible and sexual ethics. On the one hand, I have included some material that is not included in other books on sexual ethics—e.g., a chapter on gender roles. On the other hand, there are topics that receive passing attention and in some cases no attention at all—e.g., bioethics and reproductive technologies. In what I have covered, I have tried to interact with some of the more important voices in the literature, but even here the treatment is not comprehensive. My hope is that there is enough interaction with the sources to give the reader a basic idea of how the issues are being discussed *and* enough principles to guide the reader to make sound ethical judgments about the issues covered in this volume.

Second, this book is biblical. It is not philosophical. By that I mean that my primary orientation is the text of Scripture, not contemporary debates about natural law or secular ethical theories. That is not to say that these other inquiries have no value. It is just to say that this is not that kind of book. I mean to cut to the chase and take readers directly to the norm that is not normed by any other norm—the Bible. So my aim has been to make explicit what the Bible teaches about the meaning of sex. From time to time, there are statistics and other anecdotes of contemporary relevance. But these are brought in so as to see more clearly how the Scripture ought to be applied in the modern day. In the main, however, my purpose is to be as biblical as possible. Throughout this book, you will find extended exegetical discussions and interpretations of Scripture. Indeed, chapter 1 is essentially a commentary on 1 Corinthians 6:12–20. The reason for this is that it appears in a section of Scripture that is dense with material on sexual ethics. In this one passage we see how the apostle Paul uses Scripture to admonish and correct a group of philandering whoremongers in the church at Corinth. His method is a model for what I hope to achieve in this book. Paul was into the application of Scripture to sexual ethics, and that is what I want to be into as well.

Third, this book is for sinners. It is not for people who are perfect. Nor is it written by someone who is perfect. After viewing all the holy commands of God as they relate to our sexual lives, the soft heart is apt to carry away an abiding sense of his own failures and shortcomings. I have felt that many times throughout the writing of this book. I can only imagine the myriad experiences that readers will bring to this book and the despair they might feel in view of the Bible's standard of sexual holiness. So let me make an appeal to you from one broken sinner to another. The same God who issued these impossible commands also sent his Son to live the perfect life that we could not live, to die as our substitute, to pay for our failures, to be raised for our eternal life, and to enable us to walk with him through the power of the Spirit. You cannot earn these gifts by sexual holiness. You can only receive them by faith alone in Christ alone. Through Christ, he gives us everything we need for life and godliness. We are no longer slaves to our passions, but we are new creations enabled to walk in newness of life. Look away from yourself as you read this book and train your eyes on Jesus—the author and finisher of our faith.

I have already mentioned my parents and the formative influence they bring to this work. But there are others as well who must be mentioned. I have often said that John Piper has been my mentor *in absentia*. For the last fifteen years, no one has been more influential over my thinking and theology. This influence was not because I knew him or because we have ever been personal friends. Nor was it because of his books. The influence has been entirely due to his preaching ministry. I first heard John Piper preach in 1995. The sermon was on a cassette tape that someone had loaned me, and it was a message about the supremacy of God in preaching. I didn't like what I heard. After listening, I wrote Piper off as someone who needed to rely more on the sufficiency of Scripture and less on his emotions. I did not have ears to hear. But that changed in 1998.

In 1998 I attended the second annual Passion conference in Austin, Texas. I didn't come with high expectations. I had no idea that a Copernican revolution was in the offing for me spiritually. The message that the Lord used was Piper's exposition of Romans 3:25–26. Piper's exposition of the cross of Jesus Christ in these two verses made my heart soar in worship. I was gripped by the notion that Christ died not just for me but for God. The "basic riddle of the universe" had nothing to do with my rights but with God's rights. It was this exposition of the cross that gave me ears to hear that God is most glorified in us when we are most satisfied in him.

That theocentric perspective shaped my thinking through years of listening to Piper's Bible-saturated messages. I cannot begin to calculate how many hundreds of messages I have listened to since then. Yet over time, I began to see that God's glory is not something that exists elusively in the untouchable ether. God aims to manifest his glory in the gritty details of life—and that includes our sexual lives, a topic to which Piper repeatedly returned. There were messages on sexual purity, a series on marriage, sermons about homosexuality and so-called gay marriage, strategies for fighting sexual sin, exhortations against abortion, teaching on biblical manhood and womanhood, and on and on. In those years, God was giving shape to a sexual ethic rooted in the ideal of covenant marriage and oriented toward the display of God's glory. I am not exaggerating when I say that the thesis of this book has been shaped over the last fifteen years by a man I hardly know—my mentor *in absentia*.

In more recent years, another significant influence has entered the picture in the person of R. Albert Mohler Jr. I am grateful to have benefitted from his writings over the years, but I am especially grateful for the three years of weekly interaction that I had with him when I served on his cabinet as dean of Boyce College. In those years he helped me perhaps more than anyone else to understand the interface between Christian sexual ethics and the larger debate in our culture about what makes for the common good. I have never known anyone as learned and well read as he is, nor anyone with a keen sense of where the culture is going and how Christians ought to be speaking to it. He is a man of Issachar who understands the times and what the people of God ought to do.

I want to thank Russell Moore and the rest of the administration of The Southern Baptist Theological Seminary for granting me writing leave to work on this book. It was a fruitful time for this project, but it was especially fruitful for my family. We will always be grateful for that year.

Thanks are also in order to friends who read and provided feedback on early drafts of this work: Mitchell Chase, Miguel Echevarria, Joe Carter, Barry Joslin, Jim Hamilton, Tom Schreiner, Andy Naselli, and my mother, Sandra Burk. All of them had a part in knocking off the rough edges. Any rough edges that remain must be imputed wholly to my own misapprehensionalism and not to their fine editing skills.

And now I have saved the very best for last—my wife, to whom this book is dedicated. The inscription is a tag line that I have included at the end of all the anniversary poems that I have given her over our twelve years of marriage. The annual repetition of this tag has a purpose. The poems change, we change, our bodies change, the size of our family changes, our homes change, our cities change, our close friends change. But one thing does not change between us. She is still lovelier to me than anyone could ever be. I love her now more than I ever have. She is my best friend and my most trusted counselor. I can hardly imagine life without her. I am grateful to God for giving me more than I could ever have asked for in a wife. My earnest hope and prayer is that the hours spent in study for this book on marriage would bear fruit in me to make me a better husband. It will take a lifetime to realize, and that is what I am eager to give for her.

—Denny Burk
January 11, 2013

What is the chief and highest end of man?
Man's chief and highest end is to glorify God,
and fully to enjoy him forever.

—Westminster Larger Catechism, Question 1

Introduction

A few years ago I was invited to speak at a youth conference on the topic of gender confusion. At the time, I could hardly think of a more relevant theme. From television shows like *Modern Family* to Lady Gaga's pop anthem "Born This Way," our popular culture has become a reflection of the underlying confusion about what it means to live in this world as male and female. Kids today are awash in a gender-bending popular culture. So I was eager to address these students and to bring the Bible to bear upon an issue that I consider to be one of the touchstone issues of post-Christian America. So there I was in front of about one hundred junior high and high school students, and I delivered to them a message that had grown out of many hours of study and preparation. But nothing I had read before the session prepared me for the question I faced after the session.

At the conclusion of my talk, a youth minister from a small church in the area approached me for advice on how to deal with a perplexing pastoral situation that he was facing in his congregation. A young girl in his youth group had recently decided that she wanted to become a boy. My usual reaction to a pastoral conundrum like this one would be to advise the young girl of what the Bible teaches about how God created us as male and female, how Christians must embrace what God made us to be, and how God has a design for her life as a female. But there was more to this young girl's story than a spontaneous desire to change genders. There was an additional detail that would turn my usual response on its head.

This particular girl had been born with a rare biological condition that made it difficult at birth to determine whether she was a girl or a boy. The condition is known as intersex, and intersexed persons are born with reproductive or sexual anatomy that does not seem to fit the typical pattern for female or male. Until relatively recently, the most common medical treatment for intersex has been for doctors to recommend a gender, to encourage the parents to embrace that gender, to reshape the genitals and reproductive organs accordingly through surgery, and to advise parents not to express any ambiguity to the child about the selected gender. The young woman in question had undergone such surgery as an infant but now as a teenager felt that she was not really a girl after all. She felt that her parents had made the wrong choice about what sex she was, and now she was in the midst of an identity crisis. She wanted to become what she felt she was born to be. She wanted to be a boy.

So the youth minister asks me, "What should I say to them? How do I minister to this student and her family?" I confess that I was at a bit of a loss to answer his question—not because I didn't know what the Bible teaches, but because I didn't know what intersex was. As I struggled to apply Scripture to a condition I had never even heard of, it occurred to me that at the heart of this minister's query was a question about sex—not *sex* narrowly conceived as sexual acts, but sex more broadly conceived as gender and sexuality. At the root of his difficulty was a desire to know how the Bible's normative teaching about manhood and womanhood speaks to this very difficult situation.

A Collision with Reality

How would you have answered this youth minister's question? Would you have had the biblical and theological wherewithal to speak truth into this morally confounding situation? Do you know what the Bible teaches about gender? About sex? About human sexuality in general? Do you know if the Bible even addresses these issues at all? Does the existence of intersex throw into question your belief in the Bible's teaching that God created humans in his image as male and female (Gen. 1:27)?

My first conversation about intersex highlighted for me a larger issue—the need for Christians to understand what the Bible teaches and how it applies to the various ethical challenges we face. It occurred to me during that conversation that the only way to answer the question was not only to understand the problem (the child's intersex condition and all the life complications that stemmed from it) but also to understand what the Bible actually says about human sexuality. Sadly, this latter point is one that we can no longer assume. Not only has biblical literacy declined in our day, but so also has the Bible's cultural influence on sexual mores. Whereas there used to be a broad cultural consensus about gender norms and sexual morality, that is no longer the case in the contemporary West. As Christopher Ash has written, "Western societies are witnessing sexual relationships characterized by . . . lower levels of public commitment than before, which are proving more transient than previously, with fewer children, and in which a succession of public sexual partners is increasingly common."[1] We can no longer assume a consensus even among those who name themselves as Christians. From the progressive wing of evangelicalism to the more liberal mainlines, many "Christian" groups have accommodated themselves to the spirit of the age. The result has been a sustained assault on what the Bible teaches about gender and sexuality. This crisis of faith has undermined the faithfulness of many congregations. These churches and their leaders have given up on biblical sexual ethics and have turned elsewhere for guidance.

This larger cultural pressure has influenced many Bible-believing churches as well. Many pastors and teachers simply do not want to push back in a countercultural sort of way but are content to remain silent about the Bible's teaching about these

---

[1] Christopher Ash, *Marriage: Sex in the Service of God* (Vancouver, British Columbia: Regent College Publishing, 2003), 43.

flashpoints in the larger culture war. Meanwhile, their congregations are floundering in misunderstanding and false teaching about human sexuality. Many Christians have little training in what it means to be created in the image of God as male and female. It has rightly been said that where there is a mist in the pulpit, there is a fog in the pew. In the absence of clear, biblical teaching on gender and sexuality, people tend to get folded in to the Bible-ignoring *zeitgeist*. Unfortunately, that is where too many evangelical Christians have drifted.

What Is the Purpose of Sex?

The purpose of this book is to answer the underlying question put to me by that youth minister: *What is the meaning of sex?* But we cannot answer this question by coming to it in the usual way. Oftentimes when we want to explain something, we look to find out what caused it. But when it comes to ultimate meaning, we do not find answers in *causes* but in *purposes*.[2] If I want to understand a hammer, it is not enough to know its cause (i.e., where the hammer came from, the factory in which it was manufactured, who designed it, etc.). To understand a hammer, I have to know for what *purpose* it was created. A hammer's created purpose is to drive nails. I can know everything about where a hammer came from, who made it and designed it, the truck that shipped it to the store, etc. Yet if I do not know for what *purpose* it was made, I have entirely missed the point. I do not necessarily need to know anything about the hammer's origin (what caused it) in order to have a full appreciation for its purpose. It is the hammer's *purpose* that determines ultimate meaning, not the *cause*.[3] Similarly, I might know everything there is to know about theories of human origins, about human reproduction, and about the biological and

---

[2] John Piper, "Why Was This Child Born Blind?," sermon preached at Bethlehem Baptist Church, May 21, 2011, http://www.desiringgod.org/resource-library/sermons/why-was-this-child-born-blind.

[3] No analogy is perfect, and I do not wish to imply that cause is unimportant. Indeed, it is often the case that the cause or genesis of a thing reveals the purpose of that thing. As we shall see, gender and sexuality are a case in point. The biblical paradigm for sex and gender is set in Genesis 1–2.

genetic factors that determine human sexuality. But if I do not understand the *purpose* for which human sexuality was made, then I do not understand it. Nor am I prepared to give a proper ethical evaluation of its use.

Of course in the Christian worldview, the purpose of human sexuality is inexorably bound up with its origin. God's purpose for sex is revealed in the account of God's initial creation of human beings as male and female (Genesis 1–2). That account and subsequent scriptural reflection on it suggest a very clear purpose for human sexuality. A book on sexual ethics, therefore, will stand or fall on its ability to describe that purpose as it is found in Scripture. Many books on sexual ethics—including Christian ones—founder on just this point. As Andreas Köstenberger has noted, "There is a relative dearth of conscious Christian reflection on the deeper meaning of and purpose for sex."[4] To be sure, some Christian books do describe the purpose(s) of sex, but too often they do not go far enough. They do not give an adequate account of the *ultimate* purpose of sex as the Bible describes it. Even though they may suggest some purposes for sex, there is a failure to distinguish ultimate ends from subordinate ends.[5]

What is the difference between ultimate ends and subordinate ends? Why is the distinction important? I might point to an automobile and say, "That car was made for someone to sit in." Since there are doors on each side of the car and seats inside, no one could deny that one of the purposes of a car is for people to get inside and sit down. But it would be inadequate if we stopped there in describing the purpose of a car. The ultimate purpose of a car is to transport people and objects from one place to another. Sitting down in a car is a subordinate end. Transportation

---

[4] Andreas J. Köstenberger and David W. Jones, *God, Marriage, and Family: Rebuilding the Biblical Foundation*, 2nd ed. (Wheaton, IL: Crossway, 2010), 79.

[5] I am taking this distinction from Jonathan Edwards [1749], *Ethical Writings* (*WJE Online*, vol. 8), edited by Paul Ramsey, p. 405: "A subordinate end is something that an agent seeks and aims at in what he does; but yet does not seek it, or regard it at all upon its own account, but wholly on the account of a further end, or in order to some other thing which it is considered as a means of. . . . An ultimate end is that which the agent seeks in what he does for its own sake; that he has respect to, as what he loves, values and takes pleasure in on its own account, and not merely as a means of a further end." The Yale edition of Edwards's work is available at http://edwards.yale.edu.

is the ultimate end. Sitting down in the car is one of the means by which transportation ultimately comes about. Unless we account for the ultimate end of the automobile, we have not really understood the purpose of the car. Describing subordinate ends alone is insufficient.

This distinction between ultimate ends and subordinate ends is critical when thinking about sexual ethics. Sexual ethicists make a mistake when they focus attention only on subordinate ends rather than on the ultimate end. They may rightly speak of the purpose(s) of sex while giving short shrift to the ultimate purpose of sex. Dennis Hollinger's excellent book *The Meaning of Sex* focuses on the ethics of physical intimacy, and he argues rightly that understanding the purpose of sex is essential to developing a biblical sexual ethic. He writes,

> We must probe the ends or purposes of the gift of physical intimacy. Understanding these ends or purposes enables us to capture God's intentions from creation. But such understanding is also essential to guard against the abuses and unethical practices that tempt us in a fallen, sex-crazed world.[6]

Hollinger then identifies "four main purposes" for sex: consummation of marriage, procreation, love, and pleasure. He then argues that the moral legitimacy of any sexual act must be tested against the ability of that act to achieve those purposes.[7]

Hollinger's argument is good so far as it goes, but should we not take it further? The four purposes that he identifies are not ultimate ends but subordinate ends. One can find support in Scripture for all four of these "purposes," but the framework can seem a little bit arbitrary and difficult to apply if they are not properly connected to the ultimate purpose of sex.[8] Hollinger does seek

---

[6] Dennis P. Hollinger, *The Meaning of Sex: Christian Ethics and the Moral Life* (Grand Rapids, MI: Baker, 2009), 95.
[7] Ibid.
[8] To be fair to Hollinger, it is not as if Hollinger has no concern about "ultimate purposes." Clearly he does (ibid., 89–91). In my view, however, he could strengthen his case if he could connect an ultimate purpose to his fourfold framework.

to ground his four purposes in the larger narrative of Scripture,[9] but what if the Scripture itself indicates a larger motif that would integrate these four purposes?

The Scripture does in fact give us an all-encompassing motif, and we can hardly make any sense out of the Bible's sexual ethic unless we account for it.[10] James Hamilton has recently produced what I believe to be the best biblical and exegetical account of this all-encompassing motif. In his book *God's Glory in Salvation through Judgment: A Biblical Theology*, Hamilton argues that the glory of God is the central theme of biblical theology.[11] He argues that the metanarrative of Scripture can be summed up in four biblical themes: creation, fall, redemption, and restoration.[12] God *created* the world and everything in it to be holy and good as he himself is holy and good. But Adam's *fall* plunged the world and everything in it into judgment and death. God enacts a plan of *redemption* to rescue his people. This plan begins with the promise to crush the head of the Serpent in Genesis 3:15, and it reaches its fulfillment in the cross and resurrection of Christ. God will one day *restore* the world by making a new heaven and a new earth and by resurrecting his people to eternal life. Hamilton argues that "the center of biblical theology is the theme that organizes this metanarrative" and that it is "the theme out of which all others flow."[13] God manifests his glory through creation, fall, redemption, and restoration. All of these themes and every other subordinate theme that one might identify in Scripture find their unity and purpose in the glory of God.

So what is that purpose of sex? If we clear away all the subordinate purposes, we find that the ultimate purpose of sex is the

---

[9] Ibid., 95: "The ethics of any sexual act is then tested against the ability to encompass these four ends, or at least to be in the context of these ends. The full yet mysterious meaning of sex is found in these four purposes, set in the context of the larger biblical worldview."

[10] Ash, *Marriage*, 105: "Purpose is also a necessary theological undergirding to the interpretation of the Bible as a whole in its teaching about sexual ethics."

[11] We might define the glory of God as *all of who God is put on display*. Hamilton says it this way: "The glory of God is the weight of the majestic goodness of who God is, and the resulting name, or reputation, that he gains from his revelation of himself as Creator, Sustainer, Judge, and Redeemer, perfect in justice and mercy, loving-kindness and truth." James M. Hamilton Jr., *God's Glory in Salvation through Judgment: A Biblical Theology* (Wheaton, IL: Crossway, 2010), 56.

[12] Ibid.

[13] Ibid.

glory of God. Sex, gender, marriage, manhood, womanhood—all of it—exist ultimately for the glory of God. The glory of God as the ultimate purpose of sex is not merely a theological deduction. It is the explicit teaching of Scripture. In the next chapter I will show from 1 Corinthians 6 how Paul teaches that the glory of God is the ultimate purpose for sex. Before moving into that discussion, we need to say a word about ethical theories and subordinate purposes.

Ethical Theories and Biblical Ethics

In what I have argued so far, I have made a host of assumptions about the proper way to go about establishing a normative sexual ethic. But we would do well to acknowledge that not all ethical theories share the assumptions that form the basis for this work. Certain basic questions underlie every attempt to establish a framework for ethical conduct: What makes my actions good or bad? What are the standards we should use for determining moral judgments? Where do I get these standards?[14] Christians are not the only ones who have puzzled over these questions for answers. In the history of human thought, these questions have been answered differently by different people in different times and circumstances. In broad terms, there have been four main approaches to answering these questions: teleological ethics, consequentialist ethics, deontological ethics, and character/virtue ethics.

Teleological Ethics

Teleological ethics takes its name from the Greek term *telos*, which means "end" or "goal." Teleological theories tend to share the principle that human actions should be judged in light of their end or goal.[15] Natural-law theory is a prominent species[16] of teleology

---

[14] Hollinger, *Meaning of Sex*, 23.

[15] C. A. Brown, "Teleology," in *New Dictionary of Christian Ethics and Pastoral Theology*, ed. David J. Atkinson et al. (Downers Grove, IL: InterVarsity, 1995), 835.

[16] Although there are a variety of teleological theories, they divide broadly into two groups: consequentialist ethics and natural law theory. See Scott Paeth, "Teleological Theories of Ethics," in *Dictionary of Scripture and Ethics*, ed. Joel B. Green (Grand Rapids, MI: Baker, 2011), 766. For the

that is "concerned with the natural goal or end of human action rather than with particular consequences."[17] This theory relies on the observation that God created the world and everything in it with a purpose. Actions must be evaluated on the basis of their conformity to God's purpose for his creation. If God's glory is the ultimate purpose for creation (as I have argued above), then God has ordered creation so that its "natural" use promotes his glory. And God's ultimate purpose—his glory—is only realized when creatures fulfill the subordinate purposes for which they were made. Oliver O'Donovan describes a teleological approach in this way:

> The order of things that God has made is *there*. It is objective, and mankind has a place within it. Christian ethics, therefore, has an objective reference because it is concerned with man's life in accordance with this order. . . . Thus Christian moral judgments in principle address every man.[18]

As will be discussed below, teleology has special relevance for sexual ethics as so much of the biblical material appears to be based on the "natural" ends of human sexuality as they were given by God in creation (e.g., Rom. 1:26–27; cf. Gen. 2:24).[19]

Consequentialist Ethics

Consequentialist ethics bases moral judgments on the consequences that accrue from human actions.[20] This way of determining ethical behavior does not see any action as inherently good or evil. The consequences of an action determine which acts are good and which acts are evil.[21] Consequentialist theories define

---

purposes of this book, I will associate teleology with natural law ethics and will keep consequentialist ethics in its own category.

[17] Ibid., 767.

[18] Oliver O'Donovan, *Resurrection and Moral Order: An Outline for Evangelical Ethics*, 2nd ed. (Grand Rapids, MI: Eerdmans, 1994), 17.

[19] Ash, *Marriage*, 105: "The order the Creator has placed in creation is—at least in part—teleological order, order that serves a purpose. We seek therefore . . . to elucidate the purpose of the Creator in instituting marriage as a part of the good created order."

[20] Hollinger, *Meaning of Sex*, 24.

[21] John S. Feinberg and Paul D. Feinberg, *Ethics for a Brave New World*, 2nd ed. (Wheaton, IL: Crossway, 2010), 34.

moral good by whatever action produces the greatest amount of nonmoral good. The definition of what that nonmoral good may be differs from theory to theory. In some theories the nonmoral good is pleasure. In others it is power, knowledge, or self-realization.[22] There are two primary streams of consequentialist approaches—one that focuses on producing the greatest good for oneself (ethical egoism) and another that emphasizes producing the greatest good for the greatest number of people (utilitarianism). Epicurus, Bertrand Russell, and Albert Ellis have been associated with the former, while Jeremy Bentham, John Stuart Mill, and Peter Singer have been associated with the latter.[23]

There are a number of items we could point to that make it difficult to reconcile consequentialist approaches with a biblical worldview. First, consequentialist approaches elevate nonmoral goods above Scripture as the standard for evaluating ethics. Second, human nature limits our ability to calculate in every case what the consequences of an action might be. Third, there is no consensus on how to define the nonmoral good. Without some external arbiter to determine the matter, consequentialist approaches might change from person to person or situation to situation. Fourth, there is no intrinsic value in any action according to the consequentialist approach. In this way, a purely consequentialist approach is simply out of step with the Bible. As Richard Hays has it, "How strikingly indifferent is the New Testament . . . to consequentialist ethical reasoning. The New Testament teaches us to approach ethical issues not by asking 'What will happen if I do x?' but rather by asking 'What is the will of God?'"[24]

Deontological Ethics

Deontological ethics says that human actions are right or wrong to the extent that they are the fulfillment of duty.[25] Duty is often

---

[22] Ibid., 34.

[23] Hollinger, *Meaning of Sex*, 25–29.

[24] Richard B. Hays, *The Moral Vision of the New Testament: Community, Cross, New Creation, A Contemporary Introduction to New Testament Ethics* (New York: HarperOne, 1996), 455.

[25] M. T. Nelson, "Deontology," in *New Dictionary of Christian Ethics*, 297.

expressed in the form of principles or rules. Deontology takes its name from the Greek word *deon*, which means "that which is binding or obligatory."[26] This approach denies that the morality of an action can be measured in any way by the results of the action. Rather, a deontological approach holds that "there are inherent goods, rights, wrongs, and duties in life, regardless of what the consequences might be."[27] Immanuel Kant has given the classical formulation of the deontological approach by saying,

> The moral worth of an action then does not lie in the effect which is expected of it, and consequently in no principle of an action which must borrow its motive from the expected effect. . . . Of what sort can this law possibly be, the conception of which, even without regard for the effect expected from it, must determine the will, in order that the latter may without qualification be called purely and simply good? . . . I am never to act otherwise than *so that I could at the same time will my maxim should become a universal law.*[28]

Because deontologists hold that the morality of an action is known through rules or principles, this approach is sometimes called "principle ethics."[29] Deontological theories differ from one another in where they locate the basis for establishing the principles. The principle might be derived from reason, tradition, universal human experience, or divine revelation.[30]

Character Ethics

Character ethics (a.k.a., virtue ethics) takes its name from the belief that moral actions spring from the character of the person per-

---

[26] John Jefferson Davis, *Evangelical Ethics: Issues Facing the Church Today*, 3rd ed. (Phillipsburg, NJ: P&R, 2004), 16. See also H. G. Liddell and R. Scott, *A Greek-English Lexicon*, 9th ed. (Oxford, UK: Clarendon, 1996), s.v. δέον: "that which is binding, needful, right."

[27] Hollinger, *Meaning of Sex*, 30.

[28] Immanuel Kant, *The Fundamental Principles of the Metaphysics of Ethics*, trans. Otto Manthey-Zorn (New York: Appleton-Century-Crofts, 1938), 16–17. Kant also argued that "duty" must be the basis of an action for it to be considered morally good. To act out of one's self-interest ruins the morality of the action. In Kant's words, "If now, when there is no inclination to urge him to it, he nevertheless rouses himself from this deadly indifference and performs the act without any inclination, solely out of duty, then the action for the very first time has genuine moral value" (ibid.).

[29] Hollinger, *Meaning of Sex*, 29–30.

[30] Ibid., 30.

forming the action. The focus in character ethics is not to develop a long list of rules or to predict what the consequence of an action will be. Those who follow character ethics are more interested in forming moral character than moral norms. Character ethicists observe that laws and rules do very little to curb immoral behavior. Thus a focus on external standards can be an ineffective way to produce moral living.[31] Rather, they argue, what is needed is the moral formation of the individual who will be making moral choices. Moral acts can only come from upright character. Stanley Hauerwas says it this way:

> In matters of significance even involving the "hardest choices" there was no "decision" to be made. Rather, the decision makes itself if we know who we are and what is required of us. . . . I expect many of our decisions are . . . but confirmation of what we have become without realizing it.[32]

Character ethicists draw from the ethical theories of Aristotle, Augustine, and Aquinas. Its newfound popularity among theologians and philosophers, however, traces back to thinkers such as Alasdair MacIntyre and Stanley Hauerwas.

While there are some helpful emphases in character ethics, its aversion to rules and principles can set this approach at odds with Christian revelation. In the Bible, moral character and moral norms are not at odds. Indeed they complement each other. The Bible encourages us to have moral character as the basis for all of our moral actions (e.g., 2 Pet. 1:5–9). That is why one of Jesus's chief critiques of the religious leaders of his day was that they were "whitewashed tombs." On the outside they looked good, but on the inside there was only death. They performed moral actions, but they acted from hearts that were dead to the kingdom of God.

---

[31] Robert L. Brawley, ed., *Character Ethics and the New Testament: Moral Dimensions of Scripture* (Louisville, KY: Westminster, 2007), vii: "Legislation is hardly alone in reflecting a side of ethics that can only be labeled 'failure.' The same is true for some of our other preferred approaches to ethics: role models, principles, and rationality. They all may seduce us into a false optimism that these sources of morality make us adequate for the task."

[32] Stanley Hauerwas, *The Peaceable Kingdom: A Primer in Christian Ethics* (Notre Dame, IN: University of Notre Dame Press, 1983), 129–30.

Jesus and the authors of Scripture require inner transformation of the individual. But that transformation is effected in part by the Christian's interface with the principles and rules of Scripture. In character ethics, however, the question of what kind of people we ought to be takes precedence over the question of what we are to do.[33] To the extent that character ethics deemphasizes moral laws and rules, to that extent character ethics is out of step with Scripture.[34] As an ethical theory, character ethics often falls short of telling us what we need to know about the morality of a given act.[35] A sounder approach is to view character formation as the necessary condition for receiving and applying the ethical content of Scripture—which includes moral norms and rules.[36]

A Blended Approach

In this book, I am favoring a blended approach that gives a privileged place to teleology within the framework of divine revelation. Scripture is plainly concerned with the formation of moral character as the basis for moral choices (as in character ethics). Scripture is also concerned with rules and divine commands (as in deontology). But Scripture also focuses on the glory of God as the purpose of all things (as in teleology). These three theories do not contradict one another but rather complement one another.

Consider, for instance, the commands that we find scattered throughout the pages of Scripture. From the Ten Commandments in Exodus 20:1–17 to Jesus's two love commands in Matthew 22:36–40, God's commands are not ends in themselves. To be

---

[33] Nikki Coffey Tousley and Brad J. Kallenberg, "Virtue Ethics," in *Dictionary of Scripture and Ethics*, 814.

[34] I am arguing that character ethics can be out of step with the rules and principles that derive from Scripture. David W. Haddorff notes that this is a general weakness of character ethics that can and ought to be corrected. David W. Haddorff, "Can Character Ethics Have Moral Rules and Principles? Christian Doctrine and Comprehensive Moral Theory," *Horizons* 23, no. 1 (1996): 50.

[35] Feinberg and Feinberg, *Ethics for a Brave New World*, 38: "Virtue ethics focus more on the moral character of the *agent* than on the moral nature of the act."

[36] John R. Frame, *The Doctrine of the Christian Life* (Phillipsburg, NJ: P&R, 2008). Frame argues that "ethical knowledge" is the "product of sanctification" (ibid., 350). He writes, "It is wrong to suppose that we must get all the answers to ethical questions before we engage in spiritual warfare, as if the intellect were in every respect prior to life. Rather, there may well be some ethical questions . . . that we will not be able to answer (or even fully appreciate) until we have been in spiritual combat with the forces of darkness" (ibid., 359).

sure, these laws are deontological in that they expose principles for ethical conduct. But it cannot be denied that the laws also serve a larger purpose. For example, in Leviticus 10 God strikes two priests dead for breaking his law. God explains his judgment, saying, "By those who come near Me I will be treated as holy, And before all the people I will be glorified" (Lev. 10:3 AT). The breaking of the command constituted a failure to "glorify" God before his people. Clearly, the ultimate end of the command was the glory of God. But God made known *how* they were to glorify him by means of divine command.[37] So teleology is regulated by deontology. We learn *how* to glorify God by doing what he commands in Scripture.

In some ways, this approach resembles that of John Feinberg's and Paul Feinberg's in *Ethics for a Brave New World*. They argue for a "modified form of divine command theory"—a deontological model that relies on Scripture to determine ethical principles:

> Because we take our norms from Scripture and hold that Scripture is God's revealed Word, the source of our norms is revelation, not reason. However, given our view that norms reflect God's character and that there are inherently right and wrong acts, we also hold that by reflecting on God's attributes and the world he made, reason can see the reasonableness of what God has prescribed. For the same reasons, we think reason on its own can reach some perception of what should and should not be done. At this point, we find some kinship with natural law theories.[38]

Even though the Feinbergs deem their model to be deontological, notice the place they give to reason. Scripture is the absolute norm, but reason can also deduce moral principles based upon God's ordering of his universe. That is why they have sympathy for "natural law" theories, and that is what makes their own brand of

---

[37] In the case of Nadab and Abihu, they had disregarded the prohibition that God gave Moses in Exodus 30:9: "You shall not offer any strange incense on this altar, or burnt offering or meal offering; and you shall not pour out a drink offering on it."

[38] Feinberg and Feinberg, *Ethics for a Brave New World*, 37.

deontology very friendly to the kind of teleology that I am arguing for in this book.

We are not pursuing a teleological method that makes reason the judge of Scripture. We are pursuing a teleological method that is defined and guided at every turn by the ethical content of Scripture. Our method also assumes that God's expressed purposes for his creation may help us to "connect the dots" on thorny ethical questions that may not be directly addressed in Scripture. A husband and a wife, for example, may be wondering what sexual activities they may engage in within the context of their marriage. Are there ethical limits? Certainly, the Scripture defines a number of limits: no adultery, no brutality, and no rape (just to name a few). But what about activities that may not be explicitly mentioned in Scripture? One popular book recently attempted to give an ethical evaluation of such activities including sodomy, masturbation, role-playing, birth control, and cosmetic surgery (among other things).[39] The authors based their ethical evaluation of each act upon whether the Bible has an explicit prohibition concerning that act.[40] If there was no explicit prohibition, then the authors deemed the act "lawful" within marriage according to Scripture. What they never asked, however, is the teleological question: *Does this act fulfill God's purposes for the sexual union? Does this act fulfill God's ultimate purpose for marriage and sexuality—the glory of God?* This is where teleology can help us. The Scripture provides us not only with explicit ethical norms (à la "divine command" deontology) but also with the purposes for human sexuality (à la teleology). We must use the commands as well as the purposes in making ethical judgments concerning human sexuality.

John Frame's triperspectivalism is very similar to the approach that I am arguing for here. He argues that "ethical judgment in-

---

[39] Mark Driscoll and Grace Driscoll, *Real Marriage: The Truth about Sex, Friendship, and Life Together* (Nashville, TN: Thomas Nelson, 2012), 177–203.

[40] In their book *Real Marriage*, the Driscolls construct a taxonomy for evaluating the ethics of martial sex. The first question is: *"Is it lawful?* With this question we seek to ascertain whether or not something is in violation of the laws of government in the culture or the laws of God in Scripture" (ibid., 178). Because certain sexual activities are not explicitly prohibited by Scripture, they declare sodomy, masturbation, role-playing, and cosmetic surgery to be "lawful."

volves the application of a *norm* to a *situation* by a *person*."[41] Those three factors comprise three perspectives that must inform our approach to ethics. They also roughly coincide with the three different approaches to ethics that we have considered thus far. The situational perspective is the teleological perspective. It focuses on "God's actions in creation and providence" and compels us to ask what is the best means to accomplish God's purposes.[42] The normative perspective is the deontological perspective in which we are chiefly concerned with what the Scripture defines as our duty or obligation.[43] The existential perspective is the perspective of character ethics, and it focuses on the question, "How must I change if I am to do God's will?"[44] These three perspectives are interrelated, and all three must have a say in the ethical judgments that we make. God's glory is the purpose, Scripture is the norm, and sanctification is the virtue.

The Purpose(s) of Sex

So what is the purpose of sex? As I have already indicated, the *ultimate* purpose is the glory of God. But we must also understand that there are *subordinate* purposes as well. God's glory is not achieved simply by contemplation of the divine attributes. God defines *the means by which* our sexuality will glorify him, and he spells out the matter in Scripture and in natural revelation. We must pay careful attention to both if we are to discern the subordinate purposes of our sexuality. I have already mentioned Dennis Hollinger's important work defining four different purposes for sex, and I intend to adopt his approach in this book as the four subordinate purposes of sex. The four purposes are (1) the consummation of marriage, (2) procreation, (3) expression of love, and (4) pleasure.[45] These four purposes comprise the means by which we glorify God with our sexuality.

---

[41] Frame, *Doctrine of the Christian Life*, 33; emphasis original.
[42] Ibid.
[43] Ibid., 33–34.
[44] Ibid., 34.
[45] Hollinger, *Meaning of Sex*, 95.

Consummation of Marriage

The first purpose of sex is the consummation of marriage. The Scripture defines marriage as the covenanted heterosexual union of one man and one woman. Marriage is initiated by public declaration of an exclusive commitment and is ratified by the one-flesh union of sex. Without sexual union, there can be no marriage. Scripture teaches us that this has been the norm ever since Adam and Eve in the garden of Eden. After God formed the woman from the man's side and gave her to the man, the Bible says, "For this cause a man shall leave his father and his mother, and shall cleave to his wife; and they shall become one flesh" (Gen. 2:24 AT). So the first marriage began by leaving one family to start a new one and by the initiation of the one-flesh union. Sex completes the initiation of the marriage covenant, and "every sexual act after the initial consummation is an ongoing affirmation of the husband and wife's unique union."[46] It tends toward the glory of God in that it effects a union that is designed to be an image of Christ's marriage to his bride, the church (Eph. 5:32).[47]

Procreation

The second purpose of sex is procreation. Since the Bible permits sexual activity only within the covenant of marriage, it is no surprise that procreation is a purpose of both the conjugal act and the institution itself.[48] From the very beginning, God made his intention clear about his creative purposes for sex. At the original creation of the first man and woman, God commanded them: "Be fruitful and multiply, and fill the earth, and subdue it; and rule over the fish of the sea and over the birds of the sky and over every living thing that moves on the earth" (Gen. 1:26, 28). God makes Adam and Eve his vice-regents over the primeval world. They image forth God by "ruling over" every aspect of the world as God had given it to them. Their ability to "subdue" the earth is tied directly to their ability to

---

[46] Ibid., 100.
[47] See subsequent chapter on "Glorifying God with Your Marriage."
[48] Ash, *Marriage*, 107.

"fill it" with their offspring. Thus the procreation of man becomes a key part in God's intention to rule and reign over the world through his image bearers. Commenting on Genesis 1:27, Kenneth Matthews writes, "Human procreation is not intended merely as a mechanism for replication or the expression of human passion but is instrumental in experiencing covenant blessing."[49] Thus the propagation of the race is supposed to issue forth in the propagation of God's rule on earth. It is not just Adam and Eve who received this charge. God also gives the same charge to the patriarchs, which shows that the command to procreate plays a unique role in God's redemptive purposes for the world.[50] Procreation tends toward the glory of God as it is a means by which the glory of God will cover the earth through his image-bearing vice-regents.

Expression of Love

The third purpose of sex is love—in particular, the ongoing expression of marital love. The apostle Paul compares the "one flesh" union of husband and wife to the relationship of Christ and his church (Eph. 5:31–32). The love between a husband and wife, therefore, is not merely a state of mind but is expressed in part through the conjugal act. Human beings are not souls trapped in a husk. They are whole persons consisting in a unity of body and soul. Spouses cannot enter into a comprehensive union[51] nor can they express their love fully apart from the union of bodies. Just as sex consummates marriage, so also it serves as the ongoing affirmation of the husband and wife's unique love for one another. Perhaps no biblical book illustrates this truth more vividly than the Song of Solomon. No less than three times, the author uses the word *love* (אַהֲבָה) as a figure of speech for sexual union.[52]

---

[49] Kenneth A. Mathews, *Genesis 1–11:26*, vol. 1a, New American Commentary (Nashville, TN: Broadman, 1996), 174.

[50] Hamilton, *God's Glory in Salvation through Judgment*, 90. The mandate to procreate appears to the patriarchs in Gen. 8:17; 9:1, 7; 17:6; 22:17; 26:22, 24; 28:3–4; 35:11; 48:4, 16; 47:27; Ex. 1:7, 12.

[51] Sherif Girgis, Robert P. George, and Ryan T. Anderson, "What Is Marriage?," *Harvard Journal of Law and Public Policy* 34 (2010): 253.

[52] Brian P. Gault argues that the two most likely interpretations of "rousing love" say that the phrase is either a reference to anticipated coitus or coitus in progress. He opts for the latter. In either case, "love" appears as a metonymy for sexual relations. See Brian P. Gault, "An Admoni-

I adjure you, O daughters of Jerusalem,
By the gazelles or by the hinds of the field,
That you will not arouse or awaken my *love*
Until she pleases. (Song 2:7)

I adjure you, O daughters of Jerusalem,
By the gazelles or by the hinds of the field,
That you will not arouse or awaken my *love*
Until she pleases. (Song 3:5)

I want you to swear, O daughters of Jerusalem,
Do not arouse or awaken my *love*
Until she pleases. (Song 8:4)

Elsewhere the Song of Solomon speaks of the emotional love that exists between the lover and the beloved (Song 2:4; 7:7; 8:6–7). But in these three texts, it is not merely the emotion that is in view but the marital act. The sexual union is so closely associated with the emotion that the author uses the word *love* to refer to the deed itself. In this way, the Song teaches sex as a unique, bodily expression of love. How does the expression of love tend toward the glory of God? The apostle Paul says that this passionate union of spouses serves as a living metaphor of the loving union that Christ has with his church: "This mystery is great; but I am speaking with reference to Christ and the church" (Eph. 5:32).

Pleasure

The fourth purpose of sex is pleasure. Pleasure serves as a powerful inducement to achieve the other purposes of sex: consummation, procreation, and expression of love. Because sinners often pursue sex for pleasure alone—quite apart from the other ends that God has ordained—some have mistakenly concluded that pleasure itself is a carnal, ungodly concern. But this is not what the Bible

tion against 'Rousing Love': The Meaning of the Enigmatic Refrain in Song of Songs," *Bulletin for Biblical Research* 20, no. 2 (2010): 161–84. See also Brian P. Gault, "A 'Do Not Disturb' Sign? Reexamining the Adjuration Refrain in Song of Songs," *Journal for the Study of the Old Testament* 36, no. 1 (2011): 93–104.

teaches. The Scripture is clear that the pleasure of sex is a good gift from God. As Hollinger has argued,

> Despite the fact that Christians rightly reject hedonism, the pleasure-seeking principle, as the governing framework of their lives, there is a kind of Christian hedonism. The very fact that the Psalmist [16:11] can speak of eternal pleasures at God's right hand shows that he is a God of pleasure.[53]

Indeed, biblically speaking, God is not averse to pleasure. It is true that pleasure can become an idol when it is treated as an end within itself (Prov. 21:17; 1 Tim. 5:6). But when the pleasure of sex is enjoyed in keeping with God's comprehensive purposes, pleasure glorifies God. That is why the apostle Paul commands the Corinthians to "glorify God" with the use of the body for sex (1 Cor. 6:20). Sexual pleasure in the service of God is doxological. But where else is this taught in the Bible? Christopher Ash argues that the goodness of sexual pleasure in marriage is the assumption of all the relevant texts. He writes,

> Sexual desire and delight is part of the natural backdrop to all the biblical texts. It is taken for granted and alluded to as a natural part of life. It is important to be clear that this is understood and affirmed throughout Scripture, as a brief survey of examples will show.[54]

Consider, for instance, the delight of the bridegroom over his bride in Isaiah 62:5: "As the bridegroom rejoices over the bride, so your God will rejoice over you." Consider also the joyful anticipation of marital pleasure in Psalm 45:11: "The King will desire your beauty." Ecclesiastes 9:9 likewise says, "Enjoy life with the wife whom you love" (AT). Proverbs 5:18–19 commands the reader to "rejoice in the wife of your youth. As a loving hind and a graceful doe, let her breasts satisfy you at all times; be exhilarated always with her

---

[53] Hollinger, *Meaning of Sex*, 111.
[54] Ash, *Marriage*, 185.

love." Again, the Song of Solomon gives us some of the most vivid descriptions of the pleasures of marital love:

> Awake, O north wind,
> And come, wind of the south;
> Make my garden breathe out fragrance,
> Let its spices be wafted abroad.
> May my beloved come into his garden
> And eat its choice fruits! (Song 4:16)

The backdrop for all of these statements (and countless others) is the physical delight of the sexual union.[55] This "taken-for-grantedness" of the delight of the marriage bed has a larger theological purpose in the Bible. As Christopher Ash has observed, "Sexual attraction, desire and delight were as well known and accepted then as now. . . . The whole metaphorical structure of the Lord's marriage to his people would have been evacuated of meaning were this not so."[56]

Taken together, these four purposes are subordinate to the ultimate end of glorifying God. The four subordinate ends are not discreet goods but are inseparably related to one another in the covenant of marriage, which itself exists for the glory of God. The morality of any given action, therefore, must be measured by its conformity to these ends.

The Way Forward

The rest of this book will flesh out the thesis that the ultimate purpose of human sexuality is the glory of God and that the ultimate ethic is to glorify God with our sexuality. Chapter 1, "Glorify God with Your Body," consists of an exposition of 1 Corinthians 6:12–20

---

[55] Christopher Ash lists most of these texts and others in speaking about sexual pleasure in marriage (ibid., 186).

[56] Ibid. See also John Murray, *Principles of Conduct: Aspects of Biblical Ethics* (Grand Rapids, MI: Eerdmans, 1957), 56: "Sex desire is not wrong and Jesus does not say so. To cast any aspersion on sex desire is to impugn the integrity of the Creator and of his creation. Furthermore, it is not wrong to desire to satisfy sex desire and impulse in the way God has ordained. Indeed, sex desire is one of the considerations which induce men and women to marry. The Scripture fully recognizes the propriety of that motive and commends marriage as the honourable and necessary outlet for sex impulse."

in which the central command is for believers to glorify God with their bodies. Chapter 2, "Glorify God with Your Hermeneutic," seeks to discredit a hermeneutical approach that pits Paul against Jesus in the interpretation of Scripture. Chapter 3, "Glorify God with Your Marriage," defines the covenant of marriage and argues that the covenanted heterosexual union of two persons is the only context in which it is possible to glorify God with sex. Chapter 4, "Glorify God with Your Conjugal Union," explores the nature and limits of the sexual bond between married couples as well as the issue of divorce. Chapter 5, "Glorify God with Your Family Planning," examines the moral issues at stake with modern birth control methods while focusing special attention on the Pill. Chapter 6, "Glorify God with Your Gender," expounds a biblical view of manhood and womanhood in light of a number of contemporary challenges to it. Chapter 7, "Glorify God with Your Sexuality," takes on the challenge of homosexuality. This chapter highlights the Bible's consistent teaching on the moral status of same-sex relationships and argues that Christians need to learn how to minister more effectively to homosexuals. Chapter 8, "Glorify God with Your Singleness," examines the teachings of Jesus and Paul on singles and urges sexual purity for singles. The concluding chapter summarizes some of the broad conclusions of the book and contrasts them with a secular worldview concerning sexuality.

Christian faithfulness in our generation requires that we be prepared to apply the Word of God to the gritty issues of life. It demands that we be prepared to speak with clarity and conviction to ethical challenges like the one faced by the young minister at the beginning of this chapter. This book is an effort to set forth the vision of sexual wholeness that is found in the Bible. And that vision finds its coherence and impetus in the glory of God as he has revealed himself in the Scriptures. He has called us to glorify him with every aspect of our being. This book is aimed to help you understand how to do just that with respect to gender, sex, and marriage.

I believe in . . . the resurrection of the body,
and the life everlasting. Amen.

—The Apostles' Creed

1

Glorify God
with Your Body

This is not the first book to argue that sex exists for the glory of God. Others have made the same point under the generic biblical teaching that we should do everything for the glory of God. That general command appears in texts like this one: "Whether, then, you eat or drink or whatever you do, do all to the glory of God" (1 Cor. 10:31; cf. Col. 3:17). Likewise, the apostle Peter writes about the purpose of our service to God and to one another, "Whoever speaks, is to do so as one who is speaking the utterances of God; whoever serves is to do so as one who is serving by the strength which God supplies; so that in all things God may be glorified through Jesus Christ, to whom belongs the glory and dominion forever and ever. Amen" (1 Pet. 4:11). In these texts and elsewhere, the Bible provides general instruction about the glory of God being the purpose of all things. We should not minimize the value of these texts or the deductions we make from them— namely, that glorifying God in "all things" includes our sexuality. The purpose of this chapter, however, is to take this observation a step further—that is, to explore one particular text in which the apostle Paul explicitly connects human sexuality with the glory of God—1 Corinthians 6:12–20. We will find that in this text Paul offers us a teleological model of ethical reflection that is rooted in the text of Scripture. Paul confronts an ethical aberration in Corinth, he brings the Old Testament to bear upon the problem, and then he exhorts his readers to use their bodies sexually for the glory of God.

The Meaning of Sex in 1 Corinthians 6:12–20

The human heart has an uncanny ability to rationalize the evil it perpetrates. This is especially the case with sexual sins. Think with me a moment about what rationalization is. *To rationalize is to allow my mind to find reasons to excuse what my conscience knows is wrong.*[1] In other words, to rationalize is to commit the sin of suppressing the truth that God has revealed in order to justify the conscience (Rom. 1:18). Here is how this usually works out in our own hearts. We see something we want that we know is sin. Our desire for that particular sin becomes so intense that we begin to enumerate to ourselves the reasons that it is really not a sin after all. We convince ourselves that there is some mitigating circumstance that nullifies the clear commands of God.

Have you ever heard someone defend the practice of downloading copyrighted music illegally from the Internet? Here is how the rationalization typically goes: "Rock stars are rich and evil. Since I am poor and good, it's okay if I rip off their music from the Internet." The Bible is unambiguous in its prohibition on stealing (Ex. 20:15; Matt. 19:18; Rom. 13:9). Yet the thief wants the music so badly that he denies his conscience grounds for calling it what the Bible calls it—stealing. He does this through rationalization.

Sometimes we know a course of action is wrong, but we rationalize it as a "necessary evil" and do it anyway. Our problem is that once we assuage our conscience by calling something a necessary evil, it begins to look more and more necessary and less and less evil.[2] The great danger of rationalizing your sin in this way is that

---

[1] I have heard this aphorism attributed to Harlow Shapley, *Of Stars and Men: The Human Response to an Expanding Universe* (Boston: Beacon, 1958).
[2] I am not sure about the origin of this little aphorism, but I have seen it attributed to Sydney J. Harris.

if you suppress your conscience long enough, you eventually will not be able to tell good from evil. Every time you rationalize your sin, you harden your heart, you put a callus on your conscience, and you put your soul in mortal danger.

This is in part why the apostle Paul appeals so urgently in 1 Corinthians 6:12–20. In this text Paul addresses some of the most gifted rationalizers that ever walked the face of the earth. And these were people that Paul himself had evangelized and won to Christ (Acts 18:1–11). Paul spent a year and a half of his itinerant ministry with the Corinthians—plenty of time to develop significant relationships with them and to provide extensive instruction in the gospel (Acts 18:11).[3] Nevertheless, after Paul left, a group of men in the church decided to consort with prostitutes. When Paul finds out, he is appalled that these men would take the "members of Christ" and make them "members of a harlot" (1 Cor. 6:15 AT). This entire paragraph, therefore, is devoted to correcting these men and their rationalization for bad behavior. We are not so different from the Corinthians. We too are prone to set aside what we know to be right based on specious rationalizing. A closer look at verses 6:12–20 shows that Paul's response to the Corinthian church addresses our rationalizations and moves us closer to understanding the ultimate meaning of sex—the glory of God. But before that, a little more background is in order.

Slogans as Corinthian Excuses for Sin

Several times in this letter, Paul indicates that he has heard about slogans that the Corinthians have adopted to justify their misbehavior. Sometimes, Paul actually quotes their slogans back to them and then refutes them with gospel truth. One of the keys, therefore, to understanding Paul's argument is the ability to distinguish Paul's voice from the Corinthians'—to distinguish the Corinthian slogans from Paul's exhortation. Here are two examples to illustrate the point.

---

[3] Richard B. Hays, *First Corinthians*, Interpretation (Louisville, KY: Westminster, 1997).

1 Corinthians 1:12–13

Slogan: "I am of Paul," and "I of Apollos," and "I of Cephas," and "I of Christ."

Paul's Response: "Has Christ been divided? Paul was not crucified for you, was he? Or were you baptized in the name of Paul?"

1 Corinthians 7:1–2 (AT)

Slogan: "It is good for a man not to touch a woman."

Paul's Response: "But because of immoralities, let each man have his own wife, and let each woman have her own husband."

Notice that in 1:12 and in 7:1 Paul actually quotes what the Corinthians are saying, and then he refutes their words with the truth. This pattern is exactly what we have before us in verses 6:12–20.[4] In these verses Paul stages an argument between himself and the Corinthians by quoting their slogans and then refuting them. The Corinthian well has been poisoned with serious theological error, so Paul gives them the gospel as the antidote. The Corinthians need to see the emptiness of their sloganeering excuses, and Paul is going to help them to do just that. He tells them that Christian freedom has limits (6:12), that the resurrection has implications (6:13–18a), and that sex has a purpose (6:18b–20).

---

[4] A growing number of scholars are now identifying Corinthian slogans as a part of Paul's words in 1 Cor. 6:12–20. Something of a consensus is forming around the idea that verses 12 and 13 contain slogans, as is evident in an array of modern translations that put quotation marks in these verses (e.g., ESV, HCSB, NAB, NET, NIV, NLT, NRSV, RSV). For a number of years, the verdict was out on the presence of a slogan in verse 18. Recently, that has begun to change. Apparently, the first to argue that 6:18 is a slogan was W. J. Conybeare and J. S. Howson, *The Life and Epistles of St. Paul* (Grand Rapids, MI: Eerdmans, 1949), 392. For a full summary of the history of this interpretation until the pivotal work of Jerome Murphy-O'Connor, see "Corinthian Slogans in 1 Cor 6:12–20," *Catholic Biblical Quarterly* 40, no. 3 (1978): 391–96. O'Connor gave what has become the best argument for interpreting 6:18b as a Corinthian slogan. Recent translations marking a slogan in verse 18 include HCSB and NET. Recent articles and commentaries in favor of reading part of verse 18 as a slogan include Denny Burk, "Discerning Corinthian Slogans through Paul's Use of the Diatribe in 1 Corinthians 6.12–20," *Bulletin for Biblical Research* 18, no. 1 (2008): 99–121; Jay E. Smith, "The Roots of a 'Libertine' Slogan in 1 Corinthians 6:18," *Journal of Theological Studies* 59, no. 1 (2008): 63–95; Hays, *First Corinthians*, 101–7; Joseph A. Fitzmyer, *First Corinthians*, Anchor Yale Bible 32 (New Haven, CT: Yale University Press, 2008). Contra David E. Garland, *1 Corinthians*, Baker Exegetical Commentary on the New Testament (Grand Rapids, MI: Baker, 2003); Brian J. Dodd, "Paul's Paradigmatic 'I' and 1 Corinthians 6.12," *Journal for the Study of the New Testament* 59 (1995): 39–58.

Christian Freedom Has Limits (1 Corinthians 6:12)

The first Corinthian slogan appears in verse 12: "All things are lawful for me." This slogan expresses the belief that Christians are not constrained to keep the Jewish law. Paul quotes the slogan twice and immediately follows it in each case with a correction.

> Slogan: "All things are lawful for me."
> Paul: "But not all things are profitable."
> Slogan: "All things are lawful for me."
> Paul: "But I will not be mastered by anything."

On the face of it, the Corinthian slogan does not have the ring of serious theological error. As an expression of Christian freedom, "All things are lawful for me" is not at all unlike the language that Paul himself has used elsewhere to speak about the Christian's relationship to the Jewish law. Perhaps the Corinthians heard Paul say things like he said to the Romans:

> For sin shall not be master over you, for you are not under law but under grace. What then? Shall we sin because we are not under law but under grace? May it never be! (Rom. 6:14–15)

> Therefore, my brethren, you also were made to die to the Law through the body of Christ. . . . But now we have been released from the Law, having died to that by which we were bound, so that we serve in newness of the Spirit and not in oldness of the letter. (Rom. 7:4, 6)

So Paul is known to have told disciples that they were "not under law," that they had "died to the law," and that they had been "released from the law." It would not have been a far leap from such statements for the Corinthians to conclude that "all things are lawful for me."

But the Corinthians used this teaching in a way that Paul never intended. They turned Paul's law-free message into antinomianism and used it to justify their visits to prostitutes (v. 15). They turned

Paul's gospel into a license to sin. Yet this is not what Paul means when he says that Christians are no longer under law. In fact, Paul confronts this idea as a false conclusion in Romans 6:15: "Shall we sin because we are not under law but under grace? May it never be!" Paul says elsewhere that Christians are bound by "grace" (Rom. 6:14) to "serve" in the "Spirit" (Rom. 7:6). Paul's gospel cannot be fairly construed as a license to sin, but it looks like that is exactly what the Corinthians have done. In their minds, they can go to bed with whomever they like whenever they like because "all things are lawful for me."[5]

The spirit of the age has not changed much from the first century to the present day. The libertinism of these Corinthians is not unlike the license that characterizes sexual mores in the post-Christian West. The sexual revolution has enabled people to cast off all restraint. Modern people are not wrestling with the Jewish law per se, but they have by and large cast off Judeo-Christian sexual norms. The prevailing idea seems to be that when it comes to sexuality, anything goes, so long as the activity is between consenting adults. There are no boundaries, no rules, just license. If it feels good, do it. Anyone who disagrees with that approach is sexually repressed and puritanical.

Nevertheless, Paul refutes this "anything goes" attitude with two statements in verse 12: "*Not all things are profitable. . . . I will not be mastered by anything.*" With these words, Paul does not dismiss the idea of Christian freedom.[6] Instead, he tweaks the Corinthian misunderstanding of freedom in order to bring it into line with the gospel. He does this by placing two limitations on freedom.

---

[5] BDAG notes that ἔξεστιν usually carries with it a legal connotation, "all things are lawful for me" (BDAG, "ἔξεστιν," 348). However, it is difficult to tell in this context if Paul is referring specifically to the law. Fee notes the possibility that these slogans may "be closely related to the issue of idol food in chaps. 8–10. It has especially close affinities with 8:8, which also seems to reflect a Corinthian position. Whether Paul is himself bringing that argument of theirs to bear here, or whether they had used the same argument for both food and sex, cannot be known. Probably the latter." See Gordon D. Fee, *The First Epistle to the Corinthians*, New International Commentary on the New Testament (Grand Rapids, MI: Eerdmans, 1987), 254.

[6] As Murphy-O'Connor writes, "Paul does not deny the statement 'All things are lawful to me' (v. 12). He may even have said something like that himself when explaining the believer's freedom from the multiple prohibitions of Jewish law. What he does is to attach two restrictions which bring it into line with his understanding of Christian community." See Jerome Murphy-O'Connor, *1 Corinthians*, New Testament Message 10 (Wilmington, DE: Michael Glazier, 1979), 52.

In short, Paul says that Christian freedom from the law is limited by *love* and *lordship.*

Love for brothers and sisters in Christ limits Christian freedom. That limit appears in the words "not all things are profitable." What does *profitability* have to do with love? The word translated "profitable" does not denote profit to oneself but profit to others—in particular, to others within the body of Christ.[7] Paul therefore is saying that Christian freedom (that which is "lawful") is limited by the obligation to build up the body of Christ. So the ethical question we have to ask ourselves is not merely, "Is this or that activity okay for me to do?" The question is, "Will this or that activity be a help or a hindrance to my brothers and sisters in Christ?" When you are contemplating the morality of any given action, you have to ask yourself not just the law question but also the love question. We must ask not only, "What would the law have me do?" but also, "What would love have me do?" Paul says elsewhere, "Owe nothing to anyone except to love one another" (Rom. 13:8). And love manifests itself in part by setting aside selfish interests that might become a hindrance to others: "Therefore let us not judge one another anymore, but rather determine this—not to put an obstacle or a stumbling block in a brother's way" (Rom. 14:13).

The lordship of Jesus Christ also limits Christian freedom because, Paul says, "I will not be mastered by anything."[8] Any good thing can be turned into a bad thing if you make an idol out of it. The case in point for this passage is the use of the body for sex. Sex is a good thing in the eyes of God. It only becomes evil when it is idolized such that self-gratification displaces the *lordship* of Christ. Christians have sworn allegiance to King Jesus, and Jesus will suf-

---

[7] The idea of "profitability" comes from the Greek word *sumpherō,* a word that appears two other times in this book: 10:23–24 and 12:7. In 10:23, "profitable" parallels edification and seeking the good of one's neighbor. In 12:7, "profitable" is that which is for the "common good" of the whole body of Christ. If that is the meaning of *sumpherō* in those other two instances, it most likely has the same meaning in 6:12.

[8] ἔξεστιν and ἐξουσιάζω are etymologically connected, and it is likely that Paul uses this wordplay to make the point that one must not let one's freedom become a means of bondage. See also BDAG, "ἐξουσιάζω," 354; LSJ, "ἐξουσ-ία," 4.2 [p. 599]; Werner Foerster, "ἔξεστιν, ἐξουσία, ἐξουσιάζω, κατεξουσιάζω," in *Theological Dictionary of the New Testament,* vol. 2, ed. Gerhard Kittel and Geoffrey W. Bromiley, trans. Geoffrey W. Bromiley (Grand Rapids, MI: Eerdmans, 1964) 575.

fer no rivals. That means that he has to be your master and that you cannot serve anyone or anything else above him.

Even though Paul said that he was no longer under the Jewish law, he was no antinomian: "To those who are without law, [I became] as without law, though not being without the law of God but under the law of Christ, so that I might win those who are without law" (1 Cor. 9:21). Paul would agree that Christians have been set free from the Jewish law. But for Paul, freedom from one master meant becoming the slave of another—Jesus. The irony of gospel liberty is that it sets us free to become a slave of Jesus. That is why Paul viewed his own life as a vehicle for living Christ's life over again. He writes: "I have been crucified with Christ; and it is no longer I who live, but Christ lives in me; and the life which I now live in the flesh I live by faith in the Son of God, who loved me, and gave Himself up for me" (Gal. 2:20). For Paul, so-called Christian freedom had limits—love for others and the lordship of Jesus Christ. But that is not all.

The Resurrection Has Implications (1 Corinthians 6:13–18a)

The first half of verse 13 is another slogan: "Food is for the stomach, and the stomach is for food, but God will do away with both of them." The Corinthian justification for immorality consisted in two arguments: (1) teleology and (2) eschatology. Their teleological justification for immorality consisted in the observation that the human body's design reveals its purpose. This fact is no less clear with sex than it is with eating. Just as the stomach is made for food, so also sexual organs are made for sex. What could possibly be wrong with using the body according to its purpose? Paul exposes the folly of this argument with, "yet the body[9] is not for

---

[9] I agree with Gundry's balanced assessment of the meaning of σῶμα: "We conclude that in neither the Pauline epistles, nor the literature of the NT outside those epistles, nor the LXX, nor extra-Biblical ancient Greek literature does the definition 'whole person' find convincing support. This is not to deny that (outside Platonic tradition) emphasis falls on the unity of man's being. But it is a unity of parts, inner and outer, rather than a monadic unity. Ancient writers do not usually treat *sōma* in isolation. Rather, apart from its use for a corpse, *sōma* refers to the physical body in its proper and intended union with the soul/spirit. The body and its counterpart are portrayed as united but distinct—and separable, though unnaturally and unwantedly separated. The *sōma* may *represent* the whole person simply because the *sōma* lives in union with the soul/spirit. But

immorality,[10] but for the Lord, and the Lord is for the body." Paul does not question that the body is made for sex (a subordinate end), but he does say that the body exists for the Lord (the ultimate end). The Corinthians had fixated on the subordinate end of the body and had missed the ultimate end of God's glory. In doing so, they misconstrued how the subordinate end must serve the ultimate end. Sex is not to be enjoyed for its own sake but for God's sake. Enjoying sex for God's sake means shunning every sexual union outside of the covenanted union of one man and one woman. Since the body exists "for the Lord," its proper use must be under the lordship of Christ. Sleeping with prostitutes is not one of the Lord's purposes for the body.

The eschatological rationale for immorality consisted in the observation that physical bodies ultimately give way to death. The Corinthians contend that "God will destroy both the one and the other" (AT). By that they mean that God will ultimately "destroy" the body in death. Since every person must ultimately die and lose their body to the dust, God must not care much about physical bodies. If God does not think much of the body in the age to come, then why would he care what we do with our bodies now? From this, the Corinthians concluded that the physical body figured very little in God's moral economy. Herein is the foundational error of the Corinthians—the moral irrelevance of the body. The Corinthians argued that because God allows the destruction of the physical body, it follows that the physical body is morally inconsequential. As Ben Witherington has observed, "Many Corinthian Christians apparently thought that salvation did not involve the body."[11] The Corinthians' problem was that they had been swayed more by Plato than by Paul. They had imbibed the spirit of their

---

sōma does not *mean* 'whole person', because its use is designed to call attention to the physical object which is the body rather than to the whole personality. Where used of whole people, *sōma* directs attention to their bodies, not to the wholeness of their being." See Robert H. Gundry, *Sōma in Biblical Theology with Emphasis on Pauline Anthropology* (Cambridge, UK: Cambridge University Press, 1976), 79–80.

[10] I take πορνεία as any form of "unlawful sexual intercourse" (BDAG, "πορνεία," 854), although it may in this instance be a specific reference to having sex with a prostitute.

[11] Ben Witherington III, *Conflict and Community in Corinth: A Socio-Rhetorical Commentary on 1 and 2 Corinthians* (Grand Rapids, MI: Eerdmans, 1995), 164n11.

age—a Hellenistic dualism that "disdained the physical world for the 'higher' knowledge and wisdom of spiritual existence."[12] In doing so they were losing sight of the Christian hope of resurrection. But Paul attacks this logic in verse 14 with the gospel truth that death is not the ultimate end of the believer's body; *resurrection is the ultimate end for the believer.*[13] To say that God destroys the body as the Corinthians had said is to miss the point of the gospel, which promises that God will not in fact destroy the body but that he will do quite the opposite: "God has both raised the Lord and will raise us up by His power" (v. 14 AT). For Paul, as surely as the Lord was raised bodily, so also shall his people be raised bodily in the age to come. The cause of both of these resurrections is God's power.[14] The Christian is not waiting for God to destroy his body. He is waiting for God to resurrect it. To misunderstand the ultimate destiny of the body is not merely an ethical aberration but an undermining of the hope of the gospel itself.[15] The true *telos* of Christians is not death but eternal life.

---

[12] Scott J. Hafemann, "Corinthians, Letters to The," in *Dictionary of Paul and His Letters*, ed. Gerald F. Hawthorne, Ralph P. Martin, and Daniel G. Reid (Downers Grove, IL: InterVarsity, 1993), 174: "The Corinthians held on to that part of the Hellenistic body/soul or material/immaterial dualism which disdained the physical world for the 'higher' knowledge and wisdom of spiritual existence." Paul refers to the Corinthian preoccupation with "knowledge" on several occasions throughout the letter (1:5; 8:1, 7, 10, 11; 12:8; 13:2, 8; 14:6) and names it as the source of some of the abuses of liberty that were taking place (8:1–13). This *knowledge* is immaterial and is more important than the temporal, physical issues of life. Therefore, the resurrection, immorality, and other such corporeal matters can be dismissed as of little importance in the Christian life (6:13; 15:12). This dualism provided the conceptual support for the Corinthians' over-realized eschatology (Haffemann, "Corinthians," 175). The Corinthians' emphasis on the present reveals their failure to accept that a gap still existed between what they were and what they would become at the resurrection. Therefore, Paul chastises them, saying, "You are already filled, you have already become rich, you have become kings without us [apostles]" (4:8). They think that because they have the Spirit, they are participating in all the blessings of the eschaton. The only "not yet" of God's blessing is the shuffling off of the mortal coil of their spiritual existence; "they regarded their present spiritual existence as an assumption of that which is to be, minus the physical body" (Fee, *First Epistle to the Corinthians*, 12). Thus the doctrine of the bodily resurrection of believers has no place in the Corinthian mind-set (15:12–18). What will become clear in the following section is that this dualism and over-realized eschatology find expression in the slogans that the Corinthians use to justify immoral behavior.

[13] Of course ἐγείρω and ἐξεγείρω both refer in this context to the raising up in resurrection from physical death to physical life (BDAG, "ἐγείρω," 271; "ἐξεγείρω," 346).

[14] In this verse, διά with the genitive is a marker of instrumentality that signals the means by which bodily resurrection is effected (BDAG, "διά," 224). Paul elsewhere identifies the "power" of God as the efficient cause of bodily resurrection (e.g., Rom. 1:4; 1 Cor. 15:43; 2 Cor. 4:7; 13:4; Phil. 3:10).

[15] It is clear that the Corinthians were losing confidence in the Christian hope of resurrection, a point that Paul takes up more fully in chapter 15: "Now if Christ is preached, that He has been raised from the dead, how do some among you say that there is no resurrection of the dead?" (v. 12).

Verse 15 begins with two rhetorical questions: "Do you not know that your bodies are members[16] of Christ?[17] Shall I therefore take the members of Christ and make them members of a prostitute? May it never be!" (AT). With this rhetorical question, Paul suggests that the believer's physical body comprises Christ's own *members* or *limbs*. When the believer engages his *body* in sexual immorality, he is involving Christ's own *body parts* in the illicit act. That is why he asks, "Therefore, shall I take up the members of Christ and make them members of a prostitute?" Paul asks this hypothetical question in order to expose the real meaning of sleeping with a prostitute. Sleeping with a prostitute has the unconscionable result of involving Christ's body in a sinful act. So Paul answers his own rhetorical question with the Greek phrase *mē genoito*, "may it never be!"—the strongest possible way to reject a proposition in Greek.

Verse 16 begins with another rhetorical question: "Do you not know that the one who joins himself to a prostitute is one body with her?" What is the significance of the union of Christ's members with the members of a prostitute? Paul answers that question by quoting Genesis 2:24 to show that sexual intercourse effects a union between two people: "For He says, 'The two shall become one flesh'" (6:16b). It is unthinkable to Paul that a Christian should unite his own body, a member of Christ, to a harlot. The Christian's union with Christ through the Spirit makes the sin all the more grave. After all, "the one who joins himself to the Lord is one spirit with Him" (6:17).[18] Therefore, Paul issues the solemn command, "Flee immorality" (6:18a).[19]

It must not be missed that Paul grounds his sexual ethic in

---

[16] "Μέλος" is typically used to refer to the *limbs* or *parts* of the human body. However, this term is used metaphorically to refer to a *part* as a *member* of a whole. Figuratively speaking, the individual Christians are *members* of Christ, and together they form his body (BDAG, "μέλος," 628).

[17] Χριστοῦ is a partitive genitive. The genitive noun denotes the whole of which the head noun is a part. F. Blass and A. Debrunner, *A Greek Grammar of the New Testament and Other Early Christian Literature*, trans. and rev. Robert W. Funk (Chicago, University of Chicago Press, 1961), §164, 90; Daniel B. Wallace, *Greek Grammar beyond the Basics: An Exegetical Syntax of the New Testament* (Grand Rapids, MI: Zondervan, 1996), 84.

[18] "In light of vv. 19–20, Paul probably is referring to the work of the Spirit, whereby through the 'one Spirit' the believer's 'spirit' has been joined indissolubly with Christ. The believer is united to the Lord and thereby has become one S/spirit with him." Fee, *First Epistle to the Corinthians*, 260.

[19] The verb is a present imperative, which is used to commend general precepts concerning attitude and conduct; it has a durative force (Blass and Debrunner, *Greek Grammar of the New Testa-*

Genesis 2:24. When Paul (and Jesus, for that matter) sets out new-covenant norms for gender and sexuality, he never appeals to polygamist kings such as David or Solomon or to polygamist patriarchs such as Abraham, Isaac, or Jacob. For all the importance these Old Testament figures have in the history of redemption, Jesus and Paul do not look to any of them as the paradigm for understanding marriage. Instead, Jesus and Paul look back without exception to the pre-fall monogamous union of Adam and Eve in Genesis 2 as the norm of human sexuality and marriage. "For this cause a man shall leave his father and his mother and shall cling to his wife; and they shall become one flesh" (Gen. 2:24, AT; cf. Matt. 19:5; Mark 10:7–8; 1 Cor. 6:16; Eph. 5:31).

Sex Has a Purpose

In 1 Corinthians 6:18 we read, "Every sin, whatever a person may do, is outside of the body. But, the one who commits immorality sins against his own body" (AT). The King James has a similar translation: "Every sin that a man doeth is without the body; but he that committeth fornication sinneth against his own body." The interpretation represented in these two renderings is certainly a curious one. What could Paul possibly mean by "every sin" being something that is done "outside of the body" or "without the body"? How does one sin against the body while sinning "without" the body. The first clause (sinning without the body) seems to contradict the second (sinning against the body).

Commentators have attempted to alleviate the difficulty of a literal rendering by inserting the word "other" into the translation, and this interpretation is reflected in the vast majority of English translations. The ESV is a case in point: "Every *other* sin a person commits is outside the body, but the sexually immoral person sins against his own body."[20] Adding "other" to the translation suggests

---

ment, §335, §336, 172). See also Buist M. Fanning, "Approaches to Verbal Aspect," in *Biblical Greek Language and Linguistics*, ed. Stanley E. Porter and D. A. Carson (Sheffield, UK: JSOT Press, 1993), 55.
[20] There are several major translations that insert the word "other": ESV, NAB, NASB, NIV, NJB, NLT, RSV, TNIV.

that sexual immorality is a special kind of transgression. Only sexual immorality constitutes a "sin against the body." Every *other* sin is "apart from the body."[21] Even though this interpretation is a popular one, it is beset by one insurmountable difficulty. There is no word or phrase in the Greek text that corresponds to the word "other." There is absolutely no exegetical justification for adding the word "other" to the translation except that commentators have difficulty explaining the meaning of the verse without it.[22] We are on much firmer exegetical ground to drop "other" and to go with Paul's own words.[23]

Once "other" is removed, the key to interpreting this verse is to understand that we are dealing with another Corinthian slogan. It is not Paul but the Corinthians who argue that "every sin" is committed "outside of the body." With this slogan, the Corinthians contend that the physical body is morally insignificant and cannot be used as an instrument of sin.[24] The Corinthians apparently believed that sin was "apart from the body" in the sense that

---

[21] See, for instance, Will Deming, who hypothesizes the ideological roots of such a position: "Paul's contention that *porneia* is not like other sins may reflect the Stoic dispute over the equality of sins. . . . Paul, like some Stoics, may be arguing that all sins are not equal." Will Deming, "The Unity of 1 Corinthians 5–6," *Journal of Biblical Literature* 115 (1996): 304n55.

[22] Gordon Fee attempts to defend adding "other," saying that, "the *de* ('but') is exceptive, qualifying 'every sin' to mean 'every other sin' except the one spoken of in this clause" (Fee, *First Epistle to the Corinthians*, 262). Yet I have surveyed all the major grammars for information about the so-called exceptive use of δέ, and I have yet to find any who speak of it. Most of the grammars simply confirm the usage outlined in BDAG: "One of the most common Gk. particles, used to connect one clause to another, either to express *contrast* or simple *continuation*" (BDAG, "δέ," 213, italics mine). Fee may be following Robert Gundry's "exceptive contrast" interpretation of δέ (Robert H. Gundry, *Sōma in Biblical Theology*, 73–74). This is picked up by other writers such as Bruce Fisk, "PORNEUEIN as Body Violation: The Unique Nature of Sexual Sin in 1 Corinthians 6:18," *New Testament Studies* 42, no. 4 (1996): 544. Fisk appeals to BDF §480 (1) and §306 (5) to support the interpretation that ἄλλος has been omitted by ellipsis and that "other" should be added (ibid., 544n8). Thus Fisk argues that the omission is a "specifically Greek" idiom and "syntactically predictable," leaving no grounds for taking 1 Corinthians 6:18 as anything other than Paul's words (ibid.). Whatever one thinks about the possibility of an elliptical "other" in other New Testament contexts, J. William Johnston has completely overturned the possibility of that interpretation for 1 Corinthians 6:18. Johnston's massive study of πᾶς in the New Testament has shown that there can be no "exceptions" implied in 1 Corinthians 6:18. See J. William Johnston, *The Use of PAS in the New Testament*, Studies in Biblical Greek 11 (New York: Peter Lang, 2004), 148–57. Johnston writes, "To imply 'other' calls for a reading of πᾶς in 1 Cor 6:18b in the summative rather than implicative sense. The syntax of the present passage suggests a distributive sense with implicative scope" (ibid., 152). Or to put it in layman's terms, in 1 Corinthians 6:18 "all" means "all without exception."

[23] If Paul intended "other" to be understood, then we are forced to agree with Richard Hays that Paul is using language imprecisely. See Richard Hays, *First Corinthians*, 105.

[24] This reading is confirmed when we compare the phrase ἐκτὸς τοῦ σώματος to Paul's use of the same phrase in 2 Corinthians 12:2, where it is likely that ἐκτὸς τοῦ σώματος is synonymous with the phrase χωρὶς τοῦ σώματος ("apart from the body") in the following verse.

the physical body is morally irrelevant in the divine reckoning of things. As Jerome Murphy-O'Connor has so aptly put it, "This is not to say that the Corinthians denied the possibility of sin. Sin was possible but only on the level of motive and intention, and they refused to concede that these could be evaluated on the basis of the actions in which they were embodied. Hence, 'every sin which a man may commit is outside the body.'"[25]

Paul's answer to this slogan is direct: "But the one who commits immorality sins against[26] his own body." In other words, the Corinthians are wrong about the moral value of the physical body. The body does matter both now and in the age to come. Verse 14 has already shown how the resurrection makes the body matter for the age to come, but verse 19 shows why the body is morally relevant in the present as well. The reason is that the body is a temple of the Holy Spirit. "Or do you not know that your body is a temple of the Holy Spirit who is in you, whom you have from God, and [do you not know] that you are not your own?" Paul argues that because the Holy Spirit resides within the temple of the believer's body, the body matters in the present age. It has been marked out and set aside for God's purposes through the indwelling Spirit of Christ. Thus the Christian is not his own and has relinquished all claims to ownership over his body.

On what basis does Paul say that the Corinthians have renounced ownership of their bodies? On the basis of Christ's work on the cross. Verse 20 reads, "For you were bought with a price.[27] Therefore, glorify God with your body" (AT). Paul reminds the Corinthians that they do not own themselves. God owns them because he bought them at the cost of his Son. And God's Spirit dwells in the Corinthians as a guarantee of final redemption. As Paul has argued elsewhere, the presence of the indwelling Spirit is the ground

---

[25] Jerome Murphy-O'Connor, *1 Corinthians*, 51.

[26] εἰς can be taken one of three ways here: (1) as a marker of instrumentality, "by" or "with"; (2) as a marker of a specific point of reference, "for," "to," "with respect to," "with reference to"; or (3) as referring to actions or feelings directed in someone's direction in a friendly or hostile sense, "for," or "against" (BDAG, "εἰς," 290–91). However one takes it, the important thing to remember is that the *body* is indeed involved in the sin of sexual immorality, contrary to what the Corinthians held.

[27] τιμή refers to the amount at which something is valued, "price, value" (BDAG, "τιμή," 1005).

of the believers' hope that God will resurrect the body.[28] Therefore, Paul concludes with the emphatic imperative, "Therefore,[29] glorify God with your body." In context, *body* is a metonymy for the use of the body for sex.[30] In essence, Paul calls on the Corinthians to glorify God with their sex. For Paul, the only way to glorify God with sex is to enjoy it within the covenanted union of one man and one woman in marriage. Paul regards all other arrangements as immorality and as a dishonor to God.

After Paul has dealt with all the rationalizations of the Corinthians, his entire ethical exhortation to this congregation is summed up in one phrase: "Glorify God with your body." Yes, Paul forbids fornicating with prostitutes. Yes, Paul demolishes libertinism. Yes, Paul sets forth Genesis 2:24 as the model for sexual expression. But all of those exhortations are subordinate to the final one: "Glorify God with your body." The ethical error of the Corinthian Christians was that they were asking the wrong question. The ultimate ethical question concerning sexuality is not, "Is it lawful?" The final question is, "What must I do to glorify God?"

The Meaning of Sex

In 1 Corinthians 6:12–20 the apostle Paul offers us a model for recognizing and confronting ethical aberrations, and we will carry that model forward in the rest of this book. First, Paul identifies both the sinful deed and the theology/worldview that underlies it. Paul could have simply laid down the law. He could have written to the Corinthians and simply told them to stop fornicating with prostitutes. But Paul's ethical concern was more expansive than

---

[28] Rom. 8:11: "But if the Spirit of Him who raised Jesus from the dead dwells in you, He who raised Christ Jesus from the dead will also give life to your mortal bodies through His Spirit who dwells in you."

[29] δή is a marker that invites attention to what is being said. With exhortations or commands, it gives a sense of greater urgency, "now," "then," "therefore" (BDAG, "δή,"222).

[30] See David Crystal's definition of metonymy: "A figure of speech in which the name of an attribute of an entity is used in place of the entity itself." See David Crystal, *A Dictionary of Language*, 2nd ed. (Chicago: University of Chicago Press, 2001), 216. Note also Bussmann's description of the figure: "The replacement of an expression by a factually related term. The semantic connection is of a causal, spatial, or temporal nature and is therefore broader than synecdoche, but narrower than metaphor." See Hadumod Bussmann, *Routledge Dictionary of Language and Linguistics*, trans. Gregory Trauth and Kerstin Kazzazi (London: Routledge, 1996), 305.

that. He was interested not only in the deeds of the Corinthians but also in the theology that underlies those deeds. There was a worldview in play that cut against the gospel, and Paul sought to identify the deficiencies of that worldview for his readers.

Second, Paul recognizes that sexual holiness involves physical bodies. Paul understood the moral consequence of the body in the overall order of God's creation. Human beings cannot be platonically divided into soul and spirit such that the gospel relates mainly to the one and not to the other. For Paul, being human means being embodied, and God's plan for redemption involves the whole person, not just the soul. That is why he prays elsewhere, "May the God of peace Himself sanctify you entirely; and may your spirit and soul and body be preserved complete, without blame at the coming of our Lord Jesus Christ" (1 Thess. 5:23). Sexual holiness is not merely a state of mind but also a matter of the body. God intends the body to be his temple—a place where his glory is uniquely set on display. Biblical sexual ethics, therefore, will account for human actions as they are carried out in male and female bodies. God created human beings with bodily characteristics that define them as male and female, and this fact must be figured into our calculation of God's purpose for human sexuality.

Third, Paul counters Corinthian error with teleological focus on the glory of God. The main point of 1 Corinthians 6:12–20 is summed up in the command in verse 20, "Glorify God with your body." Paul's ethical instruction might have been delivered in the form of commands or principles only. But Paul does more than that in this text. He points his readers to the purpose of the commands—the glory of God.

Fourth, Paul's teleology is constrained by Scripture and the gospel. We have seen that Paul was not the only one with a teleological understanding of the body. The Corinthians had a teleology as well. They observed the sexual complementarity of male and female bodies and construed from that observation that sex was the purpose of the body. They wrongly concluded that frequent trysts with prostitutes are a legitimate way to use the body according to its purpose. They concluded that just as food is made for stomachs, so male and female bodies are made for sex. Here we see the limitations of applying reason to natural revelation. The fallen mind does not always make the correct ethical judgments based on observation of nature alone. Certainly this was the case with the Corinthians. That is why teleology and reason are ultimately subject to the witness of Scripture. Paul does not refute the obvious sexual complementarity of male and female bodies. Rather, he quotes from Genesis 2:24 to show that promiscuity is not a part of God's design for sex. He also argues on the basis of the gospel that the body is not for immorality but for the Lord Jesus who promises to raise and renew physical bodies. Paul does this by quoting Scripture (Gen. 2:24). He also does it by reasserting the gospel truth that just as Jesus has been raised from the dead so also will he raise up believers to blessedness (1 Cor. 6:14).

So Paul's teleology is constrained by his understanding of Scripture. Paul understands God's purposes for the body not merely by observing nature but also by understanding the gospel and biblical revelation. In other words, Paul recognizes the authority of the Bible and the teaching of the apostles. The gospel of Jesus Christ and the written revelation of God dictated his theological reflection. I argue that the same should be true of us. The old-covenant word and the authoritative apostolic revelation are preserved for us in the pages of the Old and New Testaments. Their witness should have a decisive influence on the ethical judgments that we make. But what are we to do when the authority of that scriptural word is challenged? In the next chapter, we will take a look at one challenge that has appeared quite frequently in connection with Christian sexual ethics.

The chief excellency of an expounder consists in *lucid brevity*. And, indeed, since it is almost his only work to lay open the mind of the writer whom he undertakes to explain, the degree in which he leads away his readers from it, in that degree he goes astray from his purpose, and in a manner wanders from his own boundaries.

—John Calvin, Introduction, *Commentary on Romans*

2

Glorify God with Your Hermeneutic

There is hardly anything more exciting in the world of pro wrestling than a cage match. These farcical spectacles offer the kind of contest that every red-blooded American male longs to see. The contests are generally fought in steel cages that completely cover the wrestling ring. Cage matches can have a number of different formats, but in one version, contestants are enclosed within the ring, and nobody goes in or out until there is a winner. It is high drama. One wrestler may decide that he has had enough and attempt to get out of the ring, but he can't. He's trapped in the ring for better or for worse. If he wants out, he has to win or be beaten.

The Cage-Match Hermeneutic

Perhaps the cage match sounds like an odd analogy for a hermeneutical point, but I think the comparison is apt. Why? Hermeneutics is the study of the principles and procedures of interpreting texts. Our hermeneutic defines the proper way for reading. Not all hermeneutical approaches are equal, and some positively contradict one another. Cage matches have a couple of features that are relevant to our hermeneutical inquiry. In some versions of the cage match, (1) the contestants are made to fight even if one or both of them decide they don't want to fight anymore, and (2) the entire confrontation is staged. In other words in spite of appearances, the fight is a fake one. The two contestants are put into the arena by other interests, and the personal conflict between them is a reflection more of those writing the script than of any real animosity between the two men.

There is an approach to reading the New Testament today that very much resembles a cage match. The two contestants are Jesus and Paul. They are put into a hermeneutical cage in which they are made to fight until one or the other says "uncle." In this approach to reading the New Testament, Jesus and Paul are fundamentally at odds over a variety of ethical issues, and only one vision can emerge victorious in the end. Will Paul and his war-loving, death penalty–supporting, patriarchal vision win out? Or will Jesus and his peace-loving, enemy-forgiving, egalitarian vision win out? It's the red letters versus the black letters. Who will win? It is no surprise that those who stage Jesus-versus-Paul cage matches arrange it in such a way that the Bible's red letters are more important than the black ones. After all, when was the last time you saw a "WWPD" bracelet? When was the last time you heard of a theopolitical activist group called "The Black Letter Christians"? Answer: never, and that is because the red-letter hermeneutic appeals to the piety of Christian readers and their wish to render all honor and deference to Jesus, the sinless Son of God. He alone is the proper focus of Christian worship, so of course his opinions are weightier than any person who has ever lived—including the opinions of Paul, the chief of sinners. Thus in the Jesus-versus-Paul cage match, Jesus always wins.

My aim in this chapter is twofold: (1) I want us to take a critical look at several expressions of the cage-match approach, and (2) I want to set forth briefly a better way of reading the Bible—one that coheres with the internal witness of Scripture and that sees every word of the New Testament as an authoritative word from Jesus. A closer look at the biblical evidence will show that Jesus, Paul, and the other authors of Scripture will not be goaded into a cage match. For all the diversity we might observe among the

New Testament authors, Jesus and Paul are not at odds. And a God-glorifying hermeneutic is one that discerns an underlying theological unity among the various witnesses of Scripture.

A Critical Look at the Cage-Match Hermeneutic

The alleged antipathy between Jesus and Paul is not merely the opinion of critical New Testament scholars. This hermeneutical approach has both scholarly and popular expressions. I am not going to attempt to give a comprehensive account of those who follow this approach or to outline the history of this way of reading the New Testament. The examples that follow are fairly contemporary, and some of them emanate from personalities associated with the evangelical movement. I will begin with a few popular examples before turning to published versions of the cage match from scholars of the Bible.

Example 1: Slate *Magazine*

In a 2012 article for *Slate* online, Will Oremus asked a provocative question: Was Jesus a homophobe? The article was occasioned by a story about a gay teenager in Ohio who was suing his high school after school officials prohibited him from wearing a T-shirt that said, "Jesus Is Not a Homophobe." Oremus was less concerned about the legal issues of the story than he was about the accuracy of the statement on the shirt. Oremus suggests that Jesus's views on homosexuality were more inclusive than Paul's. He writes,

> While it's reasonable to assume that Jesus and his fellow Jews in first-century Palestine would have disapproved of gay sex, there is no record of his ever having mentioned homosexuality, let alone expressed particular revulsion about it. . . . Never in the Bible does Jesus himself offer an explicit prohibition of homosexuality.[1]

---

[1] Will Oremus, "Wait, Was Jesus a Homophobe? What about All the Other People in Galilee?," *Slate* (April 9, 2012), http://www.slate.com/articles/news_and_politics/explainer/2012/04/was_jesus _a_homophobe_how_jews_and_early_christians_felt_about_homosexuality_.html.

Oremus seems to suggest that since Jesus never explicitly mentioned homosexuality, he must not have been very concerned about it. There are at least two reasons that we should be skeptical of this view.

First, there are many ethical issues about which Jesus made no explicit statement. That observation hardly means that his moral vision has no relevance to those issues. Jesus never said anything explicit about abortion, same-sex marriage, or child molestation. But it would be an incredible claim to conclude from that fact that Jesus's teaching is irrelevant to our ethical assessment of those issues. Second, Jesus did speak explicitly about sexual immorality in general and the nature of marriage. He denounced the former (e.g., Matt. 5:28; 15:19) and defined the latter according to Genesis 2:24: "For this cause a man shall leave his father and mother, and shall cleave to his wife; and the two shall become one flesh" (Matt. 19:5 AT; par. Mark 10:7–8). Jesus affirmed the covenanted union of one man and one woman as the only normative expression of human sexuality. It is incredible to suggest that these words from Jesus have no bearing on the question of homosexuality. They surely do.

So Oremus has misconstrued the relevance of Jesus's teaching to the homosexual question. Nevertheless, he goes on to contrast Jesus's attitude with that of the apostle Paul. He writes:

> Even if Jesus viewed homosexuality as a sin, he had a penchant for reaching out to sinners rather than shunning them. . . . Not all of Jesus' followers took such a tender view, however. In Romans 1, Paul denounced gay sex as unnatural—an egregious example of pagan decadence—and said it would bring the wrath of God.[2]

Here is another iteration of the cage match. On the one side are Jesus and his inclusion of homosexuals. On the other side are Paul and his exclusion of the same. Whereas Jesus was all love and tolerance, Paul was about "wrath" and intolerance. And so the slogan

---

[2] Ibid.

from the T-shirt appears to be vindicated. Despite the hang-ups of people like Paul, Jesus was not a homophobe.

Example 2: Candidate Barack Obama

In March of 2008 when then-candidate Barack Obama was running for president, he ran on the guarantee that he personally opposed same-sex marriage but that he supported civil unions for same-sex couples. Although he favored marriage as the union of one man and one woman, he believed that all the legal benefits of marriage should be allowed to same-sex couples. Candidate Obama based the rationale for his position in part on his interpretation of the New Testament. He argued that Jesus's Sermon on the Mount supports gay civil unions. In his own words,

> I believe in civil unions that allow a same-sex couple to visit each other in a hospital or transfer property to each other. . . . I don't think it should be called marriage, but I think that it is a legal right that they should have that is recognized by the state. If people find that controversial, then I would just refer them to the Sermon on the Mount, which I think is, in my mind, for my faith, more central than an obscure passage in Romans. That's my view. But we can have a respectful disagreement on that.[3]

For our purposes, I am not so much interested in scrutinizing the politics of this statement as I am the hermeneutical basis for it. Notice what candidate Obama has done here. He implies that Jesus's words conflict with Paul's words in both *clarity* and *priority*. In terms of clarity, he is suggesting that the apostle Paul's condemnation of homosexual acts in Romans 1 is less than transparent. In terms of the priority, he says that Paul's words—whatever they are—have to give way to Jesus's words in the Sermon on the Mount (Matthew 5–7), as if the two were somehow contradictory. Candidate Obama called Jesus's Sermon on the Mount "more central" and labeled Paul's words to the Romans as "obscure." Therein is

---

[3] Michael Foust, "Obama: Sermon on the Mount Supports Gay Civil Unions," *Baptist Press* (March 3, 2008), http://www.bpnews.net/bpnews.asp?id=27532.

the cage match. Paul and Jesus go in for the contest, and of course Jesus wins.

Two brief responses: obviously, the interpretation of Romans 1:26–27 has been fiercely contested in recent years. But I think candidate Obama was mistaken to conclude from that fact that the passage *itself* is somehow opaque. In chapter 7, we will see that the fact that the interpretation of Romans 1 is contested does not necessarily mean that the text itself is unclear.[4] Revisionist interpretations of Romans 1:26–27 are a relatively recent phenomenon and are at odds with every interpretation of this text prior to the middle of the twentieth century. If one allows the democracy of the dead to have their say (as Chesterton had it), the "obscure" interpretations are the ones coming from late modern biblical scholars who are standing against two thousand years of the history of interpretation of this passage.

What these two popular exchanges show (among other things) is that ideas have consequences. In particular, hermeneutical approaches have real-world consequences for the way that people appropriate the ethical content of Scripture. This way of reading the Bible did not originate with *Slate* magazine or President Obama. Mainline churches and theological schools have been urging this way of interpretation for many years. After all, they claim, this cage match hermeneutic is the only proper way to read a human document such as the New Testament, which is nothing more than a collection of writings representing a variety of religious perspectives that often contradict one another. Once you see the fundamental disunity of the Bible, all that is left for the reader is to choose a side. But is this not the very factionalism that Paul warned against when the Corinthians were dividing themselves according to their devotion to different teachers? "'I am of Paul,' and 'I am of Apollos,' and 'I am of Cephas,' and 'I am of Christ'"

---

[4] Denny Burk, "Why Evangelicals Should Not Heed Brian McLaren: How the New Testament Requires Evangelicals to Render a Judgment on the Moral Status of Homosexuality," *Themelios* 35, no. 2 (2010): 212–26. "The exegetical discussion has been voluminous and wide-ranging for several decades with arguments for both the revisionist view and traditional view. But the fact that it is contested does not necessarily mean that the New Testament itself is unclear."

(1 Cor. 1:12). The "I am of Christ" faction was the original red-letter Christian movement, and they claimed that the "Christ" tribe takes precedence over the "Paul" tribe.[5] So if you are going to be a partisan, by all means be a Jesus partisan.

Example 3: Tony Campolo

Tony Campolo is a sociologist and emeritus professor at Eastern University. He is a popularizer and a leading voice associated with the progressive wing of evangelicalism. He is also the founder of a group called "The Red Letter Christians." RedLetterChristians.org is a website that features a group of like-minded writers and speakers such as Jim Wallis, Shane Claiborne, Brian McLaren, Tony Jones, Peter Rollins, and many others. Tony Campolo has written a book in which he outlines the core values of red-letter Christians. The book is titled *Red Letter Christians: A Citizen's Guide to Faith and Politics*, and in it Campolo argues that red-letter Christians have three characteristics. (1) They have a theological core rooted in the Apostles' Creed. (2) They have a very high view of Scripture, especially of the words of Jesus. (3) They believe in the immanence of the historical Jesus in every single believer. Campolo writes,

> We emphasize the "red letters" because we believe that you can only understand the rest of the Bible when you read it from the perspective provided by Christ. . . . What differentiates Red Letter Christians from other Christians is our passionate commitment to social justice—hence, our intense involvement in politics. This involvement sometimes makes us controversial.[6]

As you can see, Campolo argues that red-letter Christians give hermeneutical priority to the words of Jesus in the formation of ethical norms. For this group, the red letters are a canon within the canon, and the Sermon on the Mount is a canon within a canon within the canon.

---

[5] So Richard B. Hays, *First Corinthians*, Interpretation (Louisville, KY: Westminster, 1997), 22–23.
[6] Tony Campolo, *Red Letter Christians: A Citizen's Guide to Faith and Politics* (Ventura, CA: Regal, 2008).

There is much to critique in Campolo's statement, but I would highlight one significant difficulty with his approach. Campolo says that "you can only understand the rest of the Bible when you read it from the perspective provided by Christ." Notice that there are two parts to the canon of Scripture in this formulation: (1) Christ's perspective in the red letters and (2) the rest of the Bible in the black letters. Christ's "perspective" in the red letters should become the hermeneutical control over how we read the black letters. This approach lends itself to the suppression of black-letter texts that seem to differ from the emphases of Jesus in the Sermon on the Mount. This red-letter approach provides a hermeneutical support for Christian pacifists who allow the black letters of Romans 13:1–7 to give way to the red letters of Matthew 5–7.

The main problem with this perspective, however, is that it undermines the "high view of Scripture" that the Red Letter Christians otherwise claim to uphold. Is it really true that Christ's "perspective" resides only or even chiefly in the red letters? As we shall see below, the apostolic authors of Scripture would not have accepted such a distinction. To be sure, they understood the difference between their own words and words that derived from the chain of oral tradition rooted in the sayings of Jesus. But that does not mean that Paul and the apostles thought their words to be in tension with Jesus's teaching. They believed that Jesus's perspective appeared in the apostolic black letters. It is after all "the Spirit of Christ" that enervated the prophetic word (1 Pet. 1:11), and it is the same Spirit that influenced the writers of Scripture to write what they did (2 Pet. 1:19). This means that the black letters were inspired by the spirit of Christ himself. To treat the black letters as anything other than Christ's perspective involves an implicit denial of the plenary inspiration of Scripture. I do not mean to allege that Campolo denies plenary inspiration. Nevertheless, that does appear to be the logical entailment of a view that says Christ's "perspective" can be found only in the red letters.

Example 4: A. N. Wilson

F. C. Baur stands at the head of generations of New Testament scholars who have in one way or another assumed a basic discontinuity between the teachings of Jesus and of Paul.[7] According to Baur, a great theological divide marked the earliest generation of the Christian church. Baur emphasized the differences he saw between Paul on the one hand and the Jerusalem apostles and Palestinian churches on the other. According to Baur's reconstruction, the Jerusalem community was more influenced by the original teaching of Jesus, and Paul was consciously independent of such traditions. In 1904 William Wrede expanded this thesis by proposing that Paul's conversion was a result of an encounter with the risen Christ, not the earthly Jesus, thus,

> Paul is to be regarded as *the second founder of Christianity.* . . . This second founder of Christianity has even, compared with the first, exercised beyond all doubt the stronger—not the better—influence. . . . Throughout long stretches of church history . . . [Paul] has thrust that greater person [Jesus], whom he meant only to serve, utterly into the background.[8]

In 1912, Wilhelm Heitmüller suggested that Paul's apparent disregard for the words and deeds of Jesus was a result of the influence of the Hellenistic Christian circles in which Paul was immersed. Most subsequent scholars who have maintained this line of thought take "it as axiomatic that the real Jesus was the Jesus of liberal theology, who preached simple but profound moral truths," not the lofty Hellenistic speculations found in Paul.[9] Rudolf Bultmann concurs: "When the essentially Pauline conceptions are considered, it is clear that there Paul is not dependent on Jesus. Jesus's teaching is—to all intents and purposes—irrelevant for Paul."[10] To this

---

[7] J. M. G. Barclay, "Jesus and Paul," in *Dictionary of Paul and His Letters*, ed. Gerald F. Hawthorne, Ralph P. Martin, and Daniel G. Reid (Downers Grove, IL: InterVarsity, 1993), 492 passim.

[8] William Wrede, *Paul*, trans. Edward Lummis (London: Philip Green, 1907).

[9] Barclay, "Jesus and Paul," 494.

[10] Rudolf Bultmann, *Faith and Understanding*, ed. Robert W. Funk, trans. Louise Pettibone Smith (New York: Harper and Row, 1969), 223.

day, this discussion provokes controversy among New Testament scholars as dispute continues over Paul's legitimacy as a bearer of tradition and as an apostolic witness to Jesus's life and teaching.

And that brings us to A. N. Wilson, who is but one more recent example of this older critical view that posits a basic theological disjunction between the apostle Paul and the historical Jesus. For Wilson, Paul's understanding of Christ was shaped more by pagan religion in Tarsus than by the Old Testament. Paul's interface in Tarsus with the cult of Mithras and the worship of the divine Herakles had a decisive influence on his "mythologized" interpretation of the cross.[11] The result of this interface was a distortion of the real Jesus of history. In his 1997 book *Paul: The Mind of the Apostle*, Wilson writes:

> The historicity of Jesus became unimportant from the moment Paul had his apocalypse. . . .
> The sayings of Jesus can shock us but they can scarcely represent a cohesive oral framework on which we can base our lives. The religion of Paul, by contrast, wild, ecstatic and confused as it must often appear . . . contains all the makings of a religion with universal appeal.[12]

I bring up Wilson's work because N. T. Wright made Wilson's book a focus of chapter 10 of his popular 1997 book on Paul, *What Saint Paul Really Said: Was Paul of Tarsus the Real Founder of Christianity?* Wright has a thorough critique of Wilson's book in that chapter, and one passage from Wright's remarks is worth highlighting here. Wright says,

> It is never completely clear whether Wilson likes Paul or dislikes him, whether he is commending him to us or warning us against him. Does he approve of Paul (with major reservations), or disapprove of him (with minor concessions)? Is he blaming Paul for muddling up the message of Jesus, or is he commending him for

---

[11] So N. T. Wright, *What Saint Paul Really Said: Was Paul of Tarsus the Real Founder of Christianity?* (Grand Rapids, MI: Eerdmans, 1997).
[12] A. N. Wilson, *Paul: The Mind of the Apostle* (London: Sinclair-Stevenson, 1997), 73, 239.

making it available to a wider audience? . . . Is he damning Paul
with faint praise, or praising him with faint damns?[13]

It is important to note that underlying most of the cage
matches from Baur to Wilson and beyond is the assumption that
the historical Jesus is something to be extracted from the canonical
Gospels, not something that can be identified with the witnesses
themselves. In much of this work, it is the Jesus behind the text
that is sought, not the Jesus of the text. And so the old antipathy
between the Christ of history and the Christ of faith lives on. In
this approach, the red letters themselves are still in contention,
and perhaps far fewer of them should be colored red than our
English translations would have us to believe.

But not everyone who pits the red letters against the black
letters takes such a skeptical view of the Gospel witnesses. Indeed
there are some who are much closer to the evangelical movement
and who have a high view of Scripture, but who nevertheless adopt
hermeneutical approaches that tend toward the cage-match mentality. And that brings me to my final two examples, who are both
working specifically in the area of New Testament ethics.

Example 5: Ben Witherington

Ben Witherington began a massive project with the publication
in 2009 of volume 1 of his series *The Indelible Image: The Theological
and Ethical Thought World of the New Testament*.[14] Witherington argues
that understanding the New Testament thought world must "begin
with and focus on Jesus, his words and deeds, his life and death
and resurrection—the whole package, all that we can reasonably
know."[15] In other words, the starting point for doing New Testament ethics begins with understanding the historical Jesus. Unlike
the scholars in the previous section, however, Witherington is not

---

[13] Wright, *What Saint Paul Really Said*.

[14] Ben Witherington III, *The Indelible Image: The Theological and Ethical Thought World of the New Testament*, vol. 1: *The Individual Witnesses* (Downers Grove, IL: IVP Academic, 2009).

[15] Ben Witherington III, *The Indelible Image: The Theological and Ethical Thought World of the New Testament*, vol. 2: *The Collective Witness* (Downers Grove, IL: IVP Academic, 2010).

skeptical about the canonical witness of the New Testament. He chaffs against James Dunn's work *Jesus Remembered* and anyone else who would suggest that all we have is a "mediated" Jesus and that "we have no direct access to Jesus."[16] He argues that the distance between the historical Jesus and the Jesus of the Gospels is almost nil. He writes:

> It is my view that we do indeed have eyewitness testimony, directly in the Fourth Gospel and indirectly in the other three. The chain of tradition between Jesus and the Gospel writers involved not many links, but only two or three—Jesus to the eyewitnesses to the gospel writers.[17]

Witherington goes on to reference his own book *What Have They Done with Jesus?* and Richard Bauckham's work *Jesus and the Eyewitnesses* and says, "The upshot of these two monographs is that all these Gospels are written by persons who are in touch with the eyewitnesses, if they themselves are not eyewitnesses."[18] All of this leads to the conclusion that Jesus was the decisive influence in the formation of Christianity. Witherington writes: "It is Jesus who was the source, the catalyst, and the basis for the subsequent phenomena that we call 'Christianity.' The credit should not be laid at the doorstep of Paul."[19] Because the gospel traditions comprise eyewitness testimony, we can have a high degree of confidence in their historical reliability. Witherington writes: "The historical Jesus is indeed also the Christ of Christian faith, or, better said, he became the Christ of Christian faith . . . through his death and resurrection, both of which were historical events."[20]

One would think that, with his confidence in the historical reliability of the Gospel accounts, Witherington would take the canonical witnesses as his starting point for understanding the historical Jesus. But in fact, that is not his view. He still argues in

---

[16] Ibid., 66.
[17] Ibid.
[18] Ibid., 67.
[19] Ibid., 68.
[20] Ibid., 77.

favor of a critical reconstruction of the historical Jesus. He writes, "Once one takes into account a Gospel writer's larger editorial agendas, one can feel fairly confident about what goes back to Jesus himself, especially when we have traditions recorded in several Gospels that can be compared."[21]

In his watershed work on New Testament ethics, Richard Hays famously argued against such critical reconstructions of the historical Jesus and contended instead that the best basis for ethics is in the canonical form of the text, not in the scholar's peeling away of the traditional onion from the historical Jesus. In other words, Hays argues that the task of New Testament ethics is to exegete the canonical texts as we have received them from the original authors. The point is to understand the authors' meaning, not Jesus's meaning behind the authors'. Witherington disagrees explicitly with Hays, and it is here that his focus on the historical Jesus leads him into hermeneutical difficulty:

> Arguing that we should ignore Jesus' thought because he did not write any of the New Testament books is rather like arguing that we should ignore the teachings and actions of Elijah when it comes to Old Testament ethics and theology because he did not write any Old Testament book. *The issue is not who wrote what, especially in an oral culture; rather, the issue is influence and importance,* and clearly, when it comes to theological and ethical thought in the New Testament, there is no figure more influential than Jesus. . . . *[The Gospels] are mainly the means of conveying not the Gospel writers' own thoughts and deeds, but someone else's—Jesus'.*[22]

Pay careful attention to what Witherington has just said. The goal of interpretation is not to understand the authors' thoughts but Jesus's thoughts. Witherington elsewhere affirms authorial intent,[23] but in this section I believe he undermines the authorial intent of the Gospel writers by appealing to Jesus's "influence." Of course,

---

[21] Ibid., 127.
[22] Ibid., 127 (italics mine).
[23] Ibid., 42–43.

Jesus had influence on the Gospel writers, but tracking that influence is not the goal of interpretation. The goal of interpretation should be to discern and set forth what the author meant when he wrote.

Witherington is a careful exegete, and I am thankful that this statement of hermeneutical principle is not carried out consistently in his work. But that does not keep him from commending another New Testament scholar who does carry out this hermeneutical priority more consistently.[24] And that brings us to example number 6, Richard Burridge.

Example 6: Richard Burridge

In his 2007 work *Imitating Jesus: An Inclusive Approach to New Testament Ethics*, Richard Burridge advances a biographical approach to New Testament ethics that insists "on the priority of the person of Jesus of Nazareth."[25] He says:

> The key to understanding the New Testament has to be the person of Jesus, and that therefore he is the correct person and place with which to begin as well as to end. . . . The biographical genre of the canonical gospels redirects our gaze back to begin with the historical Jesus, and in particular to a stress upon both his deeds and his words.[26]

For Burridge, reconstructing the historical Jesus requires a critical approach, and he uses the usual criteria of authenticity, "such as dissimilarity, coherence and multiple attestation."[27] Indeed, at times his use of these criteria leads him to the conclusion that some of the canonical sayings of Jesus do not come from the historical Jesus but are the invention of later redactors.[28] In any case, Burridge

---

[24] Witherington, *Indelible Image*, 2009: "I am pleased and relieved to see that Richard Burridge . . . thinks not only that one must take into account the ethics of Jesus, but also that one must start with his ethics if one is to do justice to New Testament ethics."

[25] Richard A. Burridge, *Imitating Jesus: An Inclusive Approach to New Testament Ethics* (Grand Rapids, MI: Eerdmans, 2007), 4.

[26] Ibid.

[27] Ibid., 39.

[28] It is possible to do redaction criticism without positing a disjunction between the Jesus of the Gospels and the Jesus of history, but that is not what Burridge is proposing here; e.g., "Mat-

argues that the canonical words of Jesus reveal a tension between Jesus's rigorous moral demands and his inclusive approach to sinners. This tension colors his reading of Paul in some unhelpful ways and has a decisive impact on how he approaches the black letters of Scripture as a normative basis for ethics. Burridge writes, "We need to start with Jesus and to keep the focus on both his words and deeds, his teachings and his example; when we move on to the study of both Paul and the canonical gospels, again we will always start with Jesus."[29] What is the hermeneutical upshot of this observation? When Paul emphasizes an ethical command or prohibition that Jesus does not address, then we should cast a wary eye toward Paul. Even though Burridge's book is not primarily about sexual ethics, in this instance he applies this observation to the issue of homosexuality. He argues that since Jesus never explicitly addresses the topic of homosexuality, we should take Paul's prohibitions less seriously than we otherwise might. He writes,

> It is puzzling why being against homosexuality, about which Jesus and the gospels have nothing to say and Paul has only these passing references alongside many other sins equally common to heterosexuals, should have become the acid test of what it means to be truly "biblical" in a number of quarters over the years. . . . [Paul's] few references to homosexuality, which occur only in his repetition of a couple of his vice-lists, should also be read in this context, rather than singled out as a primary test for the Christian fellowship.[30]

When Burridge says that "Jesus and the gospels have nothing to say" about these issues, he echoes the objections that revision-

---

thew's qualification 'except for immorality,' μὴ ἐπὶ πορνείᾳ (Matt. 19.9, agreeing with the more conservative Jewish tradition as Rabbi Shammai did), is likely to be later redaction, while Mark's uncompromising refusal to accept any grounds for divorce is so distinctive from both contemporary Judaism and the practice of the early church (cf. Paul's exception to Jesus's prohibition in 1 Cor. 7:12–16) that it is extremely unlikely to go back to the authentic teaching of the historical Jesus (Mark 10.2–12)." Ibid., 56.

[29] Ibid., 30.

[30] Ibid., 129, 131. The two Pauline vice lists that include homosexuality are in 1 Corinthians 6 and 1 Timothy 1. Burridge's remarks suggest, therefore, that he does not include Romans 1 among Paul's references to homosexuality. If so, Burridge has adopted an interpretation that overlooks Paul's single most important text on this subject.

ists have raised for years. Their protest is that Jesus's silence on the issue shows that homosexuality was of little or no concern to the historical Jesus.[31] Burridge marginalizes the relevant Pauline texts by saying that "Paul's ethical comments . . . are more like 'work in progress' than being the considered, final moral word."[32] The upshot of Burridge's approach, therefore, is that all the ethical content of the Pauline witness is subjugated to the "inclusive" framework of Jesus's ethics. Thus when Paul disagrees with Jesus, guess who wins? Burridge writes, "Paul's ethical teaching must always be balanced by his appeal to the imitation of Christ—and this entails accepting others as we have been accepted."[33] So Burridge wants to use the Scripture, even as he adopts a methodology that undermines the authority of Pauline texts to guide our ethical thinking. Again, this amounts to another cage match between Jesus and Paul, and as usual the historical Jesus vanquishes Paul once more.

An Alternative to the Cage-Match Hermeneutic

What are we to make of these six examples? And are the hermeneutical approaches represented in them really the best way to find a normative basis for ethics from the New Testament? I think the answer to that question has to be no. In the final section of this chapter, I will argue that Jesus and Paul have never entered the hermeneutical ring as opponents competing against each other. From the canonical witnesses, it is clear that neither of them would ever have accepted such a contest. Jesus and Paul enter the ring not as cage-match contestants but as tag-team partners working together to demolish "speculations and every lofty thing raised up against the knowledge of God" and to take "every thought captive to the obedience of Christ" (2 Cor. 10:5). So I will

---

[31] Indeed, Robert Gagnon devotes a whole section of his watershed work to refuting this revisionist myth about Jesus. He argues, "Jesus was not silent about same-sex intercourse inasmuch as the inferential data speaks loud and clear about Jesus' perspective." Robert A. J. Gagnon, *The Bible and Homosexual Practice: Texts and Hermeneutics* (Nashville, TN: Abingdon, 2001).

[32] Burridge, *Imitating Jesus*, 130.

[33] Ibid., 154.

set forth three principles that inform my reading of the various witnesses of the New Testament.

Principle 1: A Focus on the Author's Meaning

Obviously, this is not a given in biblical scholarship today. The New Criticism has given way to a variety of reader-response approaches that effectively remove the biblical authors as the ground, guide, and goal of textual meaning. All you have to do is peruse the program for the annual meeting of the Society of Biblical Literature (SBL), and you will find that the different study groups represent the spectrum of hermeneutical approaches. Some of them have a focus on traditional exegesis and authorial intent. Others have very little concern for the author's role in generating textual meaning. As the editor of the *Journal for Biblical Manhood and Womanhood*, I usually make a point to attend the LGBT/Queer Hermeneutics section at the annual SBL meeting. At the 2010 meeting, I went to hear Joseph Marchal's paper, which was about how Christians ought to think and react to the phenomenon of intersex. He noted that intersexed people are often stigmatized and traumatized by surgical treatments performed on them when they are infants. He turned to the book of Galatians to see what this text might have to say about the genital mutilation that occurs in the treatment of intersex. Marchal argued that just as Paul disapproves of circumcision in Galatians, so we also ought to oppose surgical procedures on intersex people. In my view, this was a really facile treatment of the text. So in the question-and-answer time, I asked Marchal if he thought the apostle Paul would agree with his interpretation of Galatians. Marchal responded in very clear terms that he was not interested in agreeing or disagreeing with Paul but with how he might "use" Paul. He did not care about understanding Paul. He just wanted to co-opt Paul's language for his own ethical agenda. Paul might have been rolling over in his grave, but Marchal seemed not too concerned about that.[34]

---

[34] See especially pages 168ff. in the published version of this address. Joseph A. Marchal, "Bodies Bound for Circumcision and Baptism: An Intersex Critique and the Interpretation of Galatians," *Theology and Sexuality* 16, no. 2 (2010): 163–82.

Even though there is a sector of biblical scholarship that down-plays the role of the author, I argue that an evangelical approach to Scripture must let the author have his say. Without rehearsing all the well-worn arguments in favor of an author-centered approach, I will simply say that E. D. Hirsch and more recently Kevin Van-hoozer have given a solid theoretical basis for an author-centered hermeneutic.[35]

The failure to observe an author-centered approach is the methodological error at the heart of many who stage Jesus-versus-Paul cage matches. Both Burridge and Witherington attempt to reconstruct the words and deeds of the historical Jesus, and they are not the first to attempt this. The only problem with this approach is that Jesus is not the author of any New Testament book. We have no access to an unmediated Jesus. We have witnesses: Matthew, Mark, Luke, and John. In an author-centered approach, the relevant hermeneutical question is not ultimately, "What did Jesus do?" or "What did Jesus say?" The relevant question is, "Why did the authors of the Gospels tell us what Jesus did and said?" Consider, for example, Jesus's conversation with the rich young ruler in Matthew 19:16–22. Jesus ultimately tells the man:

> "If you wish to be complete, go and sell your possessions and give to the poor, and you will have treasure in heaven; and come, follow Me." But when the young man heard this statement, he went away grieving; for he was one who owned much property.

Some people interpret this passage to suggest that all disciples must give away all their possessions in order to follow Jesus. But that interpretation misses the point. The ultimate hermeneutical question is not what Jesus meant when he spoke to the rich young ruler. The ultimate hermeneutical question is, "Why does Matthew tell his readers about Jesus's radical instructions to the rich young ruler?" It is highly unlikely that Matthew intends for all his read-

---

[35] E. D. Hirsch Jr., *Validity in Interpretation* (New Haven, CT: Yale University Press, 1967); Kevin J. Vanhoozer, *Is There a Meaning in This Text?: The Bible, the Reader, and the Morality of Literary Knowledge* (Grand Rapids, MI: Zondervan, 1998).

ers to divest themselves of all their possessions. Jesus meant that for the rich young ruler, but Matthew probably did not mean that for his readers.

The bottom line is this: we have no unmediated access to Jesus's words and deeds. All of them have been preserved for us in the written witnesses of the Gospels. It is, therefore, incorrect to appeal to Jesus as if he were the author of the Gospel texts. An author-centered approach focuses not on the words of Jesus but on the words of the apostles whose witness has been inscripturated for us in the Bible.

Principle 2: A Focus on Apostolic Authority

Those who favor the cage-match approach to reading the New Testament imply that the canonical words of Scripture are hermeneutically subservient to the actual words and deeds of the historical Jesus. The problem with this approach is that there is a sidelining of apostolic authority and reliability that (ironically!) contradicts the red letters of Scripture. In fact, it was Jesus's own words to and about the apostles that guided the early church's recognition of the canon of Scripture. The first and most important characteristic of any book making a claim to canonical status was its apostolic connection. Early Christians held in high esteem those books that were deemed to be derived from an apostle—either directly from an apostle or from someone set forth by an apostle. Their assumption was that if you wanted to know the words and deeds of Jesus, you needed to get into the mind of his apostles. In other words, if you want to know Jesus, you must know his apostles. Where did early Christians get that expectation from? They got it in part from the red letters of Scripture.

Consider, for instance, how the words of Jesus from the Upper Room Discourse would have informed the expectations of John's readers. At this point in John's narrative, it was just Jesus and the eleven (Judas had already gone out to betray Jesus). Modern readers often mistake these words as a direct guarantee of the Holy

Spirit's work of illumination in every believer. But that is not what the Upper Room Discourse is about. These red letters are directed to the eleven specifically:

> But the Helper, the Holy Spirit, whom the Father will send in My name, He will teach you all things, and bring to your remembrance all that I said to you. (John 14:26)

> When the Helper comes, whom I will send to you from the Father, that is the Spirit of truth who proceeds from the Father, He will testify about Me, and you will testify also, because you have been with Me from the beginning. (John 15:26–27)

> But when He, the Spirit of truth, comes, He will guide you into all the truth; for He will not speak on His own initiative, but whatever He hears, He will speak; and He will disclose to you what is to come. (John 16:13)

Unfortunately, modern readers often read themselves into the pronouns of this passage: "He will teach *you* . . . bring to *your* remembrance. . . . He will guide *you* into all the truth. . . . He will disclose to *you*." But that is a mistake. This text is not about the Spirit's work of illumination in the lives of *you* the modern reader. The "you" in this passage is the eleven. And this is Jesus's guarantee to them, his witnesses, that he would lead *them* into all truth and would remind *them* about what he taught them. In other words, this passage confirmed for John's readers the expectation that Jesus's Spirit would speak in a unique way to the apostles. John's readers learned from the red letters that if they wanted truth and if they wanted to know about everything that Jesus did and taught, they would have to listen to the apostolic witnesses. They should not try to get behind the witnesses to reconstruct Jesus. They just needed to listen to the apostles.

John confirms this perspective again in his first epistle:

> What was from the beginning, what *we* have heard, what *we* have seen with *our* eyes, what *we* have looked at and touched with *our*

hands, concerning the Word of Life—and the life was manifested, and *we* have seen and testify and proclaim to you the eternal life, which was with the Father and was manifested to *us*—what *we* have seen and heard *we* proclaim to you also, that you too may have fellowship with *us*; and indeed *our* fellowship is with the Father, and with His Son Jesus Christ. (1 John 1:1–3)

The we's and the our's refer to the apostles—those who had seen with their own eyes, heard with their own ears, and touched with their own hands the resurrection of Jesus Christ. John says *we* have fellowship with the Father and with his son Jesus Christ. If you want to have fellowship with the Father and with Jesus Christ, you have to have fellowship with us: "*We* proclaim to you also, that you too may have fellowship with *us*." In essence, John communicates to his readers, "If you don't know us, then you don't know Jesus."

The most stark statement of this principle is found in 1 John 4:6, where John explains to his readers how to tell the difference between the Spirit of God and the spirit of antichrist:

We are from God; he who knows God listens to *us*; he who is not from God does not listen to *us*. By this we know the spirit of truth and the spirit of error. (1 John 4:6)

If you want to know truth, if you want to know the historical Jesus who came in the flesh, you must listen to his apostolic witnesses. If you refuse to listen to their portrait of Jesus, you are listening to the spirit of antichrist. This is John's expansion of what Jesus himself said in the Upper Room Discourse. And that is why the attempt to get behind the Gospels to reconstruct a so-called historical Jesus can quickly take on the spirit of anti-Christ. The spirit of Christ is saying, "Listen to my apostles."

At this point I can anticipate an objection from the red-letter Christian who is skeptical of my argument thus far: "That's all well and good for the eleven, but what about this chief-of-sinners guy, Paul? Why should we accord his words the same authority as the apostles?" The reason is that there are other red letters that

direct you to give the same deference to the black letters of Paul.
Consider the red letters that Luke gives us in Acts 9:15–16, when
Jesus appeared to Ananias in a vision and said this concerning Paul:

> Go, for [Paul] is a chosen instrument of Mine, to bear My name be-
> fore the Gentiles and kings and the sons of Israel; for I will show
> him how much he must suffer for My name's sake. (Acts 9:15–16)

Also, consider the red letters that Luke gives us in Acts 26:15–18
concerning Paul:

> And I said, "Who are You, Lord?" And the Lord said, "I am Jesus
> whom you are persecuting. "But get up, and stand on your feet;
> for this purpose I have appeared to *you*, to appoint *you* a *minister*
> and a *witness* not only to the things which *you* have seen, but also
> to the things in which I will appear to *you*; rescuing you from the
> Jewish people and from the Gentiles, to whom I am sending you,
> to open their eyes so that they may turn from darkness to light
> and from the dominion of Satan to God, that they may receive
> forgiveness of sins and an inheritance among those who have
> been sanctified by faith in Me.'"

Jesus gave a commission to Paul that was very similar to what he
gave the other apostles. Luke's readers would have understood the
apostolic authority that Jesus gave to Paul. My challenge to the
red-letter partisans is this: If Jesus in the red letters chose and appointed Paul to bear his name among the Gentiles, then who are
we to gainsay Jesus? Shouldn't red-letter Christians allow King
Jesus to select his own spokesmen? He has chosen to reveal his
words and deeds through apostolic witnesses, and he has directed
us to listen to the likes of Paul.

Another objection from the red-letter Christian often goes like
this: "Doesn't Paul himself make a distinction in 1 Corinthians 7
between his words and Jesus's words?" On the one hand, in 1 Corinthians 7:10, Paul does say, "To the married I give instructions, *not
I, but the Lord*, that the wife should not leave her husband." Here
Paul explicitly accesses the oral tradition of Jesus's words handed

down to him. On the other hand, in 1 Corinthians 7:12, Paul says, "To the rest *I say, not the Lord*, that if any brother has a wife who is an unbeliever . . . let him not send her away" (AT). Paul distinguishes his words from Jesus's. But Paul never would have accepted a view that says his words reflect his own perspective in contrast to Jesus's perspective. Paul is not contrasting his authority with Jesus's authority. He's contrasting the commands he has accessed directly from the chain of oral tradition from the commands that he himself is giving. That is why he says in 1 Corinthians 7:25, "Now concerning virgins I have no command of the Lord, but I give an opinion as one who by the mercy of the Lord is trustworthy." Paul viewed his own opinion as "trustworthy" and as emanating from "the mercy of the Lord" Jesus himself. Paul would have conceded no theological daylight between himself and Jesus. He was an apostle who spoke for Jesus, and that is why he is "trustworthy." That means that his canonical words bear the authority of Jesus himself.

Principle 3: A Focus on Inspiration

I understand that perhaps the vast majority of biblical scholars and theologians have an aversion to red-letter editions of the English Bible. The practice seems to imply a priority to portions of the text that never would have entered the minds of the original authors. Their objection goes like this: "If the original authors wrote only in black letters, then why introduce a bi-level printing convention in our translations? Does not that printing convention suggest that Jesus's words are somehow more inspired than the black letters?" On one level, I am sympathetic with that concern. But on another level I think this objection misses the point. If we are going to focus on the color of the letters, the problem is not that we have too many red letters in our Bibles but too few. If the New Testament is an apostolic word, and if the apostles are who Jesus said that they were, then all of the letters of the New Testament should be colored red.

It was not a generic spirit that inspired the words of Scripture. It was the Spirit of *Christ* that moved the authors to write what they wrote. Jesus described the Spirit this way in John 15:26: "When the Helper comes, whom I will send to you from the Father, . . . He will bear witness of Me" (AT). This is the Spirit that *Jesus sends* to inspire the apostolic witness. It is the same Spirit that inspired the Old Testament, and it is the same Spirit that Peter calls "the Spirit of Christ":

> As to this salvation, the prophets who prophesied of the grace that *would come* to you made careful searches and inquiries, seeking to know what person or time the Spirit of Christ within them was indicating as He predicted the sufferings of Christ and the glories to follow. (1 Pet. 1:10–11).

Paul too spoke of "the Christ who speaks in me" in 2 Corinthians 13:3. Clearly, Paul would have included his own Christ-inspired words among the red letters.

Conclusion

Those who stage hermeneutical cage matches between Paul and Jesus are staging a contest that neither Jesus nor Paul would ever have tolerated. The approach tends to undermine the New Testament's claim to be a normative basis for ethics by making the black letters subservient to the red letters. At the end of the day, this argument is not about the color of letters but about the nature of Scripture. Those who wish to establish biblical authority over the long haul will avoid the cage-match approach. And those who truly wish to be red-letter Christians will heed the words of Paul and the other apostolic authors of Scripture as the very words of Christ. My approach in this book assumes the canonical form of the Old and New Testaments as the ultimate authority not only in determining ethical norms but also in properly informing teleology. Before we can apply these insights to sexual ethics, we must begin with a definition of marriage. That is the subject of the next chapter.

The *ultimate* thing to see in the Bible about marriage is that it exists for God's glory. Most foundationally, marriage is the doing of God. Most ultimately, marriage is the display of God. It is designed by God to display his glory in a way that no other event or institution does.

—John Piper, *This Momentary Marriage*

Marriage, therefore, is a good in all the things which are proper to the married state. And these are three: it is the ordained means of procreation, it is the guarantee of chastity, it is the bond of union.

—Augustine, *On Original Sin*

3

Glorify God with Your Marriage

The apostle Paul says that the "mystery" of marriage is great, "but I'm speaking with reference to Christ and the church" (Eph. 5:32). By "mystery," Paul means that the meaning of marriage is something that was once hidden in the Old Testament but that now has been revealed in the gospel. The deepest meaning of marriage is that it is an enacted parable of another marriage—the marriage of Christ to his bride. Can anyone really know *that* definition of marriage apart from God's revelation of this mystery? Perhaps the world can know penultimate purposes of marriage (procreation, social order, etc.), but what can it know of the ultimate purpose of marriage apart from the specially revealed gospel of Jesus Christ? If marriage is a gospel mystery, the answer has to be very little. The best we can do with nonreligious arguments as to the nature of marriage is to convince some people of some of the penultimate purposes of marriage. But even there, those purposes may appear less and less evident to secular people who do not accept God's law and the revelation of his ultimate purpose for marriage.

At the end of the day, it is impossible to make ethical judgments about human sexual behavior without first establishing what the Bible says about marriage. Any sexual ethic is only as sound as it is biblical. The Bible presents marriage as the only permissible context for the expression of human sexuality. So the aim of this chapter is to establish a definition of marriage that is rooted in the text of Scripture and that can serve as a norm by which we might be able to evaluate sexual behavior.

How Does the Bible Define Marriage?

The most important New Testament statements on marriage come to us from the lips of Jesus in the Gospels and from the hand of Paul in his letters. One of the striking things about Jesus's and Paul's teaching on marriage is their manifest dependence upon the Old Testament. As I pointed out earlier, when Jesus and Paul appeal to the Old Testament to define marriage, they do not point to the polygamous kings of Israel as models—not even to King David, the man after God's own heart; nor even to Solomon, the wisest king who ever lived. Nor do they appeal to the polygamist patriarchs of Israel—Abraham, Isaac, and Jacob. As important as these figures (and their marriages!) are to the Old Testament narrative and to biblical theology, Jesus and Paul never look to any of them as paradigms for understanding marriage and sex.[1] Instead, Jesus and Paul look back without exception to the pre-fall monogamous union of Adam and Eve in Genesis 1–2 as the norm of human sexuality and marriage. "For this reason a man shall leave his father and his mother, and be joined to his wife; and they shall become one flesh" (Gen. 2:24). In Jesus's remarks on divorce, he also invokes Genesis 1:27, which says, "God created man in His own image, in the image of God He created him; male and female He created them." Why do Jesus and Paul appeal to the first marriage to explain the meaning of all marriages? The answer has something to do with the fact

---

[1] Someone might highlight 1 Pet. 3:6 as an exception to this rule: "Sarah obeyed Abraham, calling him lord, and you have become her children if you do what is right." Yet even here Peter cites a single instance from Sarah's life as an example of obedience (cf. Gen. 18:12). Peter does not invoke Abraham and Sarah's marriage comprehensively as the paradigm for all subsequent marriages.

that this first marriage between Adam and Eve occurred when everything was literally right with the world—before sin contaminated everything. There was no death, no strife, no pride, no lust, nor any other foxes ruining the vineyard of marriage (Song 2:15). All was well and just as God intended it to be—one man and one woman living in perfect harmony and fellowship with God and with each other. It was the one time in human history that God could look at people and say that they were "good" (Gen. 1:31). It was the only time in human history when there was a perfect marriage operating according to God's creational intent. The marriage of the pre-fall Adam and Eve thus becomes the ideal for all marriages to follow.

Both Jesus and Paul invoked Genesis 2:24 when there was a specific ethical aberration that they were dealing with. Jesus quoted from both Genesis 1:27 and 2:24 when answering questions about divorce (Matt 19:4–5; Mark 10:6–8). Paul referred to Genesis 2:24 when addressing men visiting prostitutes (1 Cor. 6:16) and spousal roles in marriage (Eph. 5:31). Paul also brought forth the wider context of Genesis 2:18–25 when addressing the issue of women in ministry (1 Cor. 11:8; 1 Tim. 2:13). In these statements, Jesus and Paul provide a model for our own ethical reflection. Like Jesus and Paul, we need to understand first how the Scriptures define marriage and its purpose. Then and only then will we have a proper basis for a sexual ethic.

If we are going to produce a Christian sexual ethic, we must do so in the way that Jesus and the apostles direct us. That means that we, too, must consider the creational ideal that is set before us in Genesis 1–2. We must understand what these texts are saying and how they are appropriated in the New Testament. Taken together, these texts teach us that marriage is the covenanted sexual union of one man and one woman that is patterned upon the union of Christ with his church. In short, God created marriage to be covenantal, sexual, procreative, heterosexual, monogamous, nonincestuous, and symbolic of the gospel.

Marriage Is a Covenantal Union

A covenantal understanding of marriage must be distinguished from other views on the nature of marriage. There are three basic points of view: (1) marriage as a sacrament, (2) marriage as a contract, and (3) marriage as a covenant.[2] The sacramental view of marriage has its roots in the Roman Catholic tradition, and it views marriage not merely as a "sign" of the gospel but as an "efficacious sign" that brings about what it signifies. Thus the grace of the gospel is conferred upon anyone who rightly participates in the sacrament of marriage under the auspices of the church. The *Catechism of the Catholic Church* describes it this way:

> The matrimonial covenant, by which a man and a woman establish between themselves a partnership of the whole of life, is by its nature ordered toward the good of the spouses and the procreation and education of offspring; this covenant between baptized persons has been raised by Christ the Lord to the dignity of a sacrament.[3]

Pope John Paul II reiterates this traditional Roman Catholic view in his work *Theology of the Body*. Reasoning from Ephesians 5:32, he argues, "Through marriage as a sacrament (as one of the sacraments of the Church), *both of these dimensions of love, the spousal and the redemptive*, penetrate together with the grace of the sacrament into the life of the spouses."[4] This view of marriage is rooted deeply within Roman Catholic sacramental theology. Its plausibility is directly related to one's overall ecclesiological position. As much as I appreciate the Roman Catholic Church's stalwart stance on marriage and sexuality, I register fundamental disagreement with them on this point. In spite of an historic misinterpreta-

---

[2]There are other views that might be mentioned here, but this presentation follows the main views as presented by Andreas J. Köstenberger and David W. Jones, *God, Marriage, and Family: Rebuilding the Biblical Foundation*, 2nd ed. (Wheaton, IL: Crossway, 2010), 69–79.

[3]Catechism of the Catholic Church, §1601. See Catholic Church, *Catechism of the Catholic Church: Revised in Accordance with the Official Latin Text Promulgated by Pope John Paul II*, 2nd ed. (Washington, DC: Libreria Editrice Vaticana, 2000), 400.

[4]John Paul II, *Man and Woman He Created Them: A Theology of the Body*, trans. Michael Waldstein (Boston: Pauline Books and Media, 2006), 527.

tion of Ephesians 5, the Scripture never portrays marriage as a sacrament.[5]

The contractual model is the "prevailing secular view of marriage in Western culture," according to Andreas Köstenberger.[6] In this view, marriage is a "bilateral contract that is voluntarily formed, maintained, and dissolved by two individuals."[7] This view roots marriage primarily in civil law, which provides the norms for forming and dissolving marriage contracts. This view of marriage also has little basis in the text of Scripture, much less in God's created order, and would accommodate a "variety of marital arrangements that the Scripture clearly prohibits." The contractual view should be discarded as incompatible with Christian teaching as well.[8]

The covenantal view of marriage has deep roots in the story line of Scripture. Although the Hebrew term for *covenant* (בְּרִית) does not appear in Genesis 1–2, there are ample indications that Adam and Eve's marriage was a covenant. Genesis 2:24 says that a husband is to "leave his father and mother and shall cling to his wife" (AT). The Hebrew terms for "leave" (עזב) and "cling" (דבק) are commonly found in covenantal contexts in the Old Testament. Commentators have long acknowledged the significance of these two covenantal terms in Genesis 2:24. Victor Hamilton argues that the term *forsake* often describes Israel's rejection of her covenant relationship with Yahweh, while the term *cling* often designates the keeping of the covenant relationship.[9] Ham-

---

[5] A discussion of Roman Catholic sacramental theology would be well beyond the scope of this volume. For a wider discussion of the sacramental view of marriage, see Köstenberger and Jones, *God, Marriage, and Family*, 69–71. For a Protestant critique of sacramental theology in general, see Wayne Grudem, *Systematic Theology: An Introduction to Biblical Doctrine* (Grand Rapids, MI: Zondervan, 1994), 951–52; Michael Horton, *The Christian Faith: A Systematic Theology for Pilgrims on the Way* (Grand Rapids, MI: Zondervan, 2011), 771–76. It should be noted that Roman Catholics would agree with Protestants that marriage is a covenant. The key difference between the two groups is over marriage's status as a sacrament.

[6] Köstenberger and Jones, *God, Marriage, and Family*, 71.

[7] Ibid.

[8] Ibid., 71–73.

[9] Such examples of *forsaking* the covenant include Jer. 1:16; 2:13, 17, 19; 5:7; 16:11; 17:13; 19:4; 22:9. Examples of *clinging* to the covenant include Deut. 4:4; 10:20; 11:22; 15 [Eng. 4]; 30:20. See Victor P. Hamilton, *The Book of Genesis, Chapters 1–17*, New International Commentary on the Old Testament (Grand Rapids, MI: Eerdmans, 1990), 180–81.

ilton concludes, "Thus, to leave father and mother and cling to one's wife means to sever one loyalty and commence another. Already Scripture has sounded the note that marriage is a covenant rather than an ad-hoc, makeshift arrangement."[10] In this way, there are numerous covenantal texts in the Old Testament that invoke the very language of Genesis 2:24.[11] The appearance of these two terms, therefore, seems to confirm the covenantal nature of marriage even though the word *covenant* does not appear in Genesis 1–2.

The appearance of this covenantal language with reference to marriage in Genesis 2:24 may also explain why later Old Testament texts do use the word "covenant" (בְּרִית) to describe marriage.[12] Proverbs 2:17 warns against the adulteress who "leaves the companion of her youth and forgets the covenant of her God [בְּרִית אֱלֹהֶיהָ]."[13] Likewise, Malachi 2:14 indicates that God is a witness to the covenant of marriage: "The LORD has been a witness between you and the wife of your youth, against whom you have dealt treacherously, though she is your companion and your wife by covenant [בְּרִית]." Other commentators find support for a covenantal model of marriage in Ezekiel 16:8, in which God says to his people, "I also swore to you and entered into a covenant [בְּרִית] with you so that you became Mine." Of course, Ezekiel's language is metaphorical, depicting Yahweh's marriage to his people. Nevertheless, the metaphor likely derives from the

---

[10] Hamilton, *Book of Genesis, Chapters 1–17*, 181. See also Gordon J. Wenham, *Genesis 1–15*, Word Biblical Commentary (Waco, TX: Word Books, 1987), 71; Kenneth A. Mathews, *Genesis 1–11:26*, New American Commentary (Nashville, TN: Broadman, 1996), 222.

[11] Mathews, *Genesis 1–11:26*, 222n136. In Deut. 10:20 after God had reissued the Ten Commandments on tablets of stone to the children of Israel, Moses commands, "You shall fear the LORD your God; you shall serve Him and *cling* [דבק] to Him." Likewise, in announcing the rewards of obedience to this covenant, Moses writes in Deut. 11:22–23, "For if you are careful to keep all this commandment which I am commanding you, to do it, to love the LORD your God, to walk in all His ways and *cling* [דבק] to Him; then the LORD will drive out all these nations from before you." Similarly, Moses calls the children of Israel to "choose" life in Deut. 30:19–20 by "clinging" (דבק) to Yahweh. Kenneth Mathews also notes that "not leaving" (עזב) in Gen. 24:27 and 28:15 "indicates God's faithful provision for the patriarchs" (ibid., 222n136).

[12] See Christopher Ash's discussion of Mal. 2:14 and Prov. 2:16–17 in *Marriage: Sex in the Service of God* (Vancouver, British Columbia: Regent College Publishing, 2003), 341–45.

[13] See Christopher Ash's argument in favor of understanding "covenant of her God" as the marriage covenant in ibid., 344–45. So also Gordon P. Hugenberger, *Marriage as a Covenant: Biblical Law and Ethics as Developed from Malachi* (Grand Rapids, MI: Baker, 1994), 296–302.

covenantal understanding of marriage reflected in both Malachi 2:14 and Proverbs 2:17.[14]

What is the significance of viewing marriage as a covenant? The Hebrew term for *covenant* (בְּרִית) occurs some 285 times in the Old Testament, and the term signifies when two or more parties enter into a relationship with one another. Typically, a covenant binds persons together who are not already related to one another by blood. We might define *covenant* along the same lines as Paul Williamson:

> It conveys the idea of a solemn commitment, guaranteeing promises or obligations undertaken by one or both covenanting parties. While the term applies predominantly to divine-human commitments, it is also used of various agreements between humans . . . including marriage (Ezek. 16:8; Mal. 2:14; Prov. 2:17).[15]

Thus a covenant is not like a human contract that can be dissolved with little or no sanction. The covenant of marriage is a union which God himself witnesses and ratifies. Christopher Ash comments on the significance of God's witness to the covenant of marriage:

> The sanctions following breach of covenant are not merely human but divine. In marriage a man and a woman make a public agreement (or covenant) to live together in a sexual and social union until death parts them. To this agreement God stands witness. He is present when the covenant is made (and this has nothing to do with whether or not there is any ecclesiastical context for the vows, for this is irrelevant). His presence at all marriages means that he will hold each party accountable to him for the keeping of these vows. He places the whole weight of divine presence in

[14] So Daniel L. Block, *The Book of Ezekiel, Chapters 1–24*, New International Commentary on the Old Testament (Grand Rapids, MI: Eerdmans, 1997), 483. See also Gordon Hugenberger's argument about the oath that is present in this text. He writes: "While Mal. 2:14 implies the presence of an oath in marriage with its reference to Yahweh as 'witness' to the covenant, and while Prov. 2:17 similarly implies a ratificatory oath which invoked the deity since it identifies the marriage covenant as a 'covenant of God,' no other biblical text is so explicit in identifying the presence of an oath in marriage as is Ezek. 16:8 (and vs. 59)." Hugenberger, *Marriage as a Covenant*, 305.
[15] P. R. Williamson, "Covenant," in *New Dictionary of Biblical Theology*, ed. T. Desmond Alexander and Brian S. Rosner (Downers Grove, IL: InterVarsity, 2000), 420.

support of the vows and in judgment on any who threaten or break them.[16]

This covenantal nature of marriage means that marriage is to be a permanent union—a union sanctioned by almighty God—that should be dissolved only by death (Rom. 7:2). Likewise, in his comments on Genesis 2:24, Jesus himself spoke of marriage as something that "God has joined together" and thus that no man should "separate" (Matt. 19:6). Jesus viewed marriage as a covenant before God.

Marriage Is a Sexual Union

Both Genesis 1:27–28 and Genesis 2:24 indicate that marriage is fundamentally a sexual union. The first command that God gives to man and woman is this: "Be fruitful and multiply, and fill the earth" (Gen. 1:28). This, of course, is God's mandate for the man and the woman to procreate, which necessarily presupposes the sexual union of the pair. Likewise, Genesis 2:24 says that marriage consists of a "one flesh" union of man and woman. The "one flesh" language is no doubt an allusion to Adam's exclamation in verse 23, "This is now bone of my bones, and flesh of my flesh," indicating that the woman was formed from the rib of the man and that the pair now have a family bond on the order of blood relation. But the appearance of the "one flesh" language likely has other connotations as well. The "one flesh" language indicates the total union of the married partners, including their sexual union. This is certainly the way the apostle Paul reads this text in his citation of it in 1 Corinthians 6:16. Here Paul argues that even illicit sexual acts form a kind of union because of the "one flesh" norm established in Genesis 2:24.[17] He writes, "Do you not know that

---

[16] Ash, *Marriage*, 342–43.

[17] I do not believe that the union to which Paul refers in 1 Cor. 6:16 is a marriage. Rather, Paul's point is that it is immoral to engage in the physical bond of sex where the covenant of marriage is absent. However one chooses to interpret this text, one thing is clear. Paul considers the "one flesh" union of Gen. 2:24 to include the sexual union. For more on the significance of the "one flesh" union, see Richard Batey, "The MIA SARX Union of Christ and the Church," *New Testament Studies* 13 (n.d.): 270–81. Batey writes, "Paul's unique application of the 'one flesh' concept points out that a 'harlotrous' union was more than a temporary physical act" (ibid., 279).

the one who unites himself with a harlot is one body? For it says, 'The two will become one flesh'" (AT). Commenting on this text, Richard Hays observes:

> The whole argument presupposes that sexual intercourse cannot be understood merely as a momentary act that satisfies a transient natural urge. Instead, it creates a mysterious but real and enduring union between man and woman. In support of this claim, Paul cites Genesis 2:24.[18]

All of this indicates that the "one flesh" union is irreducibly sexual. While the "one flesh" union may denote more than the mere sexual union, it certainly does not denote less than the sexual union.[19]

Marriage Is a Procreative Union

As mentioned above, the first command that God gives to man and woman is the command to procreate. God blesses his newly formed creatures and gives them two assignments: procreation and dominion:[20] "Be fruitful and multiply, and fill the earth, and subdue it; and rule over the fish of the sea and over the birds of the sky and over every living thing that moves on the earth" (Gen. 1:28). In the pre-fall condition, it was God's creational intention for marriages to produce children. That this is an enduring, creational norm is confirmed by the fact that the command is reiterated at key points in the book of Genesis after the fall. For example, God establishes a covenant with Noah and his family, delivers them

---

[18] Richard B. Hays, *First Corinthians*, Interpretation (Louisville, KY: Westminster, 1997), 105. Cf. Gordon Fee who argues, "While the union of man and wife as 'one flesh' implies far more than merely physical union, Paul's concern here is strictly with the physical aspects of the union." Gordon D. Fee, *First Epistle to the Corinthians*, (Grand Rapids, MI: Eerdmans, 1987), 259.
[19] Commenting on "one flesh" in 2:24, Gordon Wenham writes, "This does not denote merely the sexual union that follows marriage, or the children conceived in marriage, or even the spiritual and emotional relationship that it involves, though all are involved in becoming one flesh. Rather it affirms that just as blood relations are one's flesh and bone . . . , so marriage creates a similar kinship relation between man and wife" (Wenham, *Genesis 1–15*, 71). So also Terence E. Fretheim, "The Book of Genesis," in *The New Interpreter's Bible*, vol. 1 (Nashville, TN: Abingdon, 1994), 354: "'One flesh' does not refer to sexual intimacy in a narrow way, but recognizes that man and woman constitute an indissoluble unit of humankind from *every* perspective. Hence the author refers to but does not focus on the sexual relationship."
[20] Hamilton, *Book of Genesis, Chapters 1–17*, 139.

from the flood, and commands the remnant to procreate and fill the earth:

> Bring out with you every living thing of all flesh that is with you, birds and animals and every creeping thing that creeps on the earth, that they may breed abundantly on the earth, and *be fruitful and multiply* on the earth. (Gen. 8:17)

> And God blessed Noah and his sons and said to them, "*Be fruitful and multiply*, and fill the earth." (Gen. 9:1)

> As for you, *be fruitful and multiply*; Populate the earth abundantly and multiply in it. (Gen. 9:7)

Likewise, when God changes Jacob's name to Israel, God commands procreation:

> I am God Almighty;
> *Be fruitful and multiply;*
> A nation and a company of nations shall come from you,
> And kings shall come forth from you. (Gen. 35:11)

All of these trace back to the original command from Genesis 1:28 to be fruitful and to multiply.

God gives mankind the responsibility of dominion in Genesis 1:26: "Let us make man in Our image, according to Our likeness; and let them rule over the fish of the sea and over the birds of the sky and over the cattle and over all the earth, and over every creeping thing that creeps on the earth." Thus the command to procreate in Genesis is not an arbitrary obligation. It is the means by which man spreads his dominion throughout the world. God intends for mankind not just to dwell on the earth but to rule it.[21]

---

[21] So Matthews, *Genesis 1–11:26*, 169–70: "The language of 1:26 reflects this idea of a royal figure representing God as his appointed ruler. This appears also to be the understanding of Psalm 8, which focuses on human dominion. . . . This is further indicated by the term 'rule' *(rāda)* in 1:26, 28, which is used commonly of royal dominion. . . . Our passage declares that all people, not just kings, have the special status of royalty in the eyes of God. . . . It was this feature of creation that so astonished the psalmist; for him the Infinite One crowned human infancy with the glory of his rule (8:5–8[6–9])."

God mediates his reign in the world through mankind's submission to God and their subsequent dominion over the earth. Thus procreation within the covenant of marriage becomes the necessary means by which God's kingdom is extended throughout the world.[22] The creational norm, therefore, indicates a very close connection between marriage, sex, and procreation.[23]

Marriage Is a Heterosexual Union

Genesis 1–2 establishes marriage as a heterosexual union. In Genesis 1 God creates mankind in his image, and the narrator emphasizes that God's image bearers are both male and female: "God created man in His own image, in the image of God He created him; male and female He created them" (Gen. 1:27). It is the male paired with the female to whom God gives the command to procreate. Thus the extension of the race and of mankind's dominion over the world will not happen apart from heterosexual pairings. Jesus alludes to Genesis 1:27 in his teaching on divorce in Matthew 19:4, "Have you not read that He who created them from the beginning made them male and female?" In this way, even Jesus interprets the Old Testament to establish "the complementarity of male and female within God's created order."[24] If Jesus is right (and we believe that he is!), then God himself defined marriage as heterosexual in the garden of Eden.[25]

Marriage Is a Monogamous Union

Genesis 2:24 establishes a principle of monogamy that is the creational norm for marriage. The text speaks of one "man" and one

---

[22] So Matthews: "Human procreation is not intended merely as a mechanism for replication or the expression of human passion but is instrumental in experiencing covenant blessing" (ibid., 174).
[23] Matthew Lee Anderson, *Earthen Vessels: Why Our Bodies Matter to Our Faith* (Minneapolis, MN: Bethany, 2011), 151: "Even while we evangelical Protestants emphasize the covenantal nature of marriage, we must not overshadow the other dimensions of marriage, namely the physical union that ratifies the covenant and the procreative aspect that depends upon sexual complementarity. . . . Marriage is a covenant between two persons, but it is a covenant that is sealed in a physical union of the kind that produces children."
[24] So R. T. France, *The Gospel of Matthew*, New International Commentary on the New Testament (Grand Rapids, MI: Eerdmans, 2007), 716.
[25] We shall have more to say about homosexuality in chapter 6, "Glorify God with Your Sexuality."

"wife" coming together to form a new family, and this norm derives from the specific example of Adam and Eve. There is no polygamy in this first marriage. Adam has one wife—Eve. The clear implication is that monogamy is the norm for all marriages that follow. The Septuagint's translation of verse 24 focuses attention on the monogamous nature of marriage by inserting the words "the two" (οἱ δύο) into its rendering.[26] Whereas the Hebrew text simply says that *they* shall become one flesh," the Septuagint translators specify that "*the two* shall become one flesh." The Greek translators clarify what was already clearly implied in the Hebrew text, that there are only two people involved in this union.[27] It is the Septuagint version of this text that appears in Matthew 19:5; Mark 10:8; 1 Corinthians 6:16; and Ephesians 5:31. Thus the apostolic witnesses confirm the monogamous reading of Genesis 2:24.[28] John Murray's comments are apt: "As it was in the case of divorce that 'from the beginning it was not so,' so it is that in the matter of bigamy or polygamy from the beginning it was not so. The indissolubility of the bond of marriage and the principle of monogamy are inherent in the verse."[29]

It is commonplace among some commentators to observe the numerous instances of polygamy in the Old Testament and to conclude that the Old Testament approves of polygamy.[30] Gordon Hugenberger has shown, however, that this conclusion is not war-

---

[26] So Ash, *Marriage*, 252.

[27] David Instone-Brewer comments on Jesus's quotation of Gen. 2:24 in Mark 10:6–9 and Matt. 19:4–6: "The use of Genesis 2:24 to prove monogamy was by this time very widespread, as indicated by the presence of the word 'two' in almost all the ancient versions except the Hebrew." See David Instone-Brewer, *Divorce and Remarriage in the Bible: The Social and Literary Context* (Grand Rapids, MI: Eerdmans, 2002), 137.

[28] Christopher Ash argues further that "the references to the overseer (*episkopos*) being 'a man of one woman' (*mias gunaikos andra*) in 1 Timothy 3:2 and Titus 1:6, and to the widow as being 'a woman of one man' (*henos Andros gunē*) in 1 Timothy 5:9 have this same sense, that moral uprightness in the sexual realm involves the union of *one* man with *one* woman" (Ash, *Marriage*, 252).

[29] John Murray, *Principles of Conduct: Aspects of Biblical Ethics* (Grand Rapids, MI: Eerdmans, 1957), 30. So also Matthews, *Genesis 1–11:26*, 222, 224: "Monogamy is clearly intended. . . . Monogamous heterosexual marriage was always viewed as the divine norm from the outset of creation."

[30] Hugenberger, *Marriage as a Covenant*, 111: "It has often been argued that the Old Testament does not merely recognize polygyny as a legal form of marriage, but that it also approves it." A recent popular example appears in Michael Coogan, *God and Sex: What the Bible Really Says* (New York: Twelve, 2010), 78: "As these narratives illustrate, polygamy—or more properly polygyny, the practice of a man having more than one wife—was acceptable in ancient Israel. . . . Polygyny continued to be practiced well into the biblical period, and it is attested among Jews as late as the second century CE."

ranted by the biblical data. Instances of Old Testament polygamy appear without any evidence of moral approval on the part of the biblical authors, and it is not clear that any of the relevant texts *require* its approval.[31] For example, 2 Samuel 12:8 is sometimes interpreted as a divine sanction of King David's many wives: "I also gave you your master's house and your master's wives into your care." Yet this statement no more approves polygamy than 2 Samuel 12:11 approves adultery. As Christopher Ash has argued, "Divine agency behind an action does not signify simple moral approval of that action."[32]

Likewise, the law of levirate marriage in Deuteronomy 25:5–10 is often brought forth as evidence that the Old Testament approves polygamy. If a husband dies leaving behind a childless widow, this law requires the deceased man's brother to marry the widow in order to produce offspring in his brother's stead. Many readers assume that this law requires the surviving brother to marry the widow even if the surviving brother is already married. But such an assumption goes beyond what the text actually says. The text never actually contemplates this eventuality or a variety of other real-life situations. For example, the law does not address the possibility of there not being a living brother. Nor does the law mention the possibility of the living brother being too young or immature to enter a levirate marriage. As Hugenberger argues, "Given this incompleteness, it is entirely possible that if a brother were already married, this too may have disqualified him from assuming the levirate obligation."[33]

In support of this conclusion, consider other texts that indicate that the levirate obligation fell only to unmarried men. In the story of Judah and Tamar in Genesis 38, Judah's sons failed to perform their levirate duty on behalf of Tamar. The narrator remarks in Genesis 38:12 that "the wife of Judah died." Then in verse 13, "it was told to Tamar." This news of Judah's wife's death seems to have triggered

[31] Hugenberger, *Marriage as a Covenant*, 111.
[32] Ash, *Marriage*, 250.
[33] Hugenberger, *Marriage as a Covenant*, 114.

Tamar's deceit to become impregnated by Judah. It is very likely that she viewed the levirate obligation as falling upon Judah himself only after his wife had passed away.[34] Likewise, consider also one early interpretation of Ruth 4:6. In the Targum for Ruth 4:6, the would-be redeemer for Ruth says, "I cannot redeem it; because I have a wife. I am not permitted to take another one in addition to her, lest the result be quarrel in my home, and I will be destroying my own possession. You redeem it, since you have no wife; for I am unable to do so."[35] Thus the next of kin excuses himself from his levirate obligation on the grounds that he is already married. Hugenberger concludes that this Targum "reveals what must have been the common understanding in its day, namely that an existing marriage would exempt one from performing the duty of the levirate."[36] These early interpretations support the view that the law of levirate marriage does not obligate a man to commit polygamy.[37]

The conclusion of the matter is that Genesis 1–2 establishes monogamy as the norm, and nothing in the rest of the Old Testament scriptures requires the overthrow of that norm. Jesus and the apostles ratified the creational norm of monogamy, and it remains binding on the Christian conscience today.[38]

Marriage Is a Nonincestuous Union

The norm of Genesis 2:24 says that a man *leaves* his father and mother and becomes one flesh with his wife. As mentioned above, this involves leaving one's family in order to form a new one. Whereas the husband is related to the old family by birth and by blood, the husband is to be related to the new family by covenant

---

[34] John Walton suggests that Tamar's expectation may have been shaped by a Hittite law regarding levirate marriage that required the father-in-law to perform the duty if his other sons were deceased. See John H. Walton, *Genesis*, NIV Application Commentary (Grand Rapids, MI: Zondervan, 2001), 668.

[35] Samson H. Levey, *The Text and I: Writings of Samson H. Levey*, ed. Stanley F. Chyet, South Florida Studies in the History of Judaism 166 (Atlanta, GA: Scholars Press, 1998), 90.

[36] Hugenberger, *Marriage as a Covenant*, 115.

[37] Hugenberger provides commentary on several other Old Testament texts that are often read as approving of polygamy (Ex. 21:10ff.; Lev. 18:17–18; Deut. 21:15–17; Jer. 3:6–13; Ezekiel 23). He convincingly shows that such readings are in error (ibid., 111–18).

[38] David Instone-Brewer argues that Gen. 1:27 and 7:9 were often linked in rabbinic literature as a proof for monogamy. See Instone-Brewer, *Divorce and Remarriage in the Bible*, 138ff.

only. The covenant union of marriage forms a bond on the same order as blood relation. This "leaving" and "cleaving" implies that a man must "leave" behind his blood relations in order to unite with a spouse who is not a blood relative. The clear implication of Genesis 2:24 is that spouses are expected to go outside their family circle to form a marriage. This fact then begs the question: What is the extent of a person's family circle? How many degrees of blood separation must there be in order to establish eligibility for marriage? Whereas Genesis 2:24 does not define the boundaries, Leviticus 18 does.

Leviticus 18 divides into four sections: (1) an exhortation to avoid the customs of the Gentiles, verses 1–5; (2) a list of unions regarded as incestuous, verses 6–18; (3) sexual deviations of the Canaanites to be avoided, verses 19–23; and (4) warning of the consequences for neglecting these rules, verses 24–30.[39] Leviticus 18:6 serves as a summary of the section dealing with incest: "None of you shall approach any close relative[40] of his to uncover nakedness; I am the LORD" (AT). The rest of the section codifies precisely which degrees of relation are prohibited under God's law. It thereby marks out the boundaries of the family circle and instructs readers not to transgress those boundaries in taking a spouse. Since men were the ones who typically initiated marriages, the degrees of relation are defined in terms of the man's choice.[41] Having noted that feature, however, we should recognize that the rules apply by implication to women as well, as they are later found to be equally culpable for the violation of these norms (cf. Lev. 20:10–21).[42] Gordon Wenham summarizes the twelve prohibited degrees of relation in a helpful table (Table 3.1).[43]

---

[39] Gordon J. Wenham, *The Book of Leviticus,* New International Commentary on the Old Testament (Grand Rapids, MI: Eerdmans, 1979), 249.

[40] "Close relative" glosses a Hebrew phrase (שְׁאֵר בְּשָׂרוֹ) that is difficult to render literally into English. A literal equivalent would be something like "flesh of his flesh." HALOT suggests "close relative," which appears in the NIV, ESV, NET, HCSB, NLT, and NAB. "Near of kin" appears in the KJV, NKJV, RSV, and NRSV, and it means the same thing as "close relative." The NASB glosses with "blood relative," but this is probably misleading. "Blood relative" is generic and does not define a concern about the boundaries of the family circle, which appears to be the point of Lev. 18:6–18.

[41] Wenham, *Book of Leviticus,* 253.

[42] Ibid.

[43] Ibid., 254.

Table 3.1

A man may not marry his . . .			
Mother (v. 7)	Aunt (vv. 12, 13), i.e., father's or mother's sister	Stepmother (v. 8)	Aunt by marriage (v. 14), i.e., uncle's wife
Sister or half-sister (v. 9)	Step-sister (v. 11) Step-daughter (v. 17)	Sister-in-law (v. 16) Daughter-in-law (v. 15)	
Granddaughter (v. 10)	Step-grand-daughter (v. 17)		

The table reveals that sexual intercourse (and thus marriage) is forbidden between people who are related to the first and second degree. A man may not marry his mother, sister, aunt, or granddaughter.[44] Why then is a man's daughter omitted from this list? It is likely that readers would have already understood the prohibition on that relation based on earlier texts from the Pentateuch (see Gen. 19:30–38).[45] Thus the twelve prohibited relations in Leviticus 18:6–18 are added to those prohibitions that were already self-evident to the original readers.[46] Moreover, the expression "close relative" in 18:6 has a close parallel in 21:2, "a relative near to him" (AT).[47] In 21:2, the close relatives are defined specifically as mother, father, son, daughter, brother, and virgin sister. This list is composed of first-degree relations only, and that should inform our understanding of "close relative" in 18:6. "Hence mother, sister and

---

[44] Ibid.: "Thus a man may not marry his mother or his sister (first-degree consanguinity, vv. 7, 9) or his aunt or his granddaughter (second-degree consanguinity, vv. 12–13, 10)." *Consanguinity* refers to blood relation, and *affinity* refers to relation by marriage. See F. L. Cross and E. A. Livingstone, eds., "Prohibited Degrees," *The Oxford Dictionary of the Christian Church* (New York: Oxford University Press, 2005), 1343.

[45] Wenham, *Book of Leviticus*, 254: "There is one striking omission from this table. Marriage with one's daughter is not proscribed. This is probably because it was already accepted that such a union was illicit (Gen. 19:30ff.). It is expressly forbidden both in the laws of Hammurabi (LH 154) and in the Hittite laws (HL 195). In other words these regulations extend the prohibitions on incest already accepted in other parts of the ancient Near East."

[46] As Nobuyoshi Kiuchi has argued, Lev. 18:6 gives the fundamental prohibition on marrying "close relatives," and prohibitions on other first degree relations would appear to be "self-evident." See Nobuyoshi Kiuci, *Leviticus*, Apollos Old Testament Commentary 3 (Downers Grove, IL: InterVarsity, 2007), 333.

[47] In Lev. 18:6 the Hebrew phrase is שְׁאֵר בְּשָׂרוֹ; in 21:2 it is שְׁאֵרוֹ הַקָּרֹב אֵלָיו.

daughter, as close kin, are automatically forbidden by Lev 18:6. The purpose of the list of Leviticus 18 is to indicate *who else* is forbidden by extension from these basic relationships."[48]

How do we know that this particular Old Testament law has any purchase under the new covenant? Does the law on incest represent an abiding norm, or has it been abrogated like the food laws and levitical codes? If Genesis 2:24 implies that one must find a spouse outside the family circle (as I have suggested above), then the incest laws would reflect a creational norm that is binding on all people at all times. The assumption of the New Testament seems to confirm this conclusion. For instance, the apostle Paul uses no uncertain terms in describing the sinfulness of a man who is sleeping with his stepmother: "It is actually reported that there is immorality among you, and immorality of such a kind as does not exist even among the Gentiles, that someone has his father's wife" (1 Cor. 5:1). Paul treats this case as an egregious violation of sexual holiness—an ethic defined by the prohibitions of Leviticus 18:7–8. As with homosexuality and adultery, the sexual ethics of the New Testament derive directly from the Old. We conclude with this observation from Christopher Ash:

> The sexual ethics of Leviticus 18 are quite different from, say, the food laws of Leviticus 11. The Canaanites were not "vomited out" of the land because they ate unclean food; they knew no better, and besides, the food laws were given to Israel as a sign of their distinctiveness. The sexual ethics, however, are taken by the New Testament as read, as a natural part of the created order.[49]

---

[48] These remarks come from Susan Rattray, who is quoted in Jacob Milgrom's commentary on Leviticus. See Susan Rattray, "Marriage Rules, Kinship Terms, and Family Structure in the Bible," in *Society of Biblical Literature 1987 Seminar Papers*, ed. Kent Harold Richards (Atlanta: Scholars Press, 1987), 542; Jacob Milgrom, *Leviticus 17–22: A New Translation with Introduction and Commentary*, Anchor Bible (New York: Doubleday, 2000), 1527.

[49] Ash, *Marriage*, 265. Ash goes on to explain why incest is prohibited: "The simplest and most persuasive principle for the prohibition of incest is that the family circle (close kin, Lev. 18:6) must be protected from the destructive effects of sexual possibility. Apart from husband and wife, the family circle needs to be protected against even the suggestion or faint future hope of sex. Once this possibility is admitted to be within the bounds of normality, the destructive jealousies and hatreds begin to destroy the security of nonsexual family intimacy. The most helpful, exegetically reasonable and pastorally realistic solution is to understand that the purpose of the incest prohibitions is to protect the family circle from the terrible disorders introduced by these sexual possibilities" (ibid., 268).

Marriage Is a Symbolic Union

Ephesians 5:21–33 is perhaps the linchpin for understanding the deepest meaning of marriage. In this text, Paul not only explains the different roles that men and women fulfill in marriage, but also the reason for those roles. At the heart of these verses is not simply the role distinctions themselves but an analogy. In short, God calls for husbands to be the "head" of their wives and for the wives to be submissive to their husbands. The husband's loving headship over his wife is patterned upon Christ's loving headship over his bride, the church: "The husband is the head of the wife, as Christ also is the head of the church. . . . Husbands, love your wives, just as Christ also loved the church" (Eph. 5:23, 25). Likewise, the wife's submission is patterned after the church's submission to Christ: "As the church submits to Christ, thus also the wives should be submissive to their own husbands in everything" (Eph. 5:24 AT). We will discuss these texts and the issue of gender roles in greater detail in the chapter on gender (chap. 6). But for now, the important thing to notice is the analogy that Paul makes between Christ's relation to the church and the husband's relation to his wife. The question remains, however, which piece of the analogy illuminates which? Does Paul appeal to Christ and the church to illuminate something about marriage, or does marriage exist to illuminate something about Christ and his church? The answer lies in verses 29–32.

Verse 29 confirms that marriage is to be patterned after Christ's marriage to his church: "For no one ever hated his own flesh, but nourishes and cherishes it, just as Christ also does the church." Why does Christ nourish and cherish his bride? Verse 30 answers, "Because we are members of His body." Because the church is Christ's own body, he cares for it as his own.

Verse 31 is a quotation of Genesis 2:24: "For this cause a man shall leave his father and mother, and shall cleave to his wife; and the two shall become one flesh" (AT). Notice that Paul does not introduce the quotation in the customary way. When Paul quotes the Old Testament elsewhere, he often introduces the quotation with a stock phrase such as, "As it is written" (e.g., Rom. 1:17; 3:4). Yet in verse 31 he quotes the verse without introduction. Why? He does it because he wants that first phrase to have its real connective force in the argument.[50] Why does a man leave his father and mother and join himself to a wife? Why does marriage exist in the world? Why is it that we have had this age-old institution that cuts across all cultures and all times and all religious groups, that one man and one woman would come together for life? Why does marriage exist? Marriage exists because of the cause indicated in verses 29–30. The logic goes like this: *Because Christ nourishes and cherishes his church* (vv. 29–30), *marriage exists* (v. 31).

God did not create marriage as an end unto itself. It exists not to tell its own story but to tell the story of Jesus's marriage to the church.[51] So Paul explains in verse 32, "This mystery is great; but I am speaking with reference to Christ and the church." Here Paul identifies Genesis 2:24 as a reference to Christ and the church.[52] This would not have been easy to see for the first readers of Genesis 2:24, but Paul is saying that the connection is clear now that the gospel has been revealed. The key to this text is to understand the word *mystery*. In common English parlance, *mystery* denotes something that is hidden and unknown, but that is not how Paul uses this word. A mystery in Paul's vocabulary is something that was once hidden under the old covenant but that has now been made known through the gospel (see Rom. 16:25; 1 Cor. 2:1, 7; 4:1; Eph. 1:9). The accent is on that which is revealed, not on that

---

[50] So Frank Thielman, *Ephesians*, Baker Exegetical Commentary on the New Testament (Grand Rapids, MI: Baker Academic, 2010), 389.

[51] So Russell D. Moore, "Southern Baptist Sexual Revolutionaries: Cultural Accomodation, Spiritual Conflict and the Baptist Vision of the Family," *Southwestern Journal of Theology* 49, no. 1 (2006): 15: "Paul is emphatically not using Christ and the church as illustrative of human marriage. To say such would be similar to saying that Jesus was crucified, buried, and raised from the dead in order to teach us the proper mode of baptism. In both instances, it is the other way around. The husband/wife union is a visible icon of the Christ/church union; a union in which, as a head with a body, Jesus is inseparable from His bride, a bride He protects, provides for, leads, disciples, and sanctifies."

[52] So Markus Barth, *Ephesians: Translation and Commentary on Chapters 4–6*, Anchor Bible (Garden City, NY: Doubleday, 1974), 641: "It is . . . almost commonly accepted that 'this' refers back to the Genesis text quoted in the preceding verse."

which is concealed.[53] The great mystery is that from the very beginning God intended marriage to be a depiction of the gospel. Marriage exists to manifest the glory of Christ's redemptive love for his bride. Thus each and every marriage is supposed to be an enacted parable of the gospel. Husbands are to love their brides in such a way that people can see Christ's love for his church. Wives are to submit to their husbands in such a way that the world can see the loveliness of Christ reflected in the obedience of his bride. In this way, God intends marriage to symbolize the gospel.

What Are the Purposes of Marriage?

The first six descriptors of marriage—covenantal, sexual, procreative, heterosexual, monogamous, nonincestuous—all point to the seventh and final descriptor, symbolic. The covenant of marriage symbolizes Christ's covenant marriage to his bride. The sexual, heterosexual, and monogamous nature of marriage symbolizes the exclusive union that Christ has with his bride (Rev. 19:7). The nonincestuous nature of marriage points to the fact that Christ took for himself a bride to whom he had no natural relation or obligation (Ezek. 16:3; Eph. 2:12). All of these components in the definition of marriage are directly related to the purposes for sex that we identified in the introduction. Marriage is a sexual union for the purposes of (1) consummation, (2) procreation, (3) the expression of love, and (4) pleasure.[54] Thus marriage as the covenanted sexual union of one man and one woman tends toward the glory of God as it symbolizes God's redemptive love for his people through Christ. In this way sexual union within marriage tends toward the glory of God.

These four purposes of sex cannot be separated from one another in developing a Christian sexual ethic. It will not do, for example, for someone to cite pleasure as one of the divine purposes

---

[53] P. T. O'Brien, "Mystery," in *Dictionary of Paul and His Letters*, ed. Gerald F. Hawthorne, Ralph P. Martin, and Daniel G. Reid (Downers Grove, IL: InterVarsity, 1993), 622: "It points not to some future event hidden in God's plan, but to his decisive action in Christ here and now. Paul normally employs the term with reference to its disclosure or its being revealed."

[54] Again, we are following Dennis Hollinger in this. See Dennis P. Hollinger, *The Meaning of Sex: Christian Ethics and the Moral Life* (Grand Rapids, MI: Baker, 2009), 95.

of sex and to thereby declare all pleasurable sex as glorifying God. No, these four purposes must be taken together, and they must find expression only within the covenant of marriage.[55] It is only within the covenant of marriage that any of these four purposes can glorify God in the ultimate sense.

For obvious reasons, the purposes of marriage overlap with what we have identified as the purposes of sex. Nevertheless, it can be useful to make a distinction because the institution of marriage draws our attention to the larger social purposes for the union of one man and one woman. Sherif Girgis, Robert George, and Ryan Anderson argue from a natural-law perspective that one of the purposes of marriage is to promote the "common good."[56] For them, the common good is bound up with what they call the "conjugal" view of marriage, defined as follows:

> Marriage is, of its essence, a comprehensive union: a union of will (by consent) and body (by sexual union); inherently ordered to procreation and thus the broad sharing of family life; and calling for permanent and exclusive commitment, whatever the spouses' preferences. It has long been and remains a personal and social reality, sought and prized by individuals, couples, and whole societies. But it is also a moral reality: a human good with an objective structure, which it is inherently good for us to live out.[57]

Even though Girgis et al. make their case with arguments that do not appeal to any religious authority, it is remarkable how similar their definition of the "common good" is to the Bible's definition. The "common good" is a penultimate purpose of marriage, and it is served only when society recognizes and honors a proper definition of marriage.

Though publicly accessible arguments are useful in the wider cultural conversation about the nature of marriage, Christians must

---

[55] Ibid., 146–55.
[56] Sherif Girgis, Robert P. George, and Ryan T. Anderson, "What Is Marriage?," *Harvard Journal of Law and Public Policy* 34 (2010): 248.
[57] Sherif Girgis, Ryan T. Anderson, and Robert P. George, *What Is Marriage? Man and Woman: A Defense* (New York: Encounter Books, 2012), 6.

give a specific scriptural accounting for the teleology of marriage. There is a long history of this in Christian thought, going back at least to Augustine.[58] Augustine argued that the Bible connects marriage to three "goods": *offspring, fidelity,* and *the sacramental bond.*[59] Augustine viewed procreation as the primary good of marriage. His view won the day in the Western church, and as a result Roman Catholicism to this day repudiates all forms of birth control and contraception.[60] Over the centuries, Protestants in particular have disagreed with Augustine's contention that the primary good of sex is procreation.[61] Thus these three goods have been modified. Christopher Ash summarizes them under three headings: (1) the procreational good, (2) the relational good, and (3) the public good.[62]

As noted above, the procreational good is implied in the Genesis texts in which God calls on Adam and Eve to be "fruitful and multiply." The propagation of the race is the means by which man's (and thereby God's) dominion is to spread throughout the world. God's ever-expanding dominion brings glory to him as his image bearers subdue the earth. There is no escaping the public consequences of procreation as a purpose of marriage. The relational good of marriage consists in the observation that the woman was given to the man in Genesis 2 in order to address the man's deepest social need. She is a helper who "corresponds" to him like no other creature in

---

[58] See especially Augustine, *On the Good of Marriage* (§32); *On Original Sin* (chaps. 39, 41); and *On Marriage and Concupiscence* (§19). See also Augustin, "On the Good of Marriage," in *Augustin: On the Holy Trinity, Doctrinal Treatises, Moral Treatises,* ed. Philip Schaff, Nicene and Post-Nicene Fathers 3 (Peabody, MA: Hendrickson, 2004), 395–413; Augustin, "On Original Sin," in *Augustin: Anti-Pelagian Writings,* ed. Philip Schaff, Nicene and Post-Nicene Fathers 5 (Peabody, MA: Hendrickson, 2004), 237–55; Augustin, "On Marriage and Concupiscence," in *Augustin: Anti-Pelagian Writings,* 257–80.
[59] *On Marriage and Concupiscence* (§19). In *On Original Sin* (chap. 39), Augustine gives three scriptural proofs for these three goods: 1 Tim. 5:14 for *procreation;* 1 Cor. 7:4 for *fidelity/chastity;* and Matt. 19:6 for *the sacramental bond.*
[60] See Pope Paul VI, *Humanae Vitae: Encyclical Letter of His Holiness Pope Paul VI on the Regulation of Births,* trans. Marc Calegari (San Francisco: Ignatius, 1998). See also F. L. Cross and E. A. Livingstone, eds., "Matrimony," *The Oxford Dictionary of the Christian Church* (New York: Oxford University Press, 1997), 1055.
[61] E.g., John S. Feinberg and Paul D. Feinberg, *Ethics for a Brave New World,* 2nd ed. (Wheaton, IL: Crossway, 2010), 300–302. The Feinbergs write, "Procreation is not the only purpose of sex within marriage. Since that is so, it must be permissible to use sex for the other purposes mentioned" (302).
[62] Ash, *Marriage,* 106–11. The Feinbergs identify six purposes for marriage: procreation, companionship, unity, pleasure, raising up a godly seed, and curbing fornication and adultery. See Feinberg and Feinberg, *Ethics for a Brave New World,* 300–302. These six purposes, however, overlap with the three listed above. It is not altogether clear that all six of these deserve their own category. Some of them could be subsumed under the three purposes listed by Ash.

the garden (Gen. 2:18). The relational good focuses on the inherent good of conjugal relations irrespective of whether there are children.[63] Christopher Ash describes the public good[64] this way:

> The public or institutional good is different in kind both from the procreational good and the relational good. It encompasses the benefits of ordered and regulated sexual relationships in human society. Undisciplined and disordered sexual behavior must be restrained, for it carries with it a high social and personal cost in family breakdown, destructive jealousies, resentments, bitterness and hurt. Ordered behavior is to be encouraged because it has benefits that extend beyond the couple to children, neighbors and the wider networks of relational society.[65]

How do all of these purposes come together to inform our assessment of ethical issues related to sex and marriage? As Christians who take the Bible seriously, we must pay attention to the different ways in which the Bible provides us direction in our ethical thinking. First, we must take seriously the clear commands and prohibitions of Scripture. When the Bible says, "You shall not commit adultery" (Ex. 20:14; Rom. 13:9), this is a clear prohibition on a certain kind of ethical behavior. One need not have a highly developed ethical system to comprehend the meaning of this prohibition, and there are many others like it in Scripture. Second, understanding the commands and prohibitions alone does not capture the Bible's total ethical teaching. As we argued in the introduction, we must also take into account the divinely disclosed purposes for our sexuality and measure all our thoughts and behaviors by their ability to encompass those purposes. As we evaluate different sexual behaviors in the remainder of this book, the commands of Scripture along with the biblical purposes of marriage will be our guide.

---

[63] Ash, *Marriage*, 107. Ash writes, "The perceived relational benefits . . . may include the comfort each gives the other, the companionship, the psychological benefits of mutual affirmation and acceptance, loving sexual relations and the experience of unconditional love. The relationship meets deep felt needs and may contribute to the healing of past hurts" (107–8).
[64] The public good corresponds to Augustine's "sacramental bond," which emphasized the permanence and inseverability of marriage.
[65] Ash, *Marriage*, 110.

They who, for slight causes, rashly allow of divorces, violate, in one single particular, all the laws of nature, and reduce them to nothing. If we should make it a point of conscience not to separate a father from his son, it is still greater wickedness to dissolve the bond which God has preferred to all others.

—John Calvin, commentary on Genesis 2:24

4

Glorify God with Your Conjugal Union

The conjugal bond of marriage is not merely for consummation. It is intended by God to be the ongoing affirmation of the husband and wife's unique union.[1]

The Necessity of Conjugal Union

The bond exists not merely for the purposes of consummation and procreation but also for the continuing health and chastity of each spouse. This is certainly the way that the apostle Paul addresses the matter in 1 Corinthians 7:1–6. Paul teaches not that couples *may* come together in regular conjugal union but that they *must* come together. Sexual intimacy is not merely a privilege of marriage but also a duty. Thus sexual intimacy within marriage becomes a touchstone for the spiritual and emotional vitality of marriage.

The Problem (1 Corinthians 7:1)

Longstanding misinterpretations have bedeviled the interpretation of 1 Corinthians 7:1–6 for centuries, and many of the errors trace back to verse 1. The 1984 NIV inscribes one common view

---

[1] Dennis P. Hollinger, *The Meaning of Sex: Christian Ethics and the Moral Life* (Grand Rapids, MI: Baker, 2009), 100.

by translating, "It is good for a man not to marry." Likewise, the New Living Translation's marginal note says, "Yes, it is good to live a celibate life." These two translations represent the mistaken view that Paul advises his readers not to get married. Other translations say that "it is good for a man not to have sexual relations with a woman" (ESV, NET, HSCB), while others say that "it is good for a man not to touch a woman" (NASB, KJV, RSV, NRSV). So which is correct? Is Paul talking about marriage? Sexual relations within marriage? Or perhaps some ascetic commitment not even to "touch" a woman? Does this passage address the behavior of spouses within marriage or the behavior of individuals before marriage? How one answers those questions all depends upon the meaning of verse 1.

The first thing to note are the opening words of the verse: "Now concerning the things about which you wrote . . ." These words indicate that Paul is about to quote from a letter that the Corinthians had written to him at some point before he penned the response that we know of as 1 Corinthians. This means that the words, "It is good for a man not to marry/touch/have sexual relations with a woman," are actually a quotation from that earlier Corinthian letter. Many modern translations enclose the phrase in quotation marks because the words in question are not Paul's words but the Corinthians'. Paul does in this text what he has already done elsewhere in the letter. He quotes a Corinthian slogan and then corrects it with the truth (see 1 Cor. 1:11–12; 6:12, 13; 10:23).

So what did the Corinthians mean by this phrase? It turns out that the word translated as "marry" in the NIV and "have sexual relations with" in the ESV literally means "to touch."[2] Nevertheless, the term appears elsewhere as a euphemism for sexual relations, and so it is in this text as well.[3] Thus, this slogan has nothing to do

---

[2] BDAG, s.v. "ἅπτω," 2.a: "touch, take hold of, hold."

[3] E.g., see the LXX version of Gen. 20:6; Ruth 2:9; and Prov. 6:29. Also see BDAG s.v. "ἅπτω," 4: "to touch intimately, *have sexual contact*." Richard B. Hays, *First Corinthians*, Interpretation (Louisville, KY: Westminster, 1997), 113. Contra the stimulating argument from Ciampa and Rosner that the euphemism was not used for sexual relations in general but for a range of sexual activities that

with whether Corinthians should get married. It has everything to do with describing what some of the Corinthians were doing while they were married—or more accurately, what they *were not* doing. Some of them were saying that it was good for married couples not to have sexual relations with one another. As many scholars have noted, this kind of asceticism was in the ideological air in Paul's day. Richard Hays writes, "Sexual abstinence was widely viewed as a means to personal wholeness and religious power."[4] It is difficult to say exactly why they were calling for a moratorium on marital sex, but clearly that is what was happening.

The Duty (1 Corinthians 7:2–4)

Sexual abstinence within marriage is a bad idea, and Paul is going to tell them why in verse 2: "on account of immoralities" (AT). Literally, the text reads "on account of *the* immoralities." The presence of the definite article likely indicates that Paul does not have in mind "immorality" generically, but "*the* immoralities" that he mentioned in chapter 6 where certain men were said to be visiting prostitutes.[5] Because of the temptation to commit such immorality, Paul says it is the duty for spouses to "have" one another sexually (v. 2). Paul's point is clear. Regular sexual union within marriage helps to ward off the temptation to adultery and fornication. Verse 3 amplifies the point, saying, "Let the husband give what is owed to his wife, and likewise let the wife give what is owed to her husband" (AT). Paul invokes a term that is used elsewhere to refer to financial debt,[6] but he now applies it to what husbands and wives *owe* one another in the bedroom. Each spouse has a sexual

---

would have been frowned upon by most Greco-Roman moralists of Paul's day. See Roy E. Ciampa and Brian S. Rosner, *The First Letter to the Corinthians*, Pillar New Testament Commentary (Grand Rapids, MI: 2010), 268. See also Hays, *First Corinthians*, 270–75.

[4] Hays, *First Corinthians*, 114.

[5] I take the definite article with πορνείας to be anaphoric. Moreover, the plural form of πορνείας would also seem to imply "individual acts of fornication" (Joseph A. Fitzmyer, *First Corinthians*, Anchor Yale Bible 32 [New Haven, CT: Yale University Press, 2008], 279), which would probably imply a reference to the illicit acts mentioned at the end of chapter 6. Cf. Matt. 15:19; Mark 7:21.

[6] Cf. Matt. 18:32; Rom. 13:7. Gordon Fee notes that the Greek phrase τὴν ὀφειλὴν ἀποδιδότω is used frequently in the papyri for the payment of debts. See Gordon D. Fee, *The First Epistle to the Corinthians*, New International Commentary on the New Testament (Grand Rapids, MI: Eerdmans, 1987), 279.

debt to pay, and each spouse is expected to pay up. The debt varies from couple to couple, but in general the debt is defined by the needs of one's spouse. As the New Living Translation paraphrases 1 Corinthians 7:3, "The husband should fulfill his wife's sexual needs, and the wife should fulfill her husband's needs." Fulfilling one another's needs is not the silver bullet against temptation, but Paul is nevertheless saying that it plays a crucial part in keeping the marriage bed pure.

In verse 4, Paul writes, "The wife does not have authority over her own body, but the husband does; and likewise also the husband does not have authority over his own body, but the wife does." Some have mistakenly interpreted this verse as a prescription for egalitarian gender roles within marriage.[7] That is not at all what Paul has in mind here. Rather, he is concerned narrowly with the obligation that husband and wife have to one another sexually. We know this not only because of Paul's teaching elsewhere on gender roles,[8] but also because Paul's words focus on the use of each spouse's "body" in the conjugal act. Verse 4 says that husbands and wives must relinquish to each other the right of control over their *bodies*.

This language of "authority" sometimes makes people un-comfortable. It sounds oppressive. To some who have experienced abuse, it may even sound kind of scary. Such concern misunder-stands what Paul is saying here. As with the debtor language in verse 3, the issue is not that "you owe me" but that "I owe you."[9] This text is not about coercing one's spouse to do what he or she does not want to do. It is about a husband and a wife giving

---

[7] Hays, *First Corinthians*, 116: "The marriage partners are neither placed in a hierarchical relation with one over the other or set apart as autonomous units each doing what he or she pleases. In-stead, the relationship of marriage is one of *mutual submission*, each partner having authority over the other." See also Mimi Haddad and Alvera Mickelsen, "Helping the Church Understand Biblical Equality," in *Discovering Biblical Equality: Complementarity without Hierarchy*, ed. Ronald W. Pierce and Rebecca Merrill Groothuis (Downers Grove, IL: InterVarsity, 2004), 490; Alan G. Padgett, *As Christ Submits to the Church: A Biblical Understanding of Leadership and Mutual Submission* (Grand Rapids, MI: Baker, 2011), 69–70; Philip B. Payne, *Man and Woman, One in Christ: An Exegetical and Theological Study of Paul's Letters*, 1st ed. (Grand Rapids, MI: Zondervan, 2009), 105–8.

[8] E.g., Eph. 5:22–31; 1 Cor. 11:3; 14:34–35.

[9] Fee, *First Epistle to the Corinthians*, 280. Fee also says that "the emphasis is not on 'possessing' the body of the other" but on the fact that "I do not have authority over my own body, to do with it as I please" (ibid.).

themselves freely to one another. It is not about insisting on one's autonomy and authority but about being a servant to one's spouse. With limited exceptions, this means that spouses are always to make themselves available to one another sexually. It is true that there are times when one or both spouses may not be "in the mood," but that is not the point. The point is for spouses to serve one another in love in the marital bed.

The Exception (1 Corinthians 7:5–6)

Paul punctuates these instructions with an emphatic prohibition at the beginning of verse 5: "Stop depriving one another." Paul's expression implies that they are to *stop* doing something that they were already doing.[10] This confirms that some spouses were in fact already denying conjugal relations to their mates at the time Paul wrote. Paul's command is for them to cease and desist the deprivation. Although many translations use the word *deprive*, Paul actually employs a term that invokes the idea of *stealing* or *defrauding*.[11] Each spouse has a conjugal debt to pay (v. 3). Any husband or wife who fails to pay the debt steals from his or her spouse. So Paul expects regular, conjugal union to be the norm.

Nevertheless, Paul does allow for an exception in verse 5. Under two conditions, married couples may go on a "sex fast" and refrain from sexual relations for the purposes of prayer. Condition number one is that both partners *must* be in agreement about the fast: "Stop depriving one another, except by agreement." Neither spouse has the authority to decree unilaterally a fast from sex.

---

[10] The present imperative often indicates action already in progress. Thus, to negate it with μή indicates that the action in progress should stop. See BDF §336 (3): "Something already existing is to continue (in prohibitions: is to stop)." This is not a hard and fast rule for present imperatives. See Stanley E. Porter, *Idioms of the Greek New Testament*, 2nd ed., Biblical Languages: Greek 2 (Sheffield, UK: Sheffield Academic Press, 1994), 225. Nevertheless it seems to be the case in this text. So Fee, *First Epistle to the Corinthians*, 281; Anthony C. Thiselton, *The First Epistle to the Corinthians*, New International Greek Testament Commentary (Grand Rapids, MI: Eerdmans, 2000), 507n126: "In spite of the force of many (but not all) claims in S. E. Porter . . . and B. M. Fanning . . . here the context seems to suggest that the negation applies to a process already begun, even if we acknowledge the place of 'viewpoint.'"

[11] BDAG, s.v. ἀποστερέω, 1: "To cause another to suffer loss by taking away through illicit means, rob, steal, despoil, defraud." The King James captures the sense better than many of the modern versions: "Defraud ye not one the other" (1 Cor. 7:5a).

If either of the partners has a qualm about a period of abstention, then it must not happen. If there is disagreement, regular
conjugal relations must continue unabated. If there is agreement,
then a second condition comes into play. Abstention can be only
for a limited period of time. Even by agreement, spouses are not
allowed to observe a permanent or indefinite period of time for a
fast from sex. The longer the abstention goes, the more vulnerable
spouses become to temptation. So Paul warns, "Come together
again lest Satan tempt you because of your lack of self-control"
(AT). Paul makes it clear that abstaining from sex within marriage is not a spiritually healthy thing to do. It is an exceptional
thing only to be entered into by agreement and for a very limited
period of time.

In verse 6, Paul says, "This I say by way of concession, not of
command." The "this" refers back to verse 5. Paul will *allow* short
periods of abstention under certain strict conditions. This concession is helpful because there are times when spouses can serve one
another by abstaining. A husband, for instance, would do well to
agree with his wife to abstain for a period of time after childbirth
or during his wife's cycle. A husband's tender concern for his wife
will include loving her enough to know what situations might
make sexual relations physically or emotionally uncomfortable
for her. Nevertheless, even though Paul makes a concession for
abstention, couples should take advantage of this concession with
caution. There is no biblical obligation for couples to abstain, but
there is an obligation for them to come together regularly.

The Boundaries of Conjugal Union

Books on sexual ethics and popular Christian books on marriage
often consider the question of sexual boundaries within marriage.
In general, the question they seek to answer is whether there are
limits on the kinds of activities married couples might engage
in.[12] On this question of limits, I have found a disturbing trend

---

[12] E.g., Hollinger, *Meaning of Sex*, 155.

in the literature. Upon finding no specific biblical prohibition of an activity, some authors are quick to categorize a given sexual activity as a matter of Christian freedom. For instance, quoting Paul's words in 1 Corinthians, "All things are permitted," Lewis Smedes argues, "Christian liberty sets us free from culturally invented 'moral' taboos; and since there is no rule from heaven, it is likely that the only restraint is the feeling of the other person."[13] Linda Dillow and Lorraine Pintus frame the issue with a question: "*Is it prohibited in Scripture?* If not, we may assume it is permitted. 'Everything is permissible for me' (1 Cor. 6:12)."[14] William Cutrer and Sandra Glahn write, "Lacking specific biblical prohibitions we must then ask, 'What is loving?' and 'What is satisfying between husband and wife?' Within the clear biblical limitations, anything is acceptable."[15]

But this approach can be reductionistic.[16] As we have seen, the Bible has much to say about God's purposes for the sexual union, and those purposes can be used to assess the morality of sexual behaviors even within marriage.[17] We ought to evaluate the ethics of any sexual act on the basis of its ability to encompass the four purposes identified above: consummation, procreation, love, and pleasure. In addition to that, we ought to consider how the act in question relates to the overall purpose of marriage and to the ultimate end of glorifying God. Christian ethical reflection has to take into account the whole counsel of God. Ethical decision mak-

---

[13] Lewis B. Smedes, *Sex for Christians: The Limits and Liberties of Sexual Living*, rev. ed. (Grand Rapids, MI: Eerdmans, 1994), 211–12.

[14] Linda Dillow and Lorraine Pintus, *Intimate Issues: 21 Questions Christian Women Ask about Sex* (Colorado Springs, CO: WaterBrook, 1999), 203.

[15] William Cutrer and Sandra Glahn, *Sexual Intimacy in Marriage*, 1st ed. (Grand Rapids, MI: Kregel, 1998), 85–86. Gilbert Meilaender appeals to freedom, but he does so within the framework of the purposes for marriage. He writes, "There is little reason to forbid husband and wife considerable scope for experimentation and play in their sexual relationship. The general rule will be that whatever nurtures and fosters the relational purpose of mutual love and companionship should be permitted, and whatever hinders or harms the growth of mutual love should be prohibited." See Gilbert C. Meilaender Jr., "Sexuality," in *New Dictionary of Christian Ethics and Pastoral Theology*, ed. David J. Atkinson et al. (Downers Grove, IL: IVP Academic, 1995), 77.

[16] In fact, the authors above draw the boundaries differently from one another.

[17] In his comments on 1 Cor. 6:12–14, John White rightly observes that Paul defines Christian freedom teleologically. Freedom has a purpose. He writes, "We live in a world where everything has a design and a function. . . . Your body was not designed for premarital sex and will never be truly free when you engage in it." See John White, *Eros Defiled: The Christian and Sexual Sin* (Downers Grove, IL: InterVarsity, 1977), 51.

ing can fall short of that ideal when Christians are quick to label something a matter of Christian freedom simply because there is no explicit prohibition in Scripture. Even without an explicit prohibition, an act may fall short of the glory of God because it does not achieve his purposes for human sexuality.

A popular example of the reductionistic approach appears in chapter 10 of Mark and Grace Driscoll's book *Real Marriage*.[18] Chapter 10 has the simple title "Can We _____?," and the Driscolls fill in the blank of the chapter title with a variety of sexual activities that are sometimes considered taboo. The chapter goes on to describe these activities in explicit detail, and then the authors give an ethical assessment of each activity for Christians. Like the other authors mentioned above, the Driscolls invoke 1 Corinthians 6:12 as the basis for the evaluation: *"All things are lawful for me, but not all things are profitable. All things are lawful for me, but I will not be mastered by anything."* From this text, the Driscolls propose a "taxonomy" of questions to assess the different activities: (1) *Is it lawful?* (2) *Is it helpful?* (3) *Is it enslaving?* If one judges a given behavior to be biblically lawful, relationally helpful, and nonaddictive, then it is permissible for Christians to participate in that activity. Among the activities that the authors deem permissible within this taxonomy are masturbation, oral sex, sodomy (on both spouses), menstrual sex, role-playing, sex toys, birth control, cosmetic surgery, cybersex, and sexual medication. The Driscolls are careful to stipulate that these are activities spouses *may* participate in by mutual agreement, but not that they *must* participate in. No spouse should be manipulated into doing anything that violates his or her conscience. The only item in the list deemed impermissible in every circumstance is sexual assault.

The value of the Driscolls' taxonomy is only as good as the exegesis that it is based on, but in this case their reading of 1 Corinthians 6:12 is fundamentally flawed. The Driscolls read "all things

---

[18] Mark Driscoll and Grace Driscoll, *Real Marriage: The Truth about Sex, Friendship, and Life Together* (Nashville, TN: Thomas Nelson, 2012). A good bit of the following material is taken from my review of *Real Marriage*. See Denny Burk, "Real Marriage: The Truth about Sex, Friendship, and Life Together [Review]," *Southern Baptist Journal of Theology* 16, no. 1 (2012): 72–79.

are lawful" as if the phrase were Paul's own declaration of Christian freedom, but that is mistaken. Almost every modern translation[19] and a near consensus of commentators[20] treat "all things are lawful" not as Paul's words but as a slogan that Corinthian men used to justify their visits to prostitutes (cf. 1 Cor. 6:15). The NIV captures the correct interpretation: *"'I have the right to do anything,' you say—but not everything is beneficial. 'I have the right to do anything'— but I will not be mastered by anything"* (1 Cor. 6:12).

As we saw in chapter 1, the Corinthians had twisted Paul's law-free gospel into a justification for bad behavior. Thus the phrase "all things are lawful" is not an expression of Christian freedom from the apostle Paul but rather an expression of antinomianism from fornicators! Paul's aim in 1 Corinthians 6:12–20 is to correct the Corinthians' misunderstanding. One of the reasons for the Corinthian error was the fact that they viewed the physical body as inconsequential in God's moral economy (see 1 Cor. 6:13b). Yet Paul refutes the Corinthians on this point and gives them an ultimate ethical norm with respect to their bodies: *"You have been bought with a price: therefore glorify God in your body"* (1 Cor. 6:20).

The Driscolls begin their ethical assessment with "Is it lawful?" and they answer the question based on whether there is an explicit prohibition of the behavior in Scripture. As we have seen, this is a misapplication of Paul's argument in 1 Corinthians 6. Paul's question is not "Is it lawful?" but "Does it glorify God with my body?" To miss this is to miss the entire point of the text. Sex exists for the glory of God, and Paul only commends activities that glorify God with the body. In order to answer the question "Does it glorify God?," one has to have an understanding of the *purposes* that God has given for sex and whether a given activity fits with

[19] ESV, HCSB, NET, NIV, NLT, NAB, NJB, RSV, NRSV.

[20] E.g., Fee, *First Epistle to the Corinthians*, 251; Hays, *First Corinthians*, 101; Fitzmyer, *First Corinthians*, 263; Thiselton, *First Epistle to the Corinthians*, 460; Craig L. Blomberg, *1 Corinthians*, NIV Application Commentary (Grand Rapids, MI: Zondervan, 1994), 125–26; C. K. Barrett, *The First Epistle to the Corinthians*, Black's New Testament Commentary (Peabody, MA: Hendrickson, 1968), 144; F. F. Bruce, *1 and 2 Corinthians*, New Century Bible Commentary (Grand Rapids, MI: Eerdmans, 1971), 62; Jerome Murphy-O'Connor, "Corinthian Slogans in 1 Cor 6:12–20" *Catholic Biblical Quarterly* 40, no. 3 (1978): 396; Jerome Murphy-O'Connor, 1 Corinthians, New Testament Message 10 (Wilmington, DE: Michael Glazier, 1979), 49–52.

those purposes. This kind of reflection is absent from chapter 10 in Driscoll's book.

As we have seen, the Driscolls are not the only persons who have ever misread 1 Corinthians 6:12. Nor are they the only ones to use a taxonomy like this one. In fact, the Driscolls' questions are almost identical to the ones that John Feinberg and Paul Feinberg use to judge the limits of Christian liberty in their book *Ethics for a Brave New World*.[21] Yet the Driscolls' use of the questions is reductionistic. Whereas the Feinbergs have eight questions, the Driscolls have only three. Consequently, the truncated assessment tool leaves out questions that would have mitigated the impact of the Driscolls' misreading of verse 12. The Feinbergs' questions are: (1) Am I fully persuaded that it is right? (2) Can I do it as unto the Lord? (3) Can I do it without being a stumbling block to my brother or sister in Christ? (4) Does it bring peace? (5) Does it edify my brother? (6) Is it profitable? (7) Does it enslave me? (8) Does it bring glory to God? Had the Driscolls used all eight of these questions in their taxonomy (especially number 8), their assessments might have been different.

The problems with the Driscolls' advice, however, are not merely exegetical. They are also pastoral. Although some Christian authors comment on the ethics of a husband's sodomizing his wife,[22] I have yet to find any who contemplate the reverse. Yet the Driscolls give explicit instructions to wives about how they might sodomize their husbands in a pleasurable way.[23] Yet where in the Bible is such an activity ever commended? The Bible contemplates such activities only in the context of homosexual relationships. The Bible condemns the "unnatural" use

---

[21] John S. Feinberg and Paul D. Feinberg, *Ethics for a Brave New World*, 2nd ed. (Wheaton, IL: Crossway, 2010), 52–55. Driscoll does not attribute his taxonomy to the Feinbergs.

[22] Even those who allow for sodomy within marriage often do so with extreme caution, both for marital and medical reasons. For instance, William Cutrer writes, "In my years of practicing medicine, I have never met a woman who engaged in anal sex because she thought it was 'the best thing going.' Most were doing it because their partners were pressuring them. . . . If couples wish to engage in this practice, they should know that at first it can be somewhat painful, cleanliness is important, anal contact followed by vaginal contact can cause infection, and anal sex carries with it the potential for damage to the sphincter" (Cutrer and Glahn, *Sexual Intimacy in Marriage*).

[23] Driscoll and Driscoll, *Real Marriage*, 188.

of bodies between persons of the same sex (Rom. 1:26–27). Why would Christian couples emulate that unnatural use in the marital bed? What about a husband for whom such an activity might stir up homosexual desires that he has never experienced before engaging in this activity with his wife? I do not think that the Driscolls have reckoned with the view that says "immorality" (*porneia*) is possible within the marital bed. The Driscolls may disagree with this point of view, but they should at least engage biblical commentators who understand sodomy as a defilement of marriage.[24]

I can think of a whole range of other pastoral problems that might be provoked by chapter 10 of the Driscolls' book. Is sexual holiness really upheld while engaging in cybersex over the Internet with one's spouse?[25] Is it really wise for Christians to upload digital, sexual images of themselves to the Internet even if it is only intended for a spouse? What if a third party were to intercept such an image and make it available to everyone with an Internet connection? How the cause of Christ would be shamed by such a result! But the Driscolls give little consideration to the potential consequences of making private pornography even though they admit that keeping such images private "can be nearly impossible"![26] Or what about the endorsement of sex toys? The Driscolls recommend purchasing them "from one of the more discreet Web

---

[24] It seems to me that the Driscolls need to engage interpretations of the biblical text that disagree with their own before declaring sodomy lawful. F. F. Bruce, for instance, thinks that Hebrews 13:4 has a bearing on this question: "Let marriage be held in honor among all, and let the marriage bed be undefiled, for God will judge the sexually immoral [*pornos*] and adulterous" (ESV). Bruce comments, "Fornication and adultery are not synonymous in the New Testament: adultery implies unfaithfulness by either party to the marriage vow, while the word translated 'fornication' covers a wide range of sexual irregularities, including unions within the bounds prohibited by law" (*The Epistle to the Hebrews*, rev. ed., New International Commentary on the New Testament [Grand Rapids, MI: Eerdmans, 1990], 373). One early Jewish commentator remarks on Lev. 18:22, "Outrage not your wife for shameful ways of intercourse. Transgress not for unlawful sex the natural limits of sexuality. For even animals are not pleased by intercourse of male with male. And let not women imitate the sexual role of men" (Pseudo-Phocylides, lines 189–92, in Pieter Willem van der Horst, *The Sentences of Pseudo-Phocylides: With Introduction and Commentary*, Studia in Veteris Testamenti Pseudepigrapha 4 [Leiden: Brill, 1978], 101). Such commentators are not inerrant, but their views have a long history in the Christian church. Christians have long studied what comprises an "unnatural" sex act, and the Driscolls need to give a better defense of the idea that sodomizing a husband fits within God's aims for human sexuality.

[25] Driscoll and Driscoll, *Real Marriage*, 184.

[26] Ibid., 200.

sites,"[27] but this seems to me a precarious proposition. How does a Christian go about finding a "discreet" seller of sex toys? The authors give no specific vendor for such objects. Specific rather than vague guidance might be better here, since a web search for sex toys is just as likely to connect Christians to pornography as it is to "discreet Web sites." Going through the list in chapter 10, it seems that law may not prohibit any number of these activities, but God's purposes for sex would.

As I argued in the previous chapter, the Bible teaches that the deepest meaning of marriage and indeed of the sexual union is to signify another marriage—Christ's marriage to his church (Eph. 5:32). In Ephesians 5 we learn that every marriage from Adam and Eve until now exists ultimately to give an enacted parable of Christ's covenant love for his bride. In other words, the purpose of marriage is to glorify Christ—to shine a light on his redemptive love for his people. It is only within that framework that we can understand the ultimate meaning of the marital act. The glory of the marital act is in the gospel union that it signifies. All the other "purposes" for the sexual union are subordinate to the ultimate end of glorifying God. Where this biblical teaching is absent, so is the framework for putting together ethical standards for sexual behavior within marriage. Again, the fundamental question is not merely "Is it lawful?" but "Does it glorify Christ?"

The Severing of Conjugal Union
Understanding the Divorce Culture

There may be no greater blight on the testimony of Christianity in our culture than the church's near total capitulation to the divorce culture. That divorce culture grows out of changing attitudes toward divorce over the last fifty years. Prior to 1969 most states regarded marriage as a contract between a man and a woman that could only be dissolved if one of the spouses committed an action incompatible with marriage. Such actions were known as a "fault

---

[27] Ibid., 193.

ground" for divorce. When a court granted a divorce, one person was found guilty and the other innocent.[28] By 1970 that legal reality began to change in America. In the 1960s and 70s, social activists argued that the introduction of no-fault divorce laws would reduce acrimonious divorce proceedings and enhance the status of women.[29] It was believed that by moving from a fault-based system to a no-fault system, women would be protected from predatory husbands who abused them. California became the first state to enact no-fault divorce with its 1969 Family Law Act (which went into effect in 1970).[30] Over the next two decades no-fault divorce laws like California's became the legal reality of every state in the union.

What followed was catastrophic for marriage in our culture. In 1960 about 393,000 marriages ended in divorce or annulment. By 1992 that number tripled to 1.2 million divorces annually.[31] Because getting a divorce got easier, more people availed themselves of the opportunity. And so the divorce rate increased precipitously. But no-fault divorce had a number of other unintended consequences. Rather than empowering couples with more freedom, it puts all the legal leverage in the hands of the spouse that wishes to dissolve the marriage. As Maggie Gallagher writes,

> The spouse who leaves learns that love dies. The spouse who is left learns that love betrays and that the courts and society side with the betrayers. In court, your marriage commitment means nothing. The only rule is: Whoever wants out, wins. By gutting the marital contract, no-fault divorce has transformed what it means to get married. The state will no longer enforce permanent legal commitments to a spouse. Formally, at least, no-fault divorce thus demotes marriage from a binding relation into some-

---

[28] For the foregoing three sentences, see Muller Davis, "Fault or No Fault? Rethinking Divorce Laws," *Christian Century* 119, no. 12 (2002): 28.
[29] Kim A. Lawton, "'No Fault' Divorce under Assault: Lawmakers Hope to Make the Road to Divorce Court More Difficult," *Christianity Today* 40, no. 4 (1996): 84.
[30] Ibid., 85.
[31] Ibid. The number has since stabilized and decreased, probably due to the growing number of unmarried couples cohabitating. See also "Table 78. Live Births, Deaths, Marriages, and Divorces: 1960 to 2008" at http://www.census.gov/compendia/statab/2012/tables/12s0078.pdf.

thing best described as cohabitation with insurance benefits. . . .
No-fault is thus something of a misnomer; a more accurate term
would be unilateral divorce on demand.[32]

What is perhaps most disconcerting is the fact that so many
Christian marriages seem to have accommodated themselves to
American divorce culture. Not only did churches say very little
when no-fault divorce became the legal reality of our land, but
they also said very little when no-fault divorce became the practical reality of the people sitting in our pews.[33] Though practicing
Christians tend to have lower divorce rates than the general population, the numbers are still very concerning. Among those who
report having been married, divorce rates are about 50 percent
for the religiously unaffiliated and about 42 percent for Christians and members of other religions. Roman Catholics are the
least likely to have divorced (35 percent), followed by mainline
Protestants (41 percent), evangelicals (46 precent), and black Protestants (54 percent). The divorce rate among evangelicals who
rarely attend church is 60 percent, while it is significantly lower
for those who regularly attend church, at 38 percent.[34] Perhaps
there is some consolation in the knowledge that church-attending
evangelicals seem to fare better than those who are less devout.
Nevertheless, it is a spiritual crisis that more than one-third of
the more committed evangelicals report having been divorced

---

[32] Maggie Gallagher and Barbara Dafoe Whitehead, "End No-Fault Divorce," First Things, no. 75 (1997): 25.

[33] W. Bradford Wilcox has this stinging indictment of the silence of church leaders: "Conservative Protestant moral discourse on divorce is muted and ambiguous—especially when compared with what is said on matters like homosexuality. It may well be that leaders and pastors are more comfortable confronting homosexuality, which probably does not affect many people in the pews, than confronting divorce, which does." See W. Bradford Wilcox, "Conservative Protestants and the Family: Resisting, Engaging, or Accommodating Modernity?," in A Public Faith: Evangelicals and Civic Engagement, ed. Michael Cromartie (Lanham, MD: Rowan and Littlefield, 2003), 63. See also W. Bradford Wilcox, Soft Patriarchs, New Men: How Christianity Shapes Fathers and Husbands (Chicago: University of Chicago Press, 2004), 70: "The conservative Protestant ambiguity and disagreement on divorce and remarriage can largely be explained by the fact that divorce rates are just as high among conservative Protestants as they are in the population at large. Thus, given that the divorce rate more than doubled from 1960 to 1990, conservative Protestant churches and pastors may be adjusting their views on divorce to the social practices they confront in pews and pulpits."

[34] The foregoing statistics are from Bradley R. E. Wright, Christians Are Hate-Filled Hypocrites . . . and Other Lies You've Been Told: A Sociologist Shatters Myths from the Secular and Christian Media (Bloomington, MN: Bethany, 2010), 132–33.

or separated. The numbers are still far too high for those who confess to believe what the Bible teaches about the sanctity of marriage. John Calvin's admonition is one that more people could stand to hear:

> They who, for slight causes, rashly allow of divorces, violate, in one single particular, all the laws of nature, and reduce them to nothing. If we should make it a point of conscience not to separate a father from his son, it is still greater wickedness to dissolve the bond which God has preferred to all others.[35]

Understanding Jesus's Teaching

The Bible knows nothing of no-fault divorce. As discussed earlier, the Bible defines marriage as the union of one man and one woman—a covenant made before God that cannot be dissolved without great injury to the meaning and purpose of marriage. And so the Scripture commends a truly countercultural ethic for Christians when it comes to marriage and divorce. The culture embraces divorce as the norm—a necessary evil that must be accommodated in the modern world. The Bible rejects divorce as something that God hates—an effacement of God's glory in marriage.[36]

Taking into account the Bible's clear denunciation of divorce, we must consider whether the Scripture recognizes any situations in which divorce would be allowed. This is the question about which Christian interpreters of Scripture have had no little disagreement. The ethical question boils down to two issues: divorce and remarriage. (1) Does the Scripture ever permit divorce? If so, what are the conditions under which divorce may be allowed? (2) Does the Scripture ever allow a divorced person to remarry? If so, under what conditions would remarriage be allowed?

The beginning point for this discussion is Jesus's teaching

---

[35] John Calvin, *Commentaries on the First Book of Moses Called Genesis*, trans. John King, vol. 1, Calvin's Commentaries (repr. Grand Rapids, MI: Baker, 1996), 136.
[36] In Malachi 2:16 the Lord says, "I hate divorce," according to traditional renderings. So David Instone-Brewer, *Divorce and Remarriage in the Bible: The Social and Literary Context* (Grand Rapids, MI: Eerdmans, 2002), 56–57, 301. Contra Gordon P. Hugenberger, *Marriage as a Covenant: Biblical Law and Ethics as Developed from Malachi* (Grand Rapids, MI: Baker, 1994), 70–73.

about marriage and divorce in the Synoptic Gospels. The relevant texts are set in parallel in Tables 4.1 and 4.2.

Table 4.1: *Abbreviated Versions of Jesus's Divorce Saying*

Matthew 5:31–32	Luke 16:18
It was said, "Whoever sends his wife away, let him give her a certificate of divorce"; but I say to you that everyone who divorces his wife, *except for the reason of unchastity*, makes her commit adultery; and whoever marries a divorced woman commits adultery.	Everyone who divorces his wife and marries another commits adultery, and he who marries one who is divorced from a husband commits adultery.

Table 4.2: *Longer Versions of Jesus's Divorce Saying*

Matthew 19:3–9	Mark 10:2–12
Some Pharisees came to Jesus, testing Him and asking, "Is it lawful for a man to divorce his wife for any reason at all?" And He answered and said, "Have you not read that He who created them from the beginning made them male and female, and said, 'For this reason a man shall leave his father and mother and be joined to his wife, and the two shall become one flesh'? So they are no longer two, but one flesh. What therefore God has joined together, let no man separate." They said to Him, "Why then did Moses command to give her a certificate of divorce and send her away?" He said to them, "Because of your hardness of heart Moses permitted you to divorce your wives; but from the beginning it has not been this way. And I say to you, whoever divorces his wife, *except for immorality*, and marries another woman commits adultery."	Some Pharisees came up to Jesus, testing Him, and began to question Him whether it was lawful for a man to divorce a wife. And He answered and said to them, "What did Moses command you?" They said, "Moses permitted a man to write a certificate of divorce and send her away." But Jesus said to them, "Because of your hardness of heart he wrote you this commandment. But from the beginning of creation, God made them male and female. For this reason a man shall leave his father and mother, and the two shall become one flesh; so they are no longer two, but one flesh. What therefore God has joined together, let no man separate. In the house the disciples began questioning Him about this again. And He said to them, "Whoever divorces his wife and marries another woman commits adultery against her; and if she herself divorces her husband and marries another man, she is committing adultery."

The passages have much in common, though there are subtle differences throughout. In all four passages, Jesus speaks to divorce and remarriage. In three of the texts, Jesus quotes the Old Testament. In two of the texts, he grounds his own teaching within the message of Genesis 1–2. Jesus's explication of marriage and divorce is, therefore, an exercise in biblical theology.

The major difference between the two texts from Matthew and the corresponding texts in Luke and Mark is the presence of Matthew's exception clauses: "Except for the matter of immorality" (Matt. 5:32 AT) and "except for immorality" (Matt. 19:9). The question that commentators puzzle over is why the exception clauses appear in Matthew's account but not in Luke's or Mark's. At first blush, it seems to put Matthew's account at odds with Luke's and Mark's. It appears that Luke and Mark give an absolute prohibition on divorce under any circumstance, while Matthew allows for divorce and possibly remarriage when one party commits immorality.

Commentators have tried to reconcile these apparently different perspectives in a number of ways. John Piper, for instance, argues that the absolute prohibitions of Mark and Luke should control the apparently qualified prohibitions of Matthew's account. He argues, therefore, that all four texts comprise absolute prohibitions on divorce and remarriage, and that the exception clauses in Matthew refer not to marriage but to betrothal.[37] Another view says that the qualified prohibitions of Matthew should control the absolute statements of Mark and Luke. In Matthew 19:3 the Pharisees ask Jesus whether it is lawful to divorce one's wife for "any cause" (AT). And Jesus eventually responds in 19:9 that anyone who divorces his wife—"except on the basis of immorality"—and marries another commits adultery. Although the phrases "any cause" and "except on the basis of immorality" are absent from the account in Mark 10, David Instone-Brewer argues

---

[37] John Piper, *What Jesus Demands from the World* (Wheaton, IL: Crossway, 2006), 309–16. Piper also advocates this view in *This Momentary Marriage: A Parable of Permanence* (Wheaton, IL: Crossway, 2009), 173–74.

that first-century Jewish readers would have understood them to have been implied by the speaker. The original readers would have understood that Jesus and the Pharisees were talking about a well-known interpretive dispute about the meaning of the divorce regulation in Deuteronomy 24:1. The school of Hillel interpreted Deuteronomy 24:1 to mean that a man could divorce his wife for "any cause." The school of Shammai held that the law allowed divorce only on the basis of "indecency." This debate and these phrases ("any cause" and "except indecency") would have been recognized as stock phrases from Jewish divorce law and would have been implied even if not stated (as in Mark and Luke).[38] R. T. France agrees:

> When in Mark and Luke Jesus forbids divorce *tout simple* this is understood to mean the voluntary breaking of a marriage which is hitherto intact, it being assumed that in the case of [immorality] by the wife the marriage was already destroyed and could not be allowed to continue. On that view, Matthew is merely making explicit what was assumed by Mark and Luke to be already obvious to their readers.[39]

Thus it is my view that Mark and Luke *imply* what Matthew makes *explicit* in the exception clauses and in the phrase "any cause."[40]

The question remains, what do these exception clauses mean with respect to Jesus's prohibition of divorce? The Greek term in question is *porneia* (here translated as "immorality"), and it is cited as the lone exception to Jesus's prohibition of divorce. In general, the term is a catchall for any kind of unlawful sexual activity, including but certainly not limited to adultery.[41] There

[38] Instone-Brewer, *Divorce and Remarriage in the Bible*, 134–36.
[39] R. T. France, *The Gospel of Matthew*, New International Commentary on the New Testament (Grand Rapids, MI: Eerdmans, 2007), 211.
[40] Robert Stein says that Jesus speaks hyperbolically in Mark 10:11–12 and Luke 16:18 and that Jesus never intended his statements in these two texts to categorically rule out exceptions. See Robert H. Stein, "Is It Lawful for a Man to Divorce His Wife?," *Journal of the Evangelical Theological Society* 22, no. 2 (1979): 119.
[41] The term *porneia* appears only three times in Matthew's Gospel: 5:32; 15:19; and 19:9. Because Matthew distinguishes *porneia* from *moicheia* ("adultery") in 15:19, we should not regard *porneia* as a synonym for "adultery" in either 5:32 or 9:9. Thus *porneia* appears in Matthew in its usual

are at least three different views on how the term should be understood within the so-called exception clauses.[42] The first view understands *porneia* as a reference to a spouse's sexual immorality that becomes a legitimate ground for *divorce and remarriage* for the innocent spouse.[43] The second view understands *porneia* as sexual immorality that becomes a legitimate basis for *divorce but not for remarriage*.[44] The third view sees *porneia* as a reference to some kind of sexual sin that would have made marriage unlawful under Jewish civil law. There are many varieties of this last view, but they hold in common that the exception clause allows *neither divorce nor remarriage*.[45]

On balance, the first view seems to fit best with the biblical evidence. In Matthew's account, Jesus sets forth first what marriage is. Jesus bases his instruction not on the text that the rabbis were disputing (Deut. 24:1) but on the creation norms that are set in place in Genesis 1–2. On that basis, Jesus says that marriage is a permanent union of one man and one woman that no person must ever dissolve. Jesus says that the divorce law in Deuteronomy 24:1 stands not as a testament to God's intention for marriage but as a

---

sense as a catch-all term for any unlawful sexual conduct. Based on context, such conduct might include adultery, but it is certainly not limited to it. See BDAG, "πορνεία," 1.

[42] The following summarizes the discussion in Andreas J. Köstenberger and David W. Jones, *God, Marriage, and Family: Rebuilding the Biblical Foundation*, 2nd ed. (Wheaton, IL: Crossway, 2010), 230.

[43] So Craig L. Blomberg, "Marriage, Divorce, Remarriage, and Celibacy: An Exegesis of Matthew 19:3–12," *Trinity Journal* 11, no. 2 (1990): 196; John Jefferson Davis, *Evangelical Ethics: Issues Facing the Church Today*, 3rd ed. (Phillipsburg, NJ: P&R, 2004), 111; Feinberg and Feinberg, *Ethics for a Brave New World*, 625; Richard B. Hays, *The Moral Vision of the New Testament: Community, Cross, New Creation, A Contemporary Introduction to New Testament Ethics* (New York: HarperOne, 1996), 372–73; Stein, "Is It Lawful for a Man to Divorce His Wife?"

[44] William A. Heth, "Divorce, but No Remarriage," in *Divorce and Remarriage: Four Christian Views*, ed. H. Wayne House (Downers Grove, IL: InterVarsity, 1990), 94: "I believe it can be shown that Jesus viewed remarriage after divorce, for whatever reason, as both a violation of the seventh commandment and contrary to God's creation design for marriage." Heth held this view in common with Gordon Wenham, with whom he coauthored the book *Jesus and Divorce* (London: Hodder and Stoughton, 1984). Heth later changed his position to the view that allows for divorce and remarriage. See William A. Heth, "Jesus on Divorce: How My Mind Has Changed," *Southern Baptist Journal of Theology* 6, no. 1 (2002): 4–29.

[45] E.g., Piper, *This Momentary Marriage*, 159: "If Christ ever abandons and discards his church, then a man may divorce his wife. And if the blood-bought church, under the new covenant, ever ceases to be the bride of Christ, then a wife may legitimately divorce her husband. But as long as Christ keeps his covenant with the church, and as long as the church, by the omnipotent grace of God, remains the chosen people of Christ, then the very meaning of marriage will include: *What God has joined, only God can separate.*" See also the discussion of the exception clause on pp. 173–74. See also Piper, *What Jesus Demands from the World*, 311–16. So also James Montgomery Boice, *The Sermon on the Mount: Matthew 5–7* (Grand Rapids, MI: Baker, 1972), 118–19.

testimony to mankind's hardness of heart. In other words, there are some situations in which man's sinfulness makes divorce the lesser of two evils. As R. T. France writes,

> It was the fact that divorce was taking place in defiance of God's stated intention for marriage that made it necessary for Moses to make appropriate provision. But it should never have been so. The existence of divorce legislation is a pointer not to divine approval of divorce but to human sinfulness.[46]

In any case, Jesus says that in such cases divorce is not *commanded* but *allowed* by Moses (Matt. 19:8; cf. Mark 10:4). The ideal is still lifelong fidelity within marriage. The exception clause indicates grounds upon which man's "hardness of heart" may become a factor in dissolving a marriage. If a married person has a sexual relationship with someone other than his spouse, the offended party would have legitimate grounds for divorce. It does not mean that the offended party must seek for a divorce; it just means that it becomes a possibility. As we shall see, this perspective coheres with what Paul teaches as well.

Understanding Paul's Teaching

The apostle Paul's main ethical instruction concerning divorce occurs in 1 Corinthians 7:10–16. In verse 10 he writes, "But to the married I give instructions, not I, but the Lord." By saying, "Not I, but the Lord," Paul means for his readers to understand that the Lord Jesus spoke directly to the issue of divorce in his earthly ministry and that Paul wishes to reiterate that teaching. Elsewhere, Paul accesses Jesus traditions that also appear in the Synoptic Gospels,[47] and that is what he is doing in these verses as well. Paul alludes to a tradition that has a great deal in common with the one that appears in Mark 10:11–12.[48]

---

[46] France, *Gospel of Matthew*, 720.
[47] Notice, for instance, that Paul's version of the words of institution at the Lord's Supper is very similar to Luke's version of the same (1 Cor. 11:24–25; Luke 22:19–20). This is in contrast to Matthew and Mark, who seem to be preserving a different tradition (Matt. 26:20–25; Mark 14:22–26).
[48] So Hays, *Moral Vision of the New Testament*, 358.

Table 4.3: Divorce Traditions in Mark and Paul

Mark 10:11–12	1 Corinthians 7:10–11
And He said to them, "Whoever divorces his wife and marries another woman commits adultery against her; and if she herself divorces her husband and marries another man, she is committing adultery."	But to the married I give instructions, not I, but the Lord, that the wife should not leave her husband (but if she does leave, she must remain unmarried, or else be reconciled to her husband), and that the husband should not divorce his wife.

Like the prohibition in Mark, Paul's words focus on both the husband's and the wife's individual responsibility not to divorce one's spouse. This contrasts with Matthew and Luke which focus solely on the man's role in divorcing and remarrying.[49] In Mark, Jesus says that those who divorce for illegitimate reasons and remarry thereby commit adultery. So also Paul says in 1 Corinthians 7:11 that one who leaves his spouse must remain unmarried. Paul seems to be reiterating in his own words that which Jesus himself taught in his earthly ministry.

In verses 12–13, Paul applies the Lord's teaching to a new situation that Jesus never actually spoke to in so many words. Paul says, "To the rest I say, not the Lord . . ." Some have taken this phrase to mean that Paul is offering an opinion that has less authority than the words of Jesus alluded to in verses 10–11. As discussed in chapter 2, that is not at all what Paul means by distinguishing his words from the Lord's words. All Paul means to say is that the Lord Jesus did not specifically address the issue of desertion in his teaching about divorce. Nevertheless, Paul will offer an apostolic word on the matter that has every bit as much authority over the consciences of his readers as anything Jesus ever said. Indeed, Paul believes that it is the spirit of Jesus himself who speaks through him.[50]

---

[49] Only Mark's Gospel mentions the possibility of a wife who divorces her husband (Mark 10:12). The other Synoptics focus solely on the man's role in divorcing and remarrying (see Matt. 5:32; 19:9; Luke 16:18).

[50] Paul connects his apostolic authority to his opinions: "Now concerning virgins I have no command of the Lord, but I give *an opinion as one who by the mercy of the Lord is trustworthy*" (7:25). Paul's

Paul aims to apply Jesus's teaching on divorce to the Corinthian situation. In particular, he wants to answer the question of how Jesus's words apply to believers who are married to unbelievers. Should they stay in their marriages? Should divorce be allowed when a believer's spouse deserts him? Those are the questions that Paul seeks to answer.

In Paul's day, when the gospel spread, sometimes it saved whole households (Acts 16:15). At other times it saved only some within the household. The Corinthians needed to know what to do when one spouse is a Christian and the other is not. Should the Christian stay in that marriage or leave? For many, it probably seemed that a concern for holiness would lead Christians out of marriages to unbelievers. After all, how could a Christian be holy and pure while being united to an impure and unbelieving spouse?[51] Paul's answer shows such thinking to be fundamentally at odds with the nature of the new covenant. Under the old covenant, when Jews touched a dead body or a leper, they became unclean. The same thing happened to an otherwise faithful Israelite who ate pork or shellfish. The principle was clear: anyone who touched something unclean became unclean.

But that principle got turned around with the coming of Jesus and the new covenant. When Jesus touched lepers, he did not become unclean. The lepers became clean and were healed (Matt. 8:3). When Jesus touched a dead body, Jesus did not become unclean. The dead body would be raised to life and be clean (Mark 5:41–42). Jesus came making the unclean clean. And now Jesus's followers are doing the same. Paul applies that new-covenant principle to marriages between believers and unbelievers. Christians should not divorce their unbelieving spouse. Christians are filled with the Holy Spirit of God. Jesus said in John 14:12 that those who believe in him would do greater works than he did. That means that a Christian is not made unclean by his marriage to an unbe-

---

opinions are established as "trustworthy" by the Lord Jesus himself. So Paul says that Jesus's authority inheres in the opinions that Paul gives to the Corinthians. See also 2 Cor. 13:3, in which Paul says, "Christ who speaks in me."

[51] Hays, *First Corinthians*, 121.

liever.[52] A Christian's marriage is made clean by his staying in it.[53] That doesn't mean that everyone in a Christian's family automatically becomes converted. It means that Christians bring a gospel influence to their marriage and family. Christians "sanctify" their spouses and children in the sense that they exert a gospel influence on them that would not otherwise be there. If the Christian leaves, then the only sanctifying influence leaves, and that family is left without a witness. And they are "unclean" (1 Cor. 7:14). This possibility of the conversion of family members is why Paul writes in 7:16: "For how do you know, O wife, whether you will save your husband? Or how do you know, O husband, whether you will save your wife?"

In all probability, Paul understood that Jesus's divorce prohibition had an exception for infidelity implied in it (along the lines discussed above).[54] But in the present case, Paul is not dealing with a situation in which one spouse cheats on the other but one in which one spouse deserts the other. Paul says that while a Christian should not divorce or desert an unbelieving spouse, the same is not true when an unbelieving spouse leaves the marriage. Paul surmises an exception in this case that allows for divorce. Paul's instruction is clear: "Yet if the unbelieving one leaves, let him leave; the brother or sister is not under bondage in such cases, but God has called us to peace" (1 Cor. 7:15).

Interpreters tend to disagree about what Paul means by saying that Christian spouses are not "bound" in such cases. Gordon Fee—who argues that Paul has disallowed remarriage altogether in verse 11—says that the marriage is not necessarily ended when it is "unbound" by desertion. "One is simply not under bondage to maintain the marriage, which the other person wishes to

---

[52] Richard Hays calls this an "extraordinary reversal of conventional Jewish conceptualities about ritual defilement." See Hays, *Moral Vision of the New Testament*, 360.
[53] This applies to believers whom God saves while they are already married to an unbeliever. God wants believers to stay in the situation in which God called them (1 Cor. 7:17, 20, 24). Unmarried persons, however, should never contemplate entering into marriage to an unbeliever (2 Cor. 6:14–18).
[54] Contra Richard Hays, who argues that Paul offers an amendment to Jesus's "unconditional prohibition of divorce." See Hays, *First Corinthians*, 121.

dissolve."[55] In Fee's view, the marriage continues, even though a separation has occurred. Though such a view might support a *no remarriage* position, it does not seem a very likely meaning of Paul's words. Paul's chosen term indicates that the deserted spouse is not "enslaved" or "in bondage" any longer to the marriage.[56] As Fitzmyer observes, "The statement . . . would make no sense, if it meant that the Christian spouse after the separation of the unbeliever were still bound" to the marriage.[57] To say that the believer is no longer bound means that the marriage has ended. The term Paul uses to say that the believer is no longer "bound" also seems to imply that remarriage is a possibility for the deserted spouse. The term is related to the one that Paul uses in 7:39, in which a widow is no longer "bound" to her husband after he dies.[58] Since the unbound widow in 7:39 is free to remarry, it seems to follow by analogy that the deserted spouse of 7:15 would have the same opportunity, since the deserted spouse is no longer "bound" either.

Understanding the New Testament on Divorce

Paul agrees with Jesus's prohibition on divorce. In the Corinthian situation, that means that believing spouses must never divorce their spouses. Just as Jesus had an exception to the divorce prohibition, so also Paul has one as well. Taken together, Jesus and Paul teach that divorce is not an option for believers. The only exceptions that they allow are in cases of immorality or desertion. Neither Jesus nor Paul says that a person *must* be divorced if there is *infidelity* or *desertion*. They are simply saying that it can be permissible in those two situations.

Nevertheless, the exceptions really aren't the accent. Christians who wish to understand the New Testament's teaching on divorce err if they emphasize that divorce is permissible. Jesus emphasized

---

[55] Fee, *First Epistle to the Corinthians*, 303.
[56] BDAG, "δουλόω," 2.
[57] Fitzmyer, *First Corinthians*, 302.
[58] The two Greek terms are δεδούλωται (7:15) and δέδεται (7:39). The former term contains the idea of enslaving a person, while the latter has the idea of binding/restraining/imprisoning. In both cases, it involves involuntary bondage.

the abiding permanence of marriage—that it is a covenant bond rooted in the creation ordinance of God. Jesus stressed that marriage must not be dissolved by man: "What therefore God has joined together, let no man separate." In Ephesians 5:32 Paul says that the mystery of marriage is that it points to the union that Christ has with his church. Thus a divorce does not merely fall short of an ideal. It says something blasphemous about the nature of Christ's commitment to his bride. For this reason, Christians must not end their ethical inquiry about divorce with, "What is allowed?" Again, the most important question is, "How can I most glorify God?" For this reason, even in cases of infidelity or desertion, believers should make every effort at reconciliation with their spouse. In a fallen world, this will not always be possible. Some wayward spouses will not return, and divorce is inevitable. Nevertheless, covenant faithfulness within marriage sends a message to the world about Christ's covenant faithfulness to his bride. For this reason, upholding this icon of the gospel ought to be a matter of first importance to every Christian spouse—even when that spouse has what would otherwise be legitimate grounds for dissolving the marriage.

What should a person do who is suffering abuse at the hands of her spouse? Abuse is not listed among the legitimate grounds for divorce. Does that mean that the abused spouse has no recourse? No, it does not. Separation is not the same thing as divorce, and abused spouses should separate from abusive situations in order to protect themselves and their children. The church should be actively involved in such circumstances and come to the defense of the one being abused. The church should make whatever provision is necessary for the safety and welfare of the victims. Oftentimes, this kind of separation will lead the offending party to repent and seek reconciliation. Or after time, the abuser will leave the marriage and the exception for desertion comes into play (1 Cor. 7:15).[59] In any case, the victim must be protected and the abuser sanctioned.[60]

---

[59] Much of the foregoing paragraph comes from Köstenberger and Jones, *God, Marriage, and Family*, 237.

[60] Threatening or intentionally causing bodily harm to a spouse is a crime that is punishable in many states by fines, imprisonment, or both. Churches should not only take steps to discipline

Conclusion

The conjugal union of marriage is a gift from God, and it exists to bring glory to God. Conjugal union is not an option in marriage. It is a mandate. Couples must be in regular physical union with one another in order to avoid temptation and as an expression of their ongoing commitment to one another. While the marriage bed should be a place of warmth and delight, the question of limits within marriage is an important one. Couples should ask themselves not merely, "What is allowed?" but also, "What glorifies Christ and God's purposes for sexual union?" The New Testament teaches that marriage is permanent. While there are exceptions for infidelity and desertion, the accent of biblical teaching is on the covenant faithfulness of each spouse. To glorify God with one's conjugal union means taking every measure to preserve the union and to pursue reconciliation, even when one partner has broken faith.

their members who are involved in such sinful activity but should also report them to appropriate authorities. See John Piper, "Clarifying Words on Wife Abuse," December 19, 2012, http://www.desiringgod.org/blog/posts/clarifying-words-on-wife-abuse.

The 1950s felt so safe and smug, the '60s so raw and raucous, the revolutions stacked one on top of another, in race relations, gender roles, generational conflict, the clash of church and state—so many values and vanities tossed on the bonfire . . . and the pill become the Pill, the means by which women untied their aprons, scooped up their ambitions and marched eagerly into the new age.

—Nancy Gibbs, "The Pill at 50," *Time* magazine

But women will be saved through childbearing—if they continue in faith, love and holiness and propriety.

—1 Timothy 2:15 (NIV)

5

Glorify God with Your Family Planning

Perhaps no single technology has been more consequential in shaping culture than the invention of modern contraception. For the first time in human history, a technology has come onto the scene which enables couples to engage in sexual activity without having to worry about the responsibility of children. These devices have presided over an enormous social change in our culture that we are still only just beginning to reckon with. In her book *Adam and Eve after the Pill*, Mary Eberstadt puts it this way:

> No single event since Eve took the apple has been as consequential for relations between the sexes as the arrival of modern contraception. . . . By rendering fertile women infertile with nearly 100 percent accuracy, the Pill and related devices have transformed the lives and families of the great majority of people born after their invention. Modern contraception is not only a fact of our time; it may even be the central fact, in the sense that it is hard to think of any other whose demographic, social, behavioral, and personal fallout has been as profound.[1]

---

[1] Mary Eberstadt, *Adam and Eve after the Pill: Paradoxes of the Sexual Revolution* (San Francisco: Ignatius, 2012).

The Misuse of Birth Control outside of Marriage

The changes in our culture over the last fifty years have indeed been profound. It is difficult to imagine that the sexual revolution of the 1960s and 1970s could ever have occurred without the birth control pill. Indeed, one could very well make the case that it occurred *because* of the birth control pill. Sex without the consequence of children was made possible by the Pill, and it enabled subsequent generations to leave behind the quaint norm of reserving sex for marriage. By severing sex from its natural connection to childbirth, people found themselves "free" to experiment with all manner of sexual activity outside of the bonds of matrimony.

The feminist movement latched onto the Pill as a fundamental value for their cause. Before the Pill, women had always borne the heavier "burden" of the decision to engage in sexual activity. Not only were women the ones who bore the stigma of having engaged in sex outside marriage, but they were also the ones to become pregnant and to care for the child. In this way, a woman's fertility made her different from a man and thereby unequal to him. Her fertility meant that she could not compete with him in the general marketplace because her advance was so often hindered by pregnancy and children. The Pill changed all of that. It fostered the feminist dream of full equality with men by rendering women infertile. It enabled them to be just as promiscuous as men without the "baggage" of a baby. It enabled married women to remain childless so that they could pursue careers outside the home. Thus a major part of the feminist program over the decades has been to "free" women from their fertility. That is why both contraception and abortion have become important "rights" for feminists. Both of them free women from their fertility and make it possible for them to compete on a more equal footing with men.

Though many people view feminist equality and sexual liberation as progress, others have made a strong case that both of these have given birth to enormous social and spiritual ills. Since modern contraception has made feminist equality and liberation possible, we must evaluate the morality of contraception within this larger framework. Has it really fostered the common good and human flourishing to separate sexual activity from its natural consequence of childbirth? It is true that more people are having sex and that they are doing so with a greater variety of partners than they were a generation ago. But is that a good thing?

From a Christian perspective, the answer is clearly no. Modern contraception has fostered a culture in which extramarital sexual activity of all kinds flourishes. The biblical norms of chastity outside of marriage and fidelity within marriage no longer seem to be the majority view. From a societal perspective, the answer is no as well. Contraception has not only "freed" women to have sex without consequence; it has also freed men from the bondage of having to take responsibility for the women they have sex with.[2] It thereby enables and rewards predatory behavior from men. It has made men more reluctant to commit to marry. As Mary Eberstadt observes, "The sexual revolution has proved a disaster for many men and women; . . . its weight has fallen heaviest on the smallest and weakest shoulders in society—even as it has given extra strength to those already strongest and most predatory."[3]

All of these social and spiritual ills seem to be a consequence of a dissipated use of modern contraception that enables users to sever sex from it natural consequence of childbearing. That separation has led to a proliferation of fornication, and the effects on society have been devastating.

The Use of Birth Control in Marriage

The question of artificial birth control used outside of marriage is preempted by the issue of fornication. The Bible clearly rejects sex outside of marriage, so Christian teaching rejects all the inducements to such behavior—including birth control measures (Rom. 13:14). Nevertheless, opinions have been divided about the use of birth control within marriage. In general, evangelical Protestants

---

[2] Ibid., 15.
[3] Ibid., 15–16.

view it as permissible while Roman Catholics do not.[4] Among evangelicals, the main concern has been whether a given birth control method causes an abortion—the destruction of a fertilized egg. Evangelicals typically reject methods that are abortifacient and permit methods that are not.[5] Roman Catholics, however, take a more restrictive view. The Roman Catholic Church agrees with evangelicals that abortion is morally wrong. They disagree with evangelicals that modern birth control technologies can ever be right.

The Roman Catholic position on birth control deserves serious consideration because it is based on natural law theory. As a species of teleological ethics, natural law ethics is concerned with sexuality's final cause or purpose—which is also the primary concern of the present work. As a natural-law approach, the Roman Catholic view aims to apply reason to the design that God has revealed in nature. The very design of the sexual organs and their procreative power suggests that their natural end is procreation. Since nature thus reveals that God created sex for procreation, any other use of sex is "unnatural and contrary to God's intended design."[6] The Roman Catholic position has a long history, going back at least to Augustine, who argued that the primary purpose of sex is procreation. Because God intends sex for procreation, any sex act that is not open to that purpose is thereby sinful. Thus, any sex act that includes contraception in the equation would violate God's will for the gift of sex.

In 1968 Pope Paul VI reiterated the Roman Catholic Church's traditional opposition to contraception in a watershed encyclical titled *Humanae Vitae*.[7] This letter has become a touchstone of official Roman Catholic doctrine as it relates to modern birth control. This document also reflects a natural-law approach to birth control, saying that husbands and wives "must conform their actions

---

[4] Stanley J. Grenz, *Sexual Ethics: An Evangelical Perspective* (Louisville, KY: Westminster, 1997), 147.

[5] E.g., John Jefferson Davis, *Evangelical Ethics: Issues Facing the Church Today*, 3rd ed. (Phillipsburg, NJ: P&R, 2004), 54; John S. Feinberg and Paul D. Feinberg, *Ethics for a Brave New World*, 2nd ed. (Wheaton, IL: Crossway, 2010), 305.

[6] Feinberg and Feinberg, *Ethics for a Brave New World*, 296.

[7] Pope Paul VI, *Humanae Vitae*.

to the creative intention of God, expressed in the very nature of marriage and of its acts, and manifested by the constant teaching of the Church."[8] *Humanae Vitae* stresses two goods or purposes of sex: the unitive significance and the procreative significance.[9] The procreative significance highlights the good of having children. The unitive significance highlights the goodness of husband and wife being joined together in heart, soul, and body in "true mutual love."[10] *Humanae Vitae* argues that the unitive and procreative purposes of sex must be held together in every sexual act. It is immoral to pursue sexual activity within marriage in a way that intentionally denies either the unitive or procreative dimensions. Those who pursue only one of these purposes to the neglect of the other "act contrary to the nature of both man and woman and of their most intimate relationship, and, therefore, contradict also the plan of God and His will."[11] The conclusion: "Each and every marriage act must remain open to the transmission of life."[12] This means that any attempt to "render procreation impossible" is prohibited. Thus artificial birth control is not allowed under Roman Catholic teaching.[13]

Humanae Vitae and Roman Catholic teaching in general are right to look to the purposes of sex in order to develop a proper ethic regarding the use of artificial birth control methods. Nevertheless, the Roman Catholic argument falls short by failing to sort out subordinate ends from ultimate ends. Procreation is not the ultimate end of sex within marriage. It is subordinated to the ultimate end of glorifying God. And there is more than one way by which the gift of sex glorifies God. As we mentioned in the introduction, procreation tends toward the glory of God as it is a means by which the glory of God will cover the earth through his image-bearing vice-

---

[8] Ibid., 14.
[9] Ibid., 15.
[10] Ibid.
[11] Ibid., 16.
[12] Ibid., 15.
[13] Catholic teaching does allow for married couples to use a "natural" birth control—the so-called rhythm method, which relies on abstaining from sex during the fertile period of a woman's monthly cycle. See ibid., 19.

regents. Procreation is not ultimate. God's glory is. Still, the unitive purpose of sex also tends toward the glory of God even when procreation is not possible. The unitive purpose of sex encompasses three of the four purposes we listed in the introduction—consummation, expression of love, and pleasure—each of which is less clearly bound to sex's procreative potential.[14] The unitive aspects of the conjugal bond point to the marriage that Christ has with his bride. In other words, the unitive aspect of a sexual encounter between spouses glorifies God even when procreation is not immediately in view. Yes, Christians must hold all of the purposes of sex together. But those purposes must hold together over the course of a married relationship, not necessarily in each and every act. It is on this point that evangelicals have a "major break" with Roman Catholics concerning the use of contraception. As Albert Mohler has argued, "That every act of marital intercourse must be fully and equally open to the gift of children . . . claims too much, and places inordinate importance on individual acts of sexual intercourse, rather than the larger integrity of the conjugal bond."[15]

So what principles can we surmise for Christian couples as they consider whether to use birth control? I will make several suggestions.[16]

First, Christians must reject the contraceptive mentality that treats pregnancy and children as "impositions to be avoided rather than gifts to be received."[17] The Bible teaches:

Behold, children are a gift of the LORD,
The fruit of the womb is a reward.
Like arrows in the hand of a warrior,
So are the children of one's youth.
How blessed is the man whose quiver is full of them.
(Ps. 127:3–5)

---

[14] Grenz, *Sexual Ethics*, 152.
[15] R. Albert Mohler Jr., "Can Christians Use Birth Control?," *Journal for Biblical Manhood and Womanhood* 18.1 (2013): 8.
[16] In this list I am following closely and expanding on the suggestions helpfully enumerated by Albert Mohler in ibid., 7–9.
[17] Ibid., 8.

This perspective stands squarely against the spirit of the age that treats children as financial burdens and as inhibitors of personal autonomy and freedom. A selfish, materialistic mind-set is often blind to the blessings that God offers through children. Christians must reject the culture's willful rejection about what makes for the good life. Throughout Scripture, children are viewed as blessings, not as curses. As Christopher Ash has said it, "There is a great moral difference between what used to be called 'planned parenthood' and 'planned *un*parenthood.'"[18] Children are blessings, and Christians should receive them as such.

Second, we must recognize all the purposes of the gift of sex and how they relate to the ultimate purpose of glorifying God. That means that we must not separate the purposes from one another in an attempt to choose only those that we desire for ourselves. It is not legitimate for couples to pursue sexual pleasure in marriage while being closed off to the possibility of children. As Albert Mohler writes,

> We are not to sever these "goods" of marriage and choose only those we may desire for ourselves. Every marriage must be open to the gift of children. Even where the ability to conceive and bear children may be absent, the will to receive children must be present. To demand sexual pleasure without openness to children is to violate a sacred trust.[19]

We must not succumb to a cultural ideal that idolizes sexual pleasure and career advancement while treating children as a personal lifestyle choice. Christians err when they play the unitive purpose of sex against the procreative, as if they can accept the one and reject the other. The Bible teaches both. Christians who want to be faithful to the Bible must submit to all of what Scripture says. Thus, every marriage must embrace all the purposes of sex.

Third, the Roman Catholic focus on "each and every marriage

---

[18] Christopher Ash, *Marriage: Sex in the Service of God* (Vancouver, British Columbia: Regent College Publishing, 2003), 183.
[19] Mohler, "Can Christians Use Birth Control?," 8.

act" goes beyond what the Bible teaches. Even *Humanae Vitae* allows for "natural" family planning—the so-called rhythm method in which couples avoid sexual activity during periods of a woman's peak fertility. The rhythm method instructs married couples to pursue sexual relations at times that they know will not lead to the procreation of children. By definition, then, Roman Catholic teaching itself does not require "each and every marriage act" to have procreative intent. For this reason, the emphasis should be less on "each and every act" than it is on a couple's openness to children over the course of a marriage. To this end, Oliver O'Donovan writes:

> What upset so many in the teaching of Paul VI's encyclical *Humanae Vitae* was that it seemed not to perceive the difference of structure between sexual relations in marriage and simple fornication. Chastity in marriage was analysed into a series of particular acts of sexual union, a proceeding which carried with it an unwitting but unmistakable hint of the pornographic. A married couple do not know each other in isolated moments or one-night stands. Their moments of sexual union are points of focus for a physical relationship which must properly be predicated of the whole extent of their life together.[20]

Realizing the procreative intent of sex does not require openness to procreation in "each and every act" but openness to the possibility that God will bless a couple's overall sexual union with children.[21]

Fourth, the Roman Catholic moral distinction between "natural" and "artificial" methods of contraception is questionable. We question whether such a distinction finds any basis in Scripture. What we do find in Scripture is that God commands humans to procreate in order that they might rule and subdue the earth (Gen. 1:28). Thus, the procreation mandate appears within the larger cultural mandate to care for and steward God's good creation. Christians can access some forms of artificial contraception as a part of this stewardship. As Dennis Hollinger argues,

---

[20] Oliver O'Donovan, *Resurrection and Moral Order: An Outline for Evangelical Ethics*, 2nd ed. (Grand Rapids, MI: Eerdmans, 1994), 210.
[21] Ash, *Marriage: Sex in the Service of God*, 182–83.

Within this framework of stewardship we can accept contraception, not in order to negate the procreative character of sex, but to steward the gifts and resources that God grants us. We can utilize nonnatural means of contraception to work with nature just as we steward many dimensions of natural life through technology and human knowledge. . . . Stewardship is not an attempt at human autonomy or self-centeredness, but is a response to the sovereignty of God who lovingly invites us to share in the care of his creation. . . . Contraceptives can be used in order to plan our families so that we can better serve them, Christ's kingdom, and the world to which God calls us.[22]

Fifth, Scripture does not order married persons to pursue the largest number of children that could possibly be conceived. But Scripture does require couples to welcome every child that God gives to them. It is not only the planned pregnancies that yield blessing but also the unplanned ones. Thus, all children should be received with open arms into the family, even though parents may not be pursuing the maximum number of children possible. Christopher Ash assigns the issue to Christian freedom:

It may indeed be a matter of Christian freedom for a couple to make responsible decisions about the number of children they intend to have (always submitting themselves humbly to the possibility that God will give them a child unintended by them, and they will welcome that child too as a gift of God). Christian ethics has no statement to make about "the right number of children a couple should have"; this is a matter of freedom and wisdom.[23]

Sixth, married couples must ensure that their chosen method of "birth control" is truly contraceptive in effect and not abortifacient. As Christians, we recognize the intrinsic value of every human life because humans alone are made in the image of God (Gen. 1:27; 9:6). For this reason, we all have a duty to protect in-

---

[22] Dennis P. Hollinger, *The Meaning of Sex: Christian Ethics and the Moral Life* (Grand Rapids, MI: Baker, 2009), 165.
[23] Ash, *Marriage: Sex in the Service of God*, 183.

nocent persons from being led away to death (Prov. 24:10–12). Our concern for innocent human life extends from conception to natural death. For this reason, surgical or chemical abortions are not a valid means of birth control, because they destroy human life at its earliest stages. Those who access abortions merely for the purposes of birth control are committing a heinous injustice because they are taking the life of an innocent human being in order to achieve some lesser "good."

The only forms of birth control that could possibly be valid are those that prevent conception. Those that cause the destruction of a fertilized egg or fetus violate the scriptural prohibition "Thou shalt not kill" (Ex. 20:13 KJV; cf. Gen. 9:6; Matt. 19:18). On this standard the intrauterine device, or IUD, would be ruled out because it destroys human life by preventing a fertilized egg from implanting in the uterine wall.[24] Even though some have recently contested this claim, morning-after pills such as Plan B and Ella should also be ruled out on the same grounds.[25] Barrier methods such as the condom, however, would not violate this standard as their mechanism of action is truly contraceptive.[26] The consideration for all Christians is to discover how a given method works, and all abortifacient mechanisms must be ruled out. But the use of hormonal methods of birth control has been highly controversial and deserves some extended comment.

Assessing the Pill

There is a debate among Christians about hormonally based chemical methods of birth control. The delivery systems for hormonal therapies include the patch, vaginal contraceptive ring, shot/injec-

[24] *Birth Control Guide* (FDA Office of Women's Health, 2012), 18–19, http://www.fda.gov/downloads/ForConsumers/ByAudience/ForWomen/FreePublications/UCM282014.pdf.

[25] The Mayo Clinic website also says that these pills may work by "keeping a fertilized egg from implanting in the uterus," though Mayo also notes the recent discussion in the literature. See Mayo Clinic Staff, "Morning-after Pill: Why It's Done," *Mayo Clinic*, May 25, 2012, http://www.mayoclinic.com/health/morning-after-pill/MY01190/DSECTION=why-its-done. There will be more discussion of the morning-after pill in the following section.

[26] *Birth Control Guide*, 4–9. The FDA's *Birth Control Guide* defines barrier methods as those which block sperm from reaching the egg. Those methods include male condom, female condom, diaphragm with spermicide, sponge with spermicide, cervical cap with spermicide, and spermicide alone (ibid.).

tion, IUD with progestin, and the implantable rod. But probably the most popular method of delivery is the oral version known as "the Pill." The Pill comes in two basic varieties: (1) the combined pill, which contains estrogen and progestin, and (2) the mini-pill, which contains progestin only. FDA-approved labels indicate that these pills work through three mechanisms of action.[27] The first is to prevent ovulation (a contraceptive mechanism). The second is to thicken cervical mucus thereby making it difficult for sperm to pass through (also a contraceptive mechanism). The third is to inhibit the uterine lining thereby preventing a fertilized egg from implanting in the uterus (an abortifacient mechanism).[28] It is this third mechanism that has caused controversy.

There are a number of pro-life Christians who believe that the existence of this third mechanism for the Pill is inconclusive.[29] The Christian Medical and Dental Associations advance this view, saying:

> CMDA has consulted many experts in the field of reproduction who have reviewed the scientific literature. While there are data that cause concern, our current scientific knowledge does not establish a definitive causal link between the routine use of hormonal birth control and abortion. However, neither are there data to deny a post-fertilization effect.[30]

---

[27] E.g., "Combination oral contraceptives act by suppression of gonadotropins. Although the primary mechanism of this action is inhibition of ovulation, other alterations include changes in the cervical mucus, which increase the difficulty of sperm entry into the uterus, and changes in the endometrium, which reduce the likelihood of implantation." See "Ortho-Cept Tablets," August 8, 2008, http://www.accessdata.fda.gov/drugsatfda_docs/label/2012/020301s027lbl.pdf (accessed December 30, 2012).

[28] Andreas J. Köstenberger and David W. Jones, *God, Marriage, and Family: Rebuilding the Biblical Foundation*, 2nd ed. (Wheaton, IL: Crossway, 2010), 126; Randy Alcorn, *Does the Birth Control Pill Cause Abortions?*, 8th ed. (Sandy, OR: Eternal Perspective Ministries, 2007), 23.

[29] In 1998, a group of pro-life doctors went beyond the notion that the matter was "inconclusive." They argued that there is no evidence that hormonal birth control pills cause the uterine lining to be resistant to implantation. They conclude that hormonal therapies should not be considered abortifacient at all. See Joseph L. DeCook et al., "Birth Control Pills: Contraceptive or Abortifacient?," January 1998, https://www.cuw.edu/departments/institutes/bioethics/assets/Birth%20Control%20file.pdf. Randy Alcorn explains the provenance of this document. It was written by twenty pro-life OB-GYNs, perhaps in response to the first edition of Alcorn's first book. See Alcorn, *Does the Birth Control Pill Cause Abortions?*, 81.

[30] Christian Medical and Dental Association, "Hormonal Birth Control," http://www.cmda.org/wcm/CMDA/Issues2/Beginning_of_Life1/Abortion1/Ethics_Statements2/Hormonal_Birth_Contr.aspx (accessed December 30, 2012).

Likewise, the American Association of Pro-Life Obstetricians and Gynecologists studied the issue and concluded,

> There are times when our knowledge of the truth is incomplete, and we must peer through the fog to make, and act upon, judgments about the information available to us. In these settings, individuals wholeheartedly committed to the truth can come to different conclusions. So it is with us.[31]

Generally, those who follow this "inconclusive" view argue that in the absence of further evidence, hormonal contraceptives should not be considered unethical. For example, Dennis Sullivan has written an analysis of the evidence on both sides of the debate and views the matter as inconclusive. Nevertheless, he concludes that "to fail to use a potentially useful intervention because of minimal evidence or theoretical concerns is not how health practitioners should live their ethical lives."[32]

On the other side of the debate are those who claim that the third mechanism is in play when women use hormonal contraceptives. Randy Alcorn has made this case at the popular level in his book *Does the Birth Control Pill Cause Abortions?*[33] Walter Larimore and Joseph Stanford made the argument in a major medical journal in 2000, contending that combined oral contraceptives thin the lining of the uterus and make the embryo less likely to implant. They conclude that informed consent requires that doctors give patients information about the potentially abortifacient effects of these drugs.[34]

The debate comes down to whether birth control pills have a post-fertilization effect on the female reproductive cycle. Of chief concern is the effect that the thinning of the uterine lining (or endometrium) has on implantation. Both sides seem to agree that

---

[31] American Association of Pro-Life Obstetricians and Gynecologists, "Oral Contraceptive Controversy," http://www.aaplog.org/position-and-papers/oral-contraceptive-controversy/ (accessed December 30, 2012).

[32] Dennis M. Sullivan, "The Oral Contraceptive as Abortifacient: An Analysis of the Evidence," *Perspectives on Science and Christian Faith* 58, no. 3 (2006): 194.

[33] Alcorn, *Does the Birth Control Pill Cause Abortions?*

[34] Walter L. Larimore and Joseph B. Stanford, "Postfertilization Effects of Oral Contraceptives and Their Relationship to Informed Consent," *Archives of Family Medicine* 9, no. 2 (2000): 126–33.

women who take oral contraceptives have a thinner and less receptive endometrium. Both sides also seem to agree that a thinner endometrium decreases the likelihood of successful implantation.[35] The difference is whether or not the endometrium remains a hostile environment after fertilization occurs. Those who oppose the birth control pill—like Alcorn and Larimore—say that it does. Those who favor the use of the Pill—like Sullivan—say that it does not. For the latter case, Sullivan explains,

> Ovulation leaves behind the corpus luteum, a rich source of estrogen and progesterone. After six days required for the embryo to travel down the uterine tube into the uterus, these hormones have transformed the endometrium, which has now become receptive for implantation.[36]

I see value and merit in the arguments that are made on both sides of this debate. Both sides have proponents who are committed to the sanctity of human life from conception to natural death. Yet the poles of this debate are not two diametrically opposed positions. On one side are those who argue conclusively that the Pill causes abortions. On the other side are those who say the evidence is inconclusive. It seems that, at best, the case in favor of the Pill has yet to be proven. In light of this, Andreas Köstenberger's conclusion with respect to the Pill seems warranted: "If the 'profound respect for life in the prenatal stages' of a child's development . . . holds the moral authority it ought to, then perhaps it is right to reevaluate whether a low chance of aborting one's child is worth the risk at all."[37] In the absence of more definitive proof, I conclude that it is not worth the risk.

Public Controversy about Morning-After Pills

The mechanism of action of so-called morning-after pills came into public focus in 2012 when the administration of US President

---

[35] Sullivan, "The Oral Contraceptive as Abortifacient," 191.
[36] Ibid., 192.
[37] Köstenberger and Jones, *God, Marriage, and Family*, 127.

Barack Obama issued a mandate that employers must provide insurance coverage for these drugs in their employee health plans. This mandate put pro-life Christian business owners in a difficult spot because it required them to either pay for abortifacients for their employees or face fines that could put them out of business. In the midst of this controversy, there were some voices that began arguing that morning-after pills were not abortifacient and that prolife concerns were unfounded. Several responses to this controversy are in order.

First, pro-lifers define *abortion* as any measure that causes a fertilized egg or fetus to be destroyed. Pro-lifers believe that all human beings have an inalienable right to life from conception to natural death. Notice that it's not from *implantation* to natural death, but from *conception* to natural death. When sperm unites with an egg, a new human life comes into being. In the normal course of events, that new human life travels down the fallopian tubes and into the mother's womb where it implants into the uterine wall. Pro-choicers often say that an abortion can occur only after implantation. Pro-lifers contend that abortion can occur before or after implantation. Human life is at stake from the time of conception, and anything that destroys that life is abortifacient.

Second, the health-care law mandates coverage not only for morning-after pills but also for intrauterine devices, also known as IUDs. As mentioned above, FDA labeling says that IUDs have three mechanisms of action, one of which is preventing the fertilized egg from implanting in the uterine wall. In other words, IUDs cause the destruction of human life before implantation. Whatever one's views are about morning-after pills, the abortifacient effect of IUDs is not in serious dispute, and the health-care law requires coverage for these devices.

Third, despite recent controversy about morning-after pills (Plan B and Ella), recent studies contesting the abortifacient effect of morning-after pills are less conclusive than some suggest.[38]

---

[38] For example, Jeffrey Lewis and Dennis Sullivan argue that evidence for a post-fertilization effect of emergency contraception is "either lacking or is shrouded in politicized rhetoric." See Jeffrey

The FDA labels say that both Plan B and Ella have more than one mechanism of action.[39] The primary mechanism is the prevention of ovulation—a truly contraceptive measure. A secondary mechanism of morning-after pills prevents a fertilized egg from implanting—an abortifacient measure. This means that morning-after pills cause the destruction of human life whenever this secondary mechanism comes into play.

During the summer of 2012, the FDA's labeling came into dispute after the *New York Times* published an article alleging that morning-after pills are not abortifacient.[40] Citing recent scientific studies, the article claimed the FDA labels are wrong. All of this came out in the midst of a heated political campaign in which President Obama was under fire for the unpopularity of his signature health-care law. One of the main lines of criticism was that the law requires citizens to purchase insurance coverage for abortifacient birth control measures. The *Times* article attempted to show that this criticism of the President's signature health-care law was ill-founded because the most recent scientific evidence says that morning-after pills are not abortifacient. Thus, there appeared to be an overt political motive behind the reporting.

Nevertheless, evidence from within the report itself showed that the scientific evidence did not conclusively favor the thesis of the article. In fact, the studies that were cited only related to Plan B, not to Ella or IUDs. Also, several of the scientists who were interviewed said that "absolute proof" was elusive. One of the scientists cited favorably in the article is James Trussell of Princeton University. Yet he coauthored a paper in September 2012 that says morning-after pills must have other mechanisms of action besides the delaying of ovulation. Even though he thinks post-fertilization effects of morning-after pills are doubtful, he nevertheless con-

D. Lewis and Dennis M. Sullivan, "Abortifacient Potential of Emergency Contraceptives," *Ethics and Medicine* 28, no. 3 (2012): 113. Nevertheless, the research in this study applies only to Plan B. It does not deal with potential abortifacient effects of Ella (or IUD's for that matter). Also, even though the authors argue that Plan B is unlikely to interfere with implantation, "the possibility has not been completely excluded" (ibid., 116).

[39] *Birth Control Guide*, 16.

[40] Pam Belluck, "No Abortion Role Seen for Morning-After Pill," *New York Times*, June 6, 2012.

cludes that one possible mechanism of action is prevention of implantation.[41] So even one of the *Times'* own experts appears less than conclusive on the matter.

Fourth, after the controversial *Times* article was published last June, the FDA updated its *Birth Control Guide* (August 2012).[42] Even after all the controversy, the updated guide continues to list the abortifacient mechanism of morning-after pills. This fact alone is telling. It calls into question the accuracy of the *New York Times'* reporting. Given the political context of a presidential campaign, one cannot help but wonder if some other agenda was in play with the *New York Times* report.

If it were ever proven that morning-after pills have no abortifacient effect, then the pro-life moral calculus would change with respect to these devices. But no such thing has ever been proven. Taking into account the best scientific research and laboratory tests, the FDA still says that morning-after pills can prevent human embryos from implanting—thus causing the death of an innocent person. For that reason, the sanctity of human life prohibits the use of these pills.

Conclusion

Married couples glorify God in their family planning when they steward their procreational powers in line with God's purposes for sex. That means embracing all of what God intended this gift to be when he created it. The mandate to procreate is a creation ordinance (Gen. 1:28), and it is the means by which God spreads his

---

[41] James Trussell and Elizabeth G. Raymond, "Emergency Contraception: A Last Chance to Prevent Unintended Pregnancy," *The Emergency Contraception Website*, September 2012, http://ec.princeton .edu/questions/ec-review.pdf. See especially p. 7. James Trussell has been a longtime advocate of emergency contraception, even though he acknowledges the post-fertilization effects these pills have. In a 2006 editorial for the journal *Contraception*, Trussell writes: "To make an informed choice, women must know that ECPs—like all regular hormonal contraceptives such as the birth control pill . . . may prevent pregnancy by delaying or inhibiting ovulation, inhibiting fertilization, or inhibiting implantation of a fertilized egg in the endometrium." See James Trussell and Beth Jordan, "Mechanism of Action of Emergency Contraceptive Pills," *Contraception* 74 (2006): 88. Trussell and his coauthor also argue that emergency contraception pills are not abortifacient. It should be pointed out, however, that they make this argument not because there is no postfertilization effect of emergency contraception, but because they define abortion only as that which interrupts an already implanted embryo (ibid., 87).

[42] *Birth Control Guide.*

dominion over the earth through his image-bearing vice-regents. Thus all marriages that wish to glorify God must embrace this mandate by welcoming any and all children that God blesses them with. Married couples may legitimately access modern contraceptive technologies under certain conditions. First, they must never use a technology that takes the life of an unborn human being. All abortifacient means of birth control are therefore ruled out. Second, they must not access contraception in order to violate the mandate to procreate. It is immoral to enter into marriage while rejecting God's purposes for sexual union, one of which is procreation. Deliberately childless marriages are an affront to God's purpose for marriage. Third, they must scrutinize a cultural preference for smaller families and welcome children as blessings from the Lord and not as burdens. Couples that desire to keep the family circle small must ask themselves if they have been unduly influenced by the spirit of the age, which treats children as a drag on personal freedom and prosperity. That is not to say that couples must have as many children as they possibly can. It is to say that couples should steward their family planning for kingdom purposes, not for selfish ends. Even the use of modern birth control methods should be for the glory of God.

When the constructed status of gender is theorized as radically independent of sex, gender itself becomes a free-floating artifice, with the consequence that man and masculine might just as easily signify a female body as a male one, and woman and feminine a male body as easily as a female one.

—Judith Butler, *Gender Trouble*

Now the meaning of the words is this: God, who created the human race, made them male and female, so that every man might be satisfied with his own wife, and might not desire more.

—John Calvin, *Commentary on a Harmony of the Evangelists, Matthew, Mark, and Luke, vol. 1*

6

Glorify God with Your Gender

Every year in December, the Pope delivers an address to the Roman Curia—a speech that has been dubbed "The State of the Union" for the Roman Catholic Church. The Pope's 2012 address caught the attention of the worldwide media when he focused at length on gender and sexuality. News reports and pundits focused a great deal of their attention on the speech's implications for gay marriage—namely, that the Pope opposes same-sex unions of any kind. Yet one could argue that this focus was a rather shallow analysis of the speech. Make no mistake—the Pope's words were nothing less than a broadside against any notion of same-sex marriage. But what he said actually goes much deeper than that.

He argues that there is a "crisis" threatening the very foundations of the family in the Western world. The crisis is not merely about a particular social construct but about what it means to be "authentically human." The family is in crisis because mankind in the Western world has forgotten what it means to be created in the image of God as male and female. The Pope takes on not merely homosexual marriage but the entire foundation of modern gender theory—the idea that gender is something that you choose, not something that you are. It is worth quoting him at length on this point:

The very notion of being—of what being human really means— is being called into question. . . . According to this philosophy, sex is no longer a given element of nature, that man has to accept and personally make sense of: it is a social role that we choose for ourselves, while in the past it was chosen for us by society. The profound falsehood of this theory and of the anthropological revolution contained within it is obvious. People dispute the idea that they have a nature, given by their bodily identity, that serves as a defining element of the human being. They deny their nature and decide that it is not something previously given to them, but that they make it for themselves. According to the biblical creation account, being created by God as male and female pertains to the essence of the human creature. This duality is an essential aspect of what being human is all about, as ordained by God. This very duality as something previously given is what is now disputed. The words of the creation account: "male and female he created them" (Gen. 1:27) no longer apply.[1]

Few people—and, I fear, far too few Christians—realize that what the Pope is talking about here is at the leading edge of the conflict over sexual ethics in the post-Christian West. The secular West has given up on God as the maker in whose image man is created. Likewise, the culture has all but given up on the idea that men and women are different and that they are so by God's design. In the West, male and female are not creation categories. They are simply identities that we learn from culture.

It would be easy to blame this devolution on feminism or queer theory,[2] but that would be too superficial, for both modern

---

[1] "Pope: Address to the Roman Curia," *The Vatican Today*, December 21, 2012, http://www.news.va /en/news/pope-address-to-the-roman-curia.

[2] Queer theory is a cross-disciplinary intellectual movement that questions the validity of sexual identity categories. Queer theorists typically hold that not only are gender roles socially constructed but so is biological gender. Categories such as male, female, gay, lesbian, and transgender are purely conventional and have no stable definition. As we shall see, Judith Butler is one of the crucial progenitors of this movement. For an introduction to Queer Theory, see Gust A. Yep, Karen E. Lovaas, and John P. Elia, "Introduction: Queering Communication: Starting the Conversation," in *Queer Theory and Communication: From Disciplining Queers to Queering the Discipline(s)*, ed. Gust A. Yep, Karen E. Lovaas, and John P. Elia (Binghamton, NY: Harrington Park, 2003), 2ff.

feminism and queer theory derive from the secular spirit of the age which denies that we are as God has made us. It is not the Spirit of God but another spirit altogether that says that male and female are completely interchangeable, not only at the level of social roles but also at the level of sexual practice. The feminists and the queer theorists hold such basic assumptions in common, and that is why their alliance in the larger culture has been so unbreakable.[3]

Many secular responses to the Pope's speech focused almost entirely on the question of gay marriage and the perception that the Pope is against "gay rights." This secular narrative defines this discussion exclusively in terms of the march of human progress and equality. It is able to do that because it has already accepted—perhaps uncritically—the notion that gender is something you learn, not something you are. If those assumptions about gender turn out to be false—and Scripture tells us that they are indeed false—then the narrative of equality that is built upon it crumbles. Those advancing the equality narrative may not realize this, but they have built their entire house on shifting sand. That house will be washed away in due time.

As a Protestant and a Baptist, I have many serious differences with the Pope. But when it comes to the ethics of gender and sexuality and the rot that is eating away at Western culture, I find that we have much in common. The Pope rings true on this because he is agreeing with Genesis 1:27: "God created man in His own image, in the image of God He created him; male and female He created them." God did in fact make us male and female. To deny this is to deny what it means to be human. For this reason, it is all the more important for Christians to understand what the Bible says about manhood and womanhood. That is what this chapter is about.

---

[3] Laurel C. Schneider, "Homosexuality, Queer Theory, and Christian Theology," *Religious Studies Review* 26, no. 1 (2000): 5–6: "Whether queer theory is something really separate from feminism is not at all clear. . . . Where queer theory diverges from feminism is . . . only where feminist theory is falsely limited to essentialist, even ontological claims about women, nature, and sexuality."

A Biblical Summary of Manhood and Womanhood

Equality in the Image of God

The foundational biblical passages for understanding manhood and womanhood are the same ones for understanding the meaning of marriage—Genesis 1–2. In fact, what we find in these texts is that God has created male and female respectively in order that they might inhabit their respective vocations to which he has called them within marriage. Men and women are different in some important respects, but they are the same in some others. The creation of mankind in Genesis 1 has a special focus on what male and female have in common. The key verses are 1:26–28:

> Then God said, "Let Us make man in Our image, according to Our likeness; and let them rule over the fish of the sea and over the birds of the sky and over the cattle and over all the earth, and over every creeping thing that creeps on the earth." God created man in His own image, in the image of God He created him; male and female He created them. God blessed them; and God said to them, "Be fruitful and multiply, and fill the earth, and subdue it; and rule over the fish of the sea and over the birds of the sky and over every living thing that moves on the earth."

There are a number of observations we might make that point to the equality between the first man and woman.

First, we dare not miss that God created sexual differentiation. The terms *male* and *female* are not cultural constructs. They are not social roles foisted upon mankind by the accretion of culture and tradition. *Male* and *female* designate the fundamental distinction that God has embedded in the very biology of the race. As Ray Ortlund has it, "Male-female equality does not constitute an undifferentiated sameness."[4] From the very opening pages of the Scripture, therefore, we find that men and women are different from one another. Their differences are rooted in sexual categories

[4] Raymond C. Ortlund Jr., "Male-Female Equality and Male Headship: Genesis 1–3," in *Recovering Biblical Manhood and Womanhood: A Response to Evangelical Feminism*, ed. John Piper and Wayne Grudem (Wheaton, IL: Crossway, 1991), 99.

that have been ordained and created by God. As we shall see, *difference* does not mean the same thing as *inequality*. For there are some fundamental equalities between these two very different creatures.

Second, God made both man and woman equally in his image. Verse 27 says, "God created man in His own image, in the image of God He created him." It is a mistake to construe the word "man" to indicate that males only are created in the image of God. The Hebrew term is *'ādam* (אָדָם), and it regularly refers to *mankind* inclusively.[5] That is the meaning of the term here (as well as in v. 26), as the following clauses make clear: "In the image of God He created him; male and female He created them" (Gen. 1:27). The text indicates no difference between male and female with respect to their being created in God's image. The woman's image bearing does not derive from the man, nor does the man's derive from the woman. The man is no more an image bearer than the woman. The woman is no more an image bearer than the man. God assigns this dignity to both of them irrespective of their sexual difference. There has been a great deal of discussion over the years about what the image of God is, and I will not attempt to resolve that debate here.[6] What is important to observe is that God crowns no other creature with image-bearing status. Human beings alone wield this honor, and man and woman share equally in the image of God.[7]

This observation has massive implications for our understanding of the precious value that God assigns to all human life—whether male or female. It also has implications for the way in which God accomplishes redemption for his people through Christ. God's image bearers share equally in the salvation that God provides through Jesus Christ. The apostle Paul would say it this way in Galatians 3:28: "There is neither Jew nor Greek, there

---

[5] HALOT, "אָדָם," 3.

[6] Kenneth Matthews has a long excursus, "Interpreting the 'Image of God,'" in his commentary on Genesis. See Kenneth A. Matthews, *Genesis 1–11:26*, New American Commentary (Nashville, TN: Broadman, 1996), 164–72.

[7] So John Calvin: "Certainly, it cannot be denied, that the woman also, though in the second degree, was created in the image of God; whence it follows, that what was said in the creation of the man belongs to the female sex." See John Calvin, *Commentaries on the First Book of Moses Called Genesis*, trans. John King, vol. 1, Calvin's Commentaries (repr. Grand Rapids, MI: Baker, 1996), 129.

is neither slave nor free man, there is neither male nor female; for you are all one in Christ Jesus." This means that there is no distinction between men and women with respect to the benefits of salvation. According to God's grace, they share equally in the grace of regeneration, justification, sanctification, indwelling, and every other benefit purchased for us through Christ. There are no second-class citizens in the kingdom of God. That is why Peter instructs husbands that their wives are "fellow heir[s] of the grace of life" (1 Pet. 3:7). God assigns deep and abiding equality between men and women with respect to their value and worth as image bearers and with respect to their share in Christ.

Third, God also assigned both man and woman the responsibility to rule over his creation. As noted in an earlier chapter, God commands male and female to "be fruitful and multiply, and fill the earth, and subdue it" (Gen. 1:28). In essence, God appoints man as his vice-regent on earth—the one who would extend God's dominion over creation by extending his own dominion over the whole earth. Notice here as well that this command is addressed not only to the man but also to the woman. That means that the mandate to rule over creation extends to men and women equally. That is not to say that they may not have different roles in extending God's dominion, but it is to say that God gives the command to both of them. The reason for this is fairly clear. Mankind's rule will extend *by means of* multiplying and filling the earth. Thus man and woman both have a necessary share in the procreation of the race and in the fulfillment of the dominion mandate. Man and woman are each vice-regents in the rule of God over creation.

Differences as Male and Female

It is in this context of equality that God introduces differences between the sexes as well. As image bearers, man and woman would have different vocations in their callings as vice-regents and rulers. These different assignments—which are rooted in God's good creation—do nothing to undermine the fundamental equalities enumerated above. But they are nevertheless differences, and they do involve a hierarchical ordering of roles between the first man and woman. Man and woman are equal in their essence as divine image bearers, but they are unequal in their social roles. The first man Adam acts as the leader in this first marriage, and Eve is called to follow his leadership. God's appointment of Adam as leader comes out in at least five ways in Genesis 2.[8]

First, God creates Adam before he creates the woman. In the modern world in which egalitarian notions of humanity dominate, the order of creation would seem to make very little difference in terms of social roles. But that would not have been the case for the original readers of Genesis for whom primogeniture was a common feature of family life.[9] The firstborn would often have special authority over those born after him, and Adam and Eve's relationship is similar. God forms Adam first and then Eve. Thus Adam is given the position of authority. As Kenneth Matthews argues, "The priority of the man's creation is important for recognizing leadership-followership in the garden."[10] Certainly by the time of the first century, readers of the Old and New Testaments would have been quite familiar with primogeniture.[11] So much so that Paul grounds his views of gender roles and church leadership in the order of Adam and Eve's creation in Genesis 2. "For Adam was formed first, then Eve" (1 Tim. 2:13 AT; cf. 1 Cor. 11:8–9). Paul views Adam's prior creation as significant for establishing Adam's

---

[8] The arguments enumerated below are an adaptation from Thomas R. Schreiner, "Women in Ministry: Another Complementarian Perspective," in *Two Views on Women in Ministry*, ed. James R. Beck, rev. ed., Counterpoints (Grand Rapids, MI: Zondervan, 2005), 289–97. These six arguments could be expanded; e.g., Wayne Grudem identifies ten arguments showing male headship before the fall. See Wayne Grudem, *Evangelical Feminism and Biblical Truth: An Analysis of More Than 100 Disputed Questions* (Wheaton, IL: Crossway, 2004), 30–42.

[9] So Schreiner, "Women in Ministry: Another Complementarian Perspective," 291. Contra Richard S. Hess, "Equality with and without Innocence: Genesis 1–3," in *Discovering Biblical Equality: Complementarity without Hierarchy*, ed. Ronald W. Pierce, Rebecca Merrill Groothuis, and Gordon D. Fee (Downers Grove, IL: InterVarsity, 2004), 84.

[10] Matthews, *Genesis 1–11:26*, 221.

[11] Thomas R. Schreiner, "An Interpretation of 1 Timothy 2:9–15: A Dialogue with Scholarship," in *Women in the Church: An Analysis and Application of 1 Timothy 2:9–15*, ed. Andreas J. Köstenberger and Thomas R. Schreiner, 2nd ed. (Grand Rapids, MI: Baker, 2005), 106. "The notion of the firstborn having authority would be easily understood by Paul's readers" (ibid., 107). Contra William J. Webb, *Slaves, Women, and Homosexuals: Exploring the Hermeneutics of Cultural Analysis* (Downers Grove, IL: InterVarsity, 2001), 257–62.

leadership, and Paul's interpretation of the text is a binding and authoritative one. God made Adam first, thereby establishing him as the leader of the pair.

Second, God holds Adam accountable first for breaking God's word. In Genesis 2:15–17, God speaks to Adam, commanding him to "cultivate" and to "keep" or "guard" the garden of Eden (v. 15). God forbids Adam from eating from the tree of the knowledge of good and evil (v. 17), and he warns him that disobedience leads to judgment. The word of God comes to Adam before Eve is even created (v. 22). This fact suggests that it was indeed Adam who communicated God's commands to Eve. Thus Adam's leadership in the first marriage is implied by his delivering God's word to Eve. This interpretation is confirmed by the fact that God seeks out Adam after the couple sins. Even though Eve was the one who was first deceived by the Serpent and who first ate of the tree, God seeks out Adam first and interrogates him alone before turning to Eve: "Then the LORD God called to the man, and said to him, 'Where are you? . . . Who told you that you were naked? Have you eaten from the tree of which I commanded you not to eat?'" (Gen. 3:9–11). God delivered the word to Adam first and held Adam to account first after God's word was broken. All of this points to Adam's special responsibility as leader in the first marriage.

Third, God designates the woman to be a "helper" to Adam. To this end, God says that the woman alone will be "suitable" for the man (Gen. 2:18, 20). The word translated as "suitable" comes from a Hebrew term indicating "correspondence" or "complementarity."[12] Unlike the newly created animals—none of whom corresponded to Adam—the woman that God formed from Adam's side would complement him like no other creature on earth could (v. 20). But she would not be like Adam in every respect. Her unique vocation would be to serve as his "helper." The Hebrew term translated as

---

[12] HALOT, "נֶגֶד," 1: "that which corresponds." So Wenham, *Genesis 1–15*, 68: "It seems to express the notion of complementarity rather than identity."

"helper" simply denotes someone who offers help or assistance.[13] Thus Eve is called to come alongside Adam to assist him in the vocation that God had given him to work and keep the garden. Some critics of this view point out that the word *helper* is elsewhere used of God (e.g., Gen. 49:25; Ex. 18:4). Thus it would appear to be improper to say that "helper" always indicates a subordinate role. In response, it must be pointed out that the word is not only used of God but is also used of those who are helpers in a subordinate role (e.g., 1 Kings 20:16; 1 Chron. 12:1, 22–23; 22:17; 2 Chron. 26:13). Thus, the context of the term determines whether the helper is a subordinate of the one being helped. David Clines may be correct to argue that in one sense even superiors become subordinates when they serve as helpers. They are subjecting themselves to a "secondary, subordinate position" in order to assist another, though they themselves may not actually *be* a subordinate.[14] In that sense, every helper is a subordinate of some sort.[15] In Genesis 2:18, Adam and Eve's roles cannot be exchanged. Eve's helping is oriented toward Adam's leadership and thus affirms her subordinate role.[16]

Fourth, Adam names Eve. After God fashions the woman from the man's side, Adam responds with poetry: "This is now bone of my bones, and flesh of my flesh; she shall be called Woman, because she was taken out of Man" (Gen. 2:23). At the end of the poem, Adam gives a name to this new creation that God has given him. In context, the very fact that Adam is the one who names her is significant, for the one who names is the one who leads. In Genesis 1 God exercises his rule by naming. He calls the light "day" and the darkness "night" (1:5). He calls the sky "heaven" and the dry land "earth" (vv. 1:8, 10). God assigns to Adam the authority to name the animals: "Out of the ground the LORD God formed every beast of the field and every bird of the sky, and brought them to

---

[13] HALOT, "עֵזֶר."
[14] David J. A. Clines, "What Does Eve Do to Help? and Other Irredeemably Androcentric Orientations in Genesis 1–3," in *What Does Eve Do to Help? and Other Readerly Questions to the Old Testament* (Sheffield, UK: Sheffield Academic Press, 1990), 30–32. See especially the first paragraph of p. 31.
[15] Contra Hess, "Equality with and without Innocence: Genesis 1–3," 86.
[16] Matthews, *Genesis 1–11:26*, 221.

the man to see what he would call them; and whatever the man called a living creature, that was its name. The man gave names to all the cattle, and to the birds of the sky, and to every beast of the field" (Gen. 2:19–20). In naming the animals, Adam exercised his authority as vice-regent over God's creation. Likewise, when Adam "called" her name to be "Woman" (Gen. 2:23; and later "Eve," 3:20), he was exerting a leadership role that God gave to him alone.[17]

Fifth, the Serpent's attack represented a subversion of God's pattern of leadership. As we have seen, there is a clear ordering of authority in Genesis 2: God→Man→Woman. God speaks to the man, and the man speaks to the woman. The Serpent enters in to subvert the order that God has established. He does not confront the man first or even God himself. Rather, the Serpent approaches the woman so that the order is reversed: Serpent→Woman→Man. The Serpent speaks to the woman, and the woman speaks to the man. And now the attack on God's rule begins from the bottom up by an overthrow of the order. The apostle Paul indicates that it was indeed the undoing of this order that was the basis for the fall of humanity into sin (1 Tim. 2:13–14).[18]

In all of these ways, the text of Genesis 2 establishes Adam's leadership role over the woman. The text sets forth this first man and woman as the paradigm for all marriages that follow. The man is the leader, and the wife is the follower. The woman's subordinate role to the man does nothing to diminish her equality with him as an image bearer. In her *humanity*, she is his equal. In her *role*, she is his subordinate. In this way, the Bible holds both equality and subordination together. Though modern people may deny that it is so, the Bible teaches that equal value is not undermined by unequal roles. In 1 Corinthians 11:3, the apostle Paul invites readers to compare man's leadership over woman to God the Father's leadership over God the Son. Man is said to be the "head" of woman in a way similar to the Father's headship over the Son. This is a useful

---

[17] So Clines, "What Does Eve Do to Help?," 37–40. Clines writes, "The name of the woman by the man, on both occasions, I conclude, signifies his authority over her" (ibid., 39).
[18] Douglas Moo, "What Does It Mean Not to Teach or Have Authority Over Men?," in *Recovering Biblical Manhood and Womanhood*, 190.

analogy because there is a lesson about gender roles embedded within intra-Trinitarian relationships. The Son and the Father are equal with one another with respect to their deity. The Son is God. The Father is God. Nevertheless, the Son submits to the Father, and the Father leads the Son. Jesus is subordinate to the Father with respect to his *role*, but he is equal with his Father with respect to his *essence* as deity. There is equality and subordination within the Godhead, and Paul points to that intra-Trinitarian reality as an analog of gender roles. Submission does not make the Son inferior to the Father. The Son's vocation is a noble and honored one. Likewise, a wife's submission to her husband does not make her inferior to him. Her vocation is a noble and honored one as well.[19]

Implications of Equality and Difference

The Scripture presents manhood and womanhood in a way that runs counter to modern notions of sexuality and gender. Gender is not merely a sociological construct that fluctuates according to one's time or culture. In the Scripture, there is an organic connection between biological sex and gender roles. And one's biological sex determines what one's gender role should be. In the first family, the leadership role belongs to the man, and the follower's role belongs to the woman. Some readers believe that Adam's leadership over the woman is a result of the fall—a part of the dissolution of God's original intention for man and woman and a feature of male oppression of women.[20] Yet Adam's headship is not owing to the fact that there is sin in the world. God established Adam's leadership in the garden of Eden before sin entered into the world.

---

[19] This view of the Trinity has become highly controversial. The point of view I am advocating here can be found at length in Bruce A. Ware, *Father, Son, and Holy Spirit: Relationships, Roles, and Relevance* (Wheaton, IL: Crossway, 2005). Contra Millard J. Erickson, *Who's Tampering with the Trinity?: An Assessment of the Subordination Debate* (Grand Rapids, MI: Kregel, 2009). My own take on the matter can be found here: Denny Burk, "Christ's Functional Subordination in Philippians 2:6: A Grammatical Note with Trinitarian Implications," in *The New Evangelical Subordinationism? Perspectives on the Equality of God the Father and God the Son*, ed. Dennis W. Jowers and H. Wayne House (Eugene, OR: Pickwick, 2012), 103–4.

[20] For a popular expression of this point of view, see Rachel Held Evans, *A Year of Biblical Womanhood: How a Liberated Woman Found Herself Sitting on Her Roof, Covering Her Head, and Calling Her Husband "Master"* (Nashville, TN: Thomas Nelson, 2012), 219.

Thus the creation ideal is one that involves equality of essence between the sexes but inequality of roles.

As we have already seen, when Jesus and Paul teach about the nature of marriage, they invariably root that teaching in the creation ideal of Genesis 1–2. That appeal is not merely to establish marriage as monogamous and heterosexual. It is also to establish role relations within marriage. The New Testament elaborates these roles primarily with respect to two spheres of human activity: the church and the home.

In the home, wives are called to submit to their husband's leadership. The pattern for her submission is the church's proper submission to Christ (Eph. 5:22–24). The husband's responsibility is to love. The pattern for his love is Christ's self-sacrificial love for his bride, the church (Eph. 5:25). His role to love his wife is not just a state of mind. This love must issue forth in certain kinds of behaviors. Biblically, this means that a man must lead, protect, and provide for his wife.[21]

In the church, these roles mean that pastoral oversight is limited to qualified male leaders. The primary responsibility for teaching and for leading falls to men who are equipped and called by God for such service (1 Tim. 2:12). Women are called to exercise their gifts within the community of faith in deference to that male leadership (1 Cor. 11:3–16).

Though the primary orientation of Scripture is on the church and the home, the Bible's teaching on gender roles has application outside of those spheres as well. Because man's relation to woman is a creation ordinance, it defines what the ideal is for all of humanity. It defines the way that husbands and wives everywhere are to function, a way that maximizes human flourishing and happiness. To the degree that men and women depart from those norms, frustration, disorder, and pain find their way into the human condition.[22]

---

[21] John Piper, "A Vision of Biblical Complementarity," in *Recovering Biblical Manhood and Womanhood*, 36–45.
[22] Ibid.

The view of gender roles that I have outlined above goes by the name *complementarianism*. Over the last century, this more traditional approach to understanding manhood and womanhood has come under fire. Criticism has come not only from outside Christianity but also from within. Within evangelicalism, the primary alternative to complementarianism is called *egalitarianism* (also known as evangelical feminism). This point of view denies that there are any gender-based role distinctions between men and women. It affirms equality of role and essence and says that women have just as much claim to leadership as men do in both marriage and church. Evangelical egalitarians distinguish themselves from other Christian feminists by invoking revisionist interpretations of Scripture rather than by denying outright the authority and inspiration of Scripture.[23]

In the next section of this chapter, I want to examine a challenge to *complementarianism* that originates from more secular sources. For the last fifty years or so, feminists and radical gender theorists have been revising mainstream opinion about what it means to be male and female. These secular approaches represent a frontal assault on the authority of Scripture and what it teaches about manhood and womanhood. Feminists have not only challenged the notion of normative gender roles; they have deconstructed the biological differences between men and women as well. That challenge has come to focus in recent literature around the phenomenon known as "intersex."

The Challenge of Intersex

In the introduction to this book, I told the story of a youth minister who asked me a probing question about a student in his youth group who was born with an intersex condition. The very existence of intersex conditions presents a challenge to the complementarian perspective that I have outlined above.[24] What are we

---

[23] For a book-length primer and exposition of egalitarianism, see Ronald W. Pierce, Rebecca Merrill Groothuis, and Gordon D. Fee, eds., *Discovering Biblical Equality: Complementarity without Hierarchy* (Downers Grove, IL: InterVarsity, 2004).

[24] It should be noted that intersex presents a challenge not just to complementarian notions of gender but also to egalitarian ones. After all, egalitarians agree with complementarians that the

to make of persons who do not fit our assumptions about male/female sexual differences? If God has created us in his image as male and female—as Genesis 1:27 teaches—then what are we to do with those for whom biological sex is not clear? This question creates a problem for complementarians who believe that gender roles—including the headship principle—are not socially constructed but biblically constructed and are assigned according to one's biological sex.[25] If biological sex is unclear, then so also is any notion of normative gender roles. That is why intersex is an ethical conundrum for complementarians. Our whole paradigm is based on the givenness of clearly indicated biological sex. What are we to do when that is missing?

Some have suggested that we need to rethink our assumptions about the givenness of biological sex. Yes, the Bible teaches that in the beginning God made us in his image as male and female (Gen. 1:27). And this would seem to support the notion of sexual dimorphism—the idea that sex should be viewed through the binary categories of male and female. But those who don't share our faith in God's revelation are telling a different story. In her 1990 book *Gender Trouble*, feminist scholar Judith Butler interacts extensively with Michel Foucault's commentary on the journals of a nineteenth-century hermaphrodite name Herculine Barbin.[26] Barbin was raised as a female, but later in life was redesignated a male after an affair with a woman and an examination by a doctor. Barbin eventually recorded his memoirs and shortly after

---

Bible teaches a normative biological complementarity of the sexes. As egalitarian Cynthia Neal Kimball writes: "The physiological differences between the sexes are clear: body build, muscular development, hormonal patterns, childbearing capacity and longevity. Social differences include level of aggression, language styles and same-sex segregation. It is clear from the crosscultural genetic gender studies that God has fashioned men and women with certain differences." See Cynthia Neal Kimball, "Nature, Culture and Gender Complementarity," in *Discovering Biblical Equality*, 469–70. Indeed, egalitarians embrace social complementarity as well so long as it is construed without any hierarchy. See Rebecca Merrill Groothuis and Ronald W. Pierce, "Introduction," in *Discovering Biblical Equality*, 15.

[25] Contra Groothuis and Pierce, who argue, "Biblical equality, therefore, denies that there is any created or otherwise God-ordained hierarchy *based solely on gender*" (Groothuis and Pierce, "Introduction," 13).

[26] Judith Butler, *Gender Trouble* (New York: Routledge, 1990), 31–32: "Foucault suggests that the category of sex, prior to any categorization of sexual difference, is itself constructed through a historically specific mode of *sexuality*."

committed suicide. Butler writes, "In editing and publishing the journals of Herculine Barbin, Foucault is clearly trying to show how an hermaphroditic or intersexed body implicitly exposes and refutes the regulative strategies of sexual categorization."[27] In other words, Foucault argues—and Butler agrees—that intersexed bodies confound the dimorphic paradigm for understanding sex. Butler argues that "the immutable character of sex is contested" and that "this construct called 'sex' is as culturally constructed as gender."[28] She concludes, "Indeed, perhaps it was always already gender, with the consequence that the distinction between sex and gender turns out to be no distinction at all."[29]

Foucault and Butler may seem far afield from evangelical theology, but that is not at all the case. In her 2011 book *The End of Sexual Identity*, Jenell Williams Paris agrees that the binary categories of male and female are socially constructed, even when applied to our understanding of biological sex.[30] While admitting that there is some validity to such categories in terms of human reproductive capacity, she also argues that there is more than one Christian way to understand human sexual difference. Sexual dimorphism is one paradigm. Another is to view biological sex along a spectrum.[31] At one of end of the spectrum is male and at the other end is female. In the middle is intersex.[32] On this view, all people find themselves somewhere along that spectrum. You are biologically male, female, or something in between. Paris writes, "I believe that any of the three options for understanding sex—rigidly held sexual dimorphism, openly held sexual dimorphism or sex as a spectrum—could fit with a Christian understanding of creation."[33]

For feminists and queer theorists alike (and to some extent for self-identified evangelicals such as Paris), intersexed persons

---

[27] Ibid., 130.
[28] Ibid., 9.
[29] Ibid., 9–10.
[30] Jenell Williams Paris, *The End of Sexual Identity: Why Sex Is Too Important to Define Who We Are* (Downers Grove, IL: InterVarsity, 2011), 31: "Sexual dimorphism and even the words *male* and *female* are cultural creations."
[31] Ibid., 34.
[32] Ibid., 33.
[33] Ibid., 34.

challenge the received wisdom that human beings are created as male and female. Their very existence calls into question the dimorphic paradigm as they appear physiologically to be something in between male and female. The challenge to a complementarian view of gender ought to be clear at this point. Complementarians assume the dimorphic paradigm in establishing gender roles. If that assumption is taken away, then the whole system collapses. If biological sex is rendered ambiguous or something to be graphed on a spectrum, then the assignment of God-ordained gender roles is rendered ambiguous as well. On this paradigm, the order of creation cannot be normative, and the sexual complementarity of man and woman becomes but one expression of human sexual potential.

So the question that must be asked and answered is this: Are the feminists and the queer theorists right in that the phenomenon of intersex implies the demise of a biblical view of gender? In order to answer that question, we will have to explore exactly what intersex is and relate that phenomenon to biblical teaching.

What Is Intersex?

For most people, identifying one's biological sex is no great mystery. At birth or perhaps at the twenty-week ultrasound, the doctor inspects the external genitalia of the baby and based on that declares either, "It's a girl" or, "It's a boy." Nevertheless, every day "somewhere in the United States, an infant is born for whom gender assignment is not obvious."[34] In her 2008 book *Fixing Sex: Intersex, Medical Authority, and Lived Experience*, Katrina Karkazis writes, "These infants may have any one of numerous diagnoses, but their common feature is gender-atypical anatomy—a combination of what are typically considered male and female chromosomal, gonadal, and genital characteristics—which is often signaled by the presence of what clinicians call ambiguous

---

[34] Katrina Karkazis, *Fixing Sex: Intersex, Medical Authority, and Lived Experience* (Durham, NC: Duke University Press, 2008), 6.

genitalia."[35] As this definition indicates, it's actually a misnomer to describe intersex as a condition. Intersex is actually a term that describes a whole range of conditions affecting the development of the human reproductive system. Indeed, some suggest that the term "disorder of sex development" (a.k.a., DSD conditions) may be a more useful term to account for the range of conditions that we know about.

There is no little bit of controversy over how frequently intersex occurs in newborn infants. That disagreement is due in no small part to differences of opinion over how to define intersex. One estimate suggests that 1.7 percent of all live births exhibit some measure of "non-dimorphic sexual development."[36] Another estimate says that the figure is more like two out of every 10,000.[37] The wide variance in the numbers is due to disagreement about what should be included as an intersex condition. One well-respected researcher says that 87 percent of the 1.7 percent estimate includes a variety of infants who are not born with "atypical genitalia." When these cases are deducted, the actual estimate comes out to about 1 in 1,000.[38]

The most common intersex condition is known as CAH—Congenital Adrenal Hyperplasia.[39] Infants with this condition are actually born with two X chromosomes—as is the norm with all females—but there is an overproduction of testosterone, which can cause the external reproductive organs to look more masculine [enlarged clitoris or fused labia].[40] It occurs in about 1 in every 10,000 live births.

Androgen Insensitivity Syndrome (a.k.a., AIS) is the second most common diagnosis. In the developmental stage, these infants do not to respond properly to androgens. Even though they have a normal male XY chromosome, they develop male internal re-

---

[35] Ibid., 6–7.
[36] Ibid., 23.
[37] Ibid.
[38] Ibid., 24.
[39] Ibid., 23.
[40] Susannah Cornwall, *Sex and Uncertainty in the Body of Christ: Intersex Conditions and Christian Theology*, Gender, Theology and Spirituality (London: Equinox, 2010), 239.

productive organs and external organs that look female. Complete AIS occurs anywhere from 1 in 13,000 births to 1 in 20,000 births. Partial AIS is about 1 in 130,000 births.

Klinefelter's Syndrome is another disorder of sex development that is often designated as an intersex condition. In this condition, there is an XY chromosome combination with one or more extra Xs (47-XXY [80 percent], 48-XXXY, 49-XXXXY, 48-XXYY).[41] The extra chromosomes cause males to have very small external reproductive organs. Some have low levels of testosterone and take on other feminine characteristics (growing breasts, laying fat in a more 'feminine' pattern).[42] This condition occurs in 1 in 500 to 1 in 1,000 males with the majority of cases going undiagnosed.[43] It should be noted that the Klinefelter's Syndrome Association states that Klinefelter's Syndrome is not an intersex condition. They believe that people with this condition are unequivocally male—a perspective I happen to agree with.[44]

Turner's syndrome is also a chromosomal abnormality. Females usually have XX chromosomes, but persons with Turner's syndrome are missing one sex chromosome. Sometimes they are categorized as XO or X.[45] Susannah Cornwall describes the condition this way: "Their external genitalia usually appear unambiguously female, but their gonads may be extremely underdeveloped or effectively absent. Where gonads are present, they may stop functioning early in life."[46] About 1 in 2,000 to 1 in 3,000 female infants are born with Turner's syndrome.

There are a variety of other intersex conditions that I could describe. But these should suffice to show the kinds of disorders of sex development that can occur. They can involve chromosomal abnormalities, ambiguous genitalia, hormonal difficulties, or all of them together.

---

[41] Ibid., 243.
[42] Ibid., 243.
[43] Ibid., 244.
[44] Ibid.
[45] Ibid.
[46] Ibid.

In the 1950s, a doctor by the name of John Money developed a set of treatment protocols that have since become very controversial. In his method, clinicians determine the cause of the disorder and assign a sex for the infant, "and then surgeons modify the infant's body, especially the genitals, to conform to the assigned sex."[47] As noted earlier, parents were encouraged to embrace the chosen gender and to raise the child accordingly without showing any doubt about the child's gender assignment. The problem with this approach is that it is obviously carried out without the consent of the child. The surgeries had long-term repercussions, some of which resulted in infertility and loss of sexual sensation. Also, the treatment protocol seems to assume that gender is a social construct—it's something that we learn, not something that we are. So if an infant born with the chromosomal makeup of a boy (XY) happened to have malformed sexual organs, doctors would sometimes recommend surgery to make the boy into a "girl." Some of these surgeries involve castration, yet the thought was that normal sexual functionality was to be desired above all else. Sometimes despite chromosomal makeup and based on what doctors had to work with, doctors would choose the gender that offered the most promise surgically. If it looked impossible to reconstruct a male anatomy, for example, then a female anatomy was surgically formed even if the child had an XY chromosomal makeup. Some of these children—like the one that I heard about from the youth minister—grew up to feel that their parents had chosen the wrong gender for them.

Recent approaches to intersex have shifted away from Money's protocol. Indeed, it is common today for clinicians to be chromosomal essentialists—meaning that the chromosomes do not lie about male or female gender assignment. Katrina Karkazis interviewed a number of doctors and clinicians about how they treat intersex. She writes, "Many clinicians I interviewed view chromosomes as indicative of the essence of the person and construe

---

[47] Karkazis, *Fixing Sex*, 7.

176 WHAT IS THE MEANING OF SEX?

one's identity as inborn, natural, and unalterable, thus establishing gender categories based on a seemingly essential truth about the body."[48] One researcher put it this way: "If there is a Y chromosome, you have to be very worried about raising the child as female."[49] In short, these doctors hold to gender dimorphism even if there's ambiguity in the externals. They believe that sexual dimorphism is encoded in our chromosomal makeup.

What Does Scripture Say about Sex as a Spectrum?

How do we assess all of this from a biblical perspective? And what are the implications for a complementarian view of gender? Is it true that intersex puts the lie to any normative notion of binary sex categories? Does intersex teach us that we are all on a spectrum of male, female, or something in between?

The foundational text for our purposes is Genesis 1:27: "God created man in His own image, in the image of God He created him; male and female He created them." A prima facie reading of this text seems to suggest a binary understanding of biological sex. Indeed, the creation norm described in Genesis involves biological complementarity for the purposes of procreation. Hence, God commands the couple, "Be fruitful and multiply" (Gen. 1:28). There is no spectrum here. There is a functioning biological dichotomy between male and female that enables procreation.[50] In other words, what God calls "good" is binary sexual complementarity. This original situation does not present us with a spectrum. Rather,

---

[48] Ibid., 105–6.

[49] Quoted in ibid., 83. Karkazis interviewed a pediatric urologist about what to do with a boy born with a normal XY chromosomal makeup but who had no external organ. The doctor responded: "I can picture all of the painful, emotional scenarios down the road because he has no phallus, but it's not any easier the other way. At least this way you're working hard to accept the truth, whereas the other way you're constantly doing things to *hide* the truth that the sex is a genetic XY. They're boys. It's really as if my penis fell off. I would be a very frustrated male, but I will not die. But God forbid that somebody tried to give me a girl's name and a vagina just because my penis fell off" (ibid., 107–8).

[50] Matthews, *Genesis 1–11:26*, 172–73: "The third colon specifies that 'ādām ('man'), created in the image of God, refers to both male and female human life. By the occurrence of 'them,' clearly referring to two distinct sexual persons, after the singular 'him,' the old misconception of an original androgynous (bisexual) man is unfounded (see 2:22 discussion). 'Them' also is found in 1:28, where procreation is its primary interest, obviously assuming the sexual differentiation of two persons, male and female."

it presents us with sexual dimorphism. Jesus himself seems to have affirmed this in his teaching in Matthew 19:4 when he alludes to Genesis 1:27, saying, "Have you not read, that He who created them from the beginning made them male and female?" As R. T. France has commented on this text, "God . . . first designed humanity in two sexes."[51] These two sexes exist so that they can come together in the one-flesh union of marriage for the purposes of procreation. This procreative capacity implies the binary view of sex.

Of course this isn't all that Jesus has to say about the matter, for it is in this passage that the disciples observe that perhaps it would be better for people not to get married, to which Jesus responds,

> Not all men can accept this statement, but only those to whom it has been given. For there are eunuchs who were born that way from their mother's womb; and there are eunuchs who were made eunuchs by men; and there are *also* eunuchs who made themselves eunuchs for the sake of the kingdom of heaven. He who is able to accept this, let him accept it. (Matt. 19:11–12)

John Nolland says that "eunuchs who were born that way" refers to "children [who] were occasionally born with defective genitals and subsequently would fail to develop male secondary characteristics as they grew up."[52] In other words, Jesus describes a group of people that seem to have similar characteristics to what we would identify today as intersex. Could it be that Jesus himself was aware of a third sex? A gendered possibility that exists somewhere between male and female? Is it significant that Jesus raises this possibility in the same conversation that he alludes to man being created as male and female? Does this not suggest that even Jesus knew that biological sex was on a spectrum?[53]

I think the answer to that last question has to be no. A eunuch

[51] R. T. France, *The Gospel of Matthew*, New International Commentary on the New Testament (Grand Rapids, MI: Eerdmans, 2007), 717.
[52] John Nolland, *The Gospel of Matthew*, New International Greek Testament Commentary (Grand Rapids, MI: Eerdmans, 2005), 778.
[53] William Loader, *Sexuality in the New Testament: Understanding the Key Texts* (Louisville, KY: Westminster, 2010), 107: "The saying may indicate awareness that not all people fit the usual categories, male and female, but need not."

in Jesus's day was not someone who was sexless but someone who lacked the ability to procreate. Indeed, those who are made eunuchs by men are not sexless. They are castrated males. Those who make themselves eunuchs for the sake of the kingdom are not sexless. They are males who have voluntarily set aside the possibility of marriage and thus of procreation.[54] Likewise, those who are born eunuchs are not sexless. They are biological males who for whatever reasons are born without the capacity to procreate. They don't stop being males because of a disorder of sex development. The point is that all three categories of eunuchs are viewed as males, not as ambiguously sexed. The result is that the text still relies on a binary conception of sex even when talking about eunuchs. Those who suggest that eunuchs are sexless are not paying close attention to the text.

The conclusion of all this is that the Bible does not present biological sex as a spectrum of possibilities. The possibilities are two: male or female.

Is Sex Defined by "Born This Way" or by New Creation?

The Lady Gaga school of gender assignment says that whatever is natural is normative. If you are born with an immutable characteristic, then that is normative and good. It is the old is/ought fallacy. The observation of what *is* becomes what *ought to be*. If a person is ambiguously sexed, then that too becomes a normative expression of human sexuality. But this perspective overlooks the fact that the creation has been cursed and is groaning. It is not what it will be in the age to come. And we too as part of creation are not what we will be. We are born with birth defects, predispositions to cancer, heart disease, and all manner of physical maladies. These conditions are not normative; they are a result of the curse. These conditions are not what ought to be but are what we long

---

[54] Citing the hyperbolic "mutilations" of Matt. 5:29–30 and 18:8–9, R. T. France says that "most subsequent interpretation has understood the 'making oneself a eunuch' here not as a literal prescription but as a metaphor for making the choice to remain unmarried. See France, *Gospel of Matthew*, 724.

to be set free from. Indeed we groan within ourselves longing for the redemption of our bodies (Rom. 8:23). We long for the new creation in which we will be set free from cancer, heart disease, and disorders of sex development.

The binary reality of sex is what existed before the fall in Adam and Eve, and it will be a part of the restoration of creation in the age to come. In his 1990 book *Everything You Ever Wanted To Know about Heaven*, Peter Kreeft asked the question, "Is there sex in Heaven?" He answered the question with a yes. Why? Because the new creation defines what we will be, not the fallenness that we observe now. The new creation restores what was normative in Eden before any sin entered into the world. On the assumption that our persons are a psychosomatic unity, Kreeft writes, "If sexuality is part of our inner essence, then it follows that there is sexuality in Heaven, whether or not we 'have sex' and whether or not we have sexually distinct social roles in Heaven."[55] Quoting Aquinas, Kreeft writes, "If sexual differences are natural, they are preserved in Heaven, for 'grace does not destroy nature but perfects it.'"[56]

This is certainly the perspective of Scripture, though some have misconstrued the nature of the new creation based on such texts as Matthew 22:30 and Galatians 3:28. In Matthew 22:30 Jesus says, "For in the resurrection they neither marry nor are given in marriage, but are like angels in heaven." Some have construed from this text that angelic genderlessness is the paradigm for what humans will be in the new creation. But that is not what this text says. It simply says that we won't be married and thus won't procreate in the resurrection. It says nothing to indicate the elimination of sexual distinctions between male and female. Likewise, Galatians 3:28 is sometimes cited as evidence that binary sexual distinctions disappear in the new creation: "There is neither male nor female; for you are all one in Christ Jesus." Yet this text re-

---

[55] Peter Kreeft, *Everything You Ever Wanted to Know about Heaven—But Never Dreamed of Asking* (San Francisco: Ignatius, 1990), 120.
[56] Ibid., 121.

fers not just to the resurrection but also to the world we live in now. We are in Christ now, and we are male or female now. Our in-Christness doesn't destroy sexual distinctions either now or in the age to come.[57] To say that there is neither male nor female in Christ is to say that God does not make distinctions between genders with respect to the benefits of redemption. Male and female share equally in the redemptive grace of God.

To understand human gender, we have to look beyond what we observe in fallen creation, for fallen creation is just that—fallen. "Born this way" does not equal "Ought to be this way." What defines our humanity is the binary sexual ideal that existed in the garden and that is to be restored in the new creation.

Is There Really a Third Sex?

As we have seen, the Scriptures seem to indicate a binary sexual ideal that existed in the garden and that will be renewed in the new creation. It is not surprising, therefore, that researchers and clinicians are retreating back into a biological essentialism when it comes to understanding disorders of sexual development. Even when external genitalia are ambiguous, there is an underlying dimorphism encoded in our cells. Even when abnormalities occur in chromosomes, they still comprise some combination of Xs and Ys. The reproductive possibilities for intersex persons seem to align with the chromosomes. Male reproductive capacity comes only from those who have Y chromosomes. Female reproductive capacity comes only from those who have no Y chromosome. Is this not reflective of the dimorphic paradigm of Scripture?

Conclusion about Intersex

Does the phenomenon of intersex undermine a complementarian view of gender? No, it does not. Scripture defines what's normative for us, not any anomaly that we find in fallen creation. The phenomenon of intersex should call forth our compassion and

---

[57] Ibid., 122.

our love for our neighbors who carry in their persons a painful reminder of the groaning creation. It should not call forth from us a revision of the binary ideal of Scripture. That binary ideal is the matrix from which a binary ideal of gender roles emerges as well.

How should parents deal with a child born with an intersex condition? There is no one-size-fits-all strategy, given the complexity of the possible conditions. Nevertheless, here are some guiding principles I suggest for parents caring for a child with this condition. The first set of principles I recommend are more theologically oriented. First, everyone needs know what the creation ideal of Scripture is. According to Genesis 1–2, man's unfallen state is a clearly gendered state, and this is the norm. Second, the entrance of sin into the world and God's subsequent curse means that all kinds of physical difficulties afflict the human condition. Disorders of sex development are included in that. Third, the gospel of Jesus Christ not only frees from the penalty and power of sin in the present; it also promises eternal life in the future. That life involves the resurrection of our physical bodies. It means a renewal and restoration of what was lost in the garden of Eden. In the resurrection, all disorders of sex development will be swept away, and intersex people will be healed and made whole. That hope of restoration should be held out to the child throughout his life even if some ambiguities about his condition remain unresolved.

Here are some principles I suggest with respect to medical treatments. First, parents should be extremely reluctant about—if not altogether against—corrective surgery when the child is an infant. This is especially the case when the surgery would involve the modification of the child's genitals or reproductive organs. Perhaps surgical procedures would be in order at some point during the child's life, but do not rush a child into surgery simply out of a desire to make the child "normal." Second, try to determine as soon as possible the chromosomal makeup of the child. If there is a Y chromosome present, that would strongly militate against raising the child as a female, regardless of the appearance of the genitals and other secondary sex characteristics. It would also suggest that medical treatments designed to make the child into a female are out of line. Third, understand that not all doctors and medical professionals share your biblical convictions. Worldviews affect the treatment of intersex conditions. Some doctors may view gender as a social construct and therefore would not let biological markers (such as a Y chromosome) determine the child's gender. Fourth, parents need to take an active role in understanding the condition and pursuing treatment options in keeping with their biblical convictions.

Conclusion

The truth about gender is that God made us male and female. This sexual differentiation finds its roots in God's good creation. Thus sexual complementarity finds its genesis in the garden of Eden in the context of the only human marriage that has ever been flawless and without error—Adam and Eve's union before the fall. Just as the Serpent mounted an assault on this ideal by subverting God's created order, so the Enemy attempts to subvert God's truth about human gender in the present day. It is no wonder that marriage is under assault in the post-Christian West. God created the covenant of marriage to be an icon of Christ's love for the church. God made marriage to depict the gospel to the world—to be a little parable of how Jesus loves his bride. From Eden until now, the Serpent has been trying to destroy that icon with every subversive scheme at his fingertips. If biblical notions of gender can be destroyed, then so can the icon of marriage. It should be no surprise, therefore, that there is such confusion abroad about what it means to be male and female. The whole world lies in the power of the evil one (1 John 5:19). It is a reminder that at the end of the day, we do not war merely against flesh and blood. Our battle is not merely with the feminists and the queer theorists. Our battle is with the subversive forces that animate their raging against creation. Our battle is ultimately against "the rulers, against the powers, against the world forces of this darkness, against the spiritual forces of wickedness in the heavenly places" (Eph. 6:12). Our war is not with the captives that the Serpent has taken to do his will. Our war is with the Adversary who has enslaved them.[58] That means that a Christian sexual ethic must include right living and right thinking about gender and sexuality. We must bear witness with our lives and our words that in the beginning God made us male and female. Manhood and womanhood biblically defined are designed to glorify God. And that is why we must contend for them no matter how much the spirit of the age turns against them.

---

[58] Russell D. Moore, "Southern Baptist Sexual Revolutionaries: Cultural Accommodation, Spiritual Conflict and the Baptist Vision of the Family," *Southwestern Journal of Theology* 49, no. 1 (2006): 17–20.

Sexuality isn't about what we do in bed. Sexuality encompasses a whole range of needs, demands, and desires. Sexuality is more a symptom of our life's condition than a cause, more a consequence than an origin. . . . Homosexuality—like all sin—is symptomatic and not causal—that is, it tells us where our heart has been, not who we inherently are or what we are destined to become.

—Rosaria Champagne Butterfield,
The Secret Thoughts of an Unlikely Convert

When God acts climactically to reclaim the world and raise our dead bodies from the grave, there will be no more homosexuality. But until then, we hope for what we do not see. Washed and waiting. That is my life—my identity as one who is forgiven and spiritually cleansed and my struggle as one who perseveres with a frustrating thorn in the flesh, looking forward to what God has promised to do.

—Wesley Hill, *Washed and Waiting*

7

Glorify God with
Your Sexuality

In the year 2012 the ongoing normalization of homosexuality reached new milestones that never would have seemed possible even five years before. For the first time in American history, a sitting president of the United States announced his support for gay marriage. Even though he was opposed to gay marriage in his first run for office in 2008, President Barack Obama said that he had been evolving on the issue. By May of 2012, his evolution was complete. In an interview with ABC News, the president reported to the nation his conversion on the issue of marriage: "It is important for me to go ahead and affirm that I think same sex couples should be able to get married."[1] Many people thought that the announcement would damage the president's prospects for reelection later that November, but that speculation turned out to be incorrect. The president was reelected handily and seemed to pay no cost in popular support for his views. This was a remarkable political reversal in a relatively short amount of time. In 2004 President Bush won reelection in part by *opposing* gay marriage. Only eight years later, President Obama won reelection in part by *supporting* it. President Obama's reelection reflects the

---

[1] Rick Klein, "Obama: 'I Think Same-Sex Couples Should Be Able to Get Married,'" *ABC News*, May 9, 2012, http://abcnews.go.com/blogs/politics/2012/05/obama-comes-out-i-think-same-sex -couples-should-be-able-to-get-married/.

fact that Americans' views about homosexuality have fundamentally shifted.

Another important milestone occurred during the election of 2012, and it too seemed to confirm Americans' changing attitudes. Before 2012 gay marriage had been legalized in several states across the country, but state-sanctioned gay marriage had always emerged from either a court decision or from legislative action. Every time that gay marriage was put to a statewide popular vote, it failed. Yet that all changed in November 2012. Maine, Maryland, and Washington State all passed laws legalizing gay marriage through statewide votes. In addition, Minnesota rejected a constitutional ban on same-sex marriage, also through popular vote. Before this time, traditional marriage supporters had pointed to the fact that gay marriage had spread because it had been imposed by courts or state legislatures, never by popular demand. In 2012 that narrative ended. Gay marriage won in popular votes. The public's increasing acceptance of homosexuality was undeniable, and the terrain of public debate fundamentally shifted.

A New Normal

Homosexuality and gay marriage are perhaps the most controversial moral issues of our time. Whereas homosexual behavior was once widely regarded as deviant, it has now been introduced into the mainstream of American life. A great deal of this is demographic. Older Americans tend to be more conservative in their attitudes toward homosexuality, while emerging generations tend to be more liberal. If demographics are destiny, then it would seem that the issue will not be controversial for very much longer. Those who oppose gay marriage are dying out with each passing year, and the generations replacing them by and large accept homosexuality as valid.[2]

---

[2] Gallup reports a disparity among different age groups when it comes to acceptance of homosexuality and gay marriage. On gay marriage, only 40 percent of Americans fifty-five and over support gay marriage. Only 47 percent of those aged thirty-five to fifty-four said that they supported gay marriage. Yet 66 percent of young adults ages eighteen to thirty-four support gay marriage. See Lydia Saad, "U.S. Acceptance of Gay/Lesbian Relations Is the New Normal," *Gallup*, May 14, 2012, http://www.gallup.com/poll/154634/Acceptance-Gay-Lesbian-Relations-New-Normal.aspx.

There can be no question that Americans have been undergoing a steady change in attitudes about homosexuality over the last decade. As a result, gay relationships have become accepted by more and more Americans. According to Gallup polling in 2001, only 40 percent of Americans viewed homosexuality as morally acceptable, while 53 percent said that it was morally wrong. By 2012 those numbers had flipped, with 53 percent calling it morally acceptable and only 42 percent saying that it is morally wrong. This growing acceptance of homosexuality has coincided with a sea change in American views on so-called gay marriage. In 2004 only 42 percent of Americans said that same-sex marriage should be legalized. By 2011 support for gay marriage had risen to 53 percent.[3] At some point in the last decade, America went from being a majority anti-gay-marriage country to a majority pro-gay-marriage country.

How did this massive change come about, and what made it happen so quickly? In her 2012 book *Victory: The Triumphant Gay Revolution*, Linda Hirshman argues that the gay rights movement began in a weaker position culturally than either the civil rights or women's rights movements that preceded it. Nevertheless, gay activists were able to achieve far more in far less time than either of those other groups. Hirshman says, "The movement succeeded, uniquely and in large part because, at the critical moments, its leaders made a moral claim. 'Gay . . . is good.'"[4] Hirshman is right. The gay rights movement has been making a fundamentally moral claim. It is the triumph of that moral claim that has advanced the wider homosexual agenda as quickly as it has. The public is increasingly seeing the issue as a civil rights issue—the next step in society's march toward greater freedom and equality. To oppose such progress is increasingly seen as backwards and irrational. That is why gay rights advocates are not asking for tolerance. They are insisting on endorsement. Because "gay is good," the public space can no longer tolerate those who say it is *not* good. Those

---

[3] Ibid.
[4] Linda Hirshman, *Victory: The Triumphant Gay Revolution / How a Despised Minority Pushed Back, Beat Death, Found Love, and Changed America for Everyone* (New York: HarperCollins, 2012), xvi.

who say gay is not good are throwbacks who stand in the way of human rights and social progress.

And herein is the fundamental clash between Christianity and the massive changes that are happening in the wider culture. The Christian view of human sexuality has become a minority position in our day. Because of this, there is now enormous pressure from outside Christian churches (and sometimes within) to revise Christianity's ancient sexual ethic in order to bring it into conformity with the new spirit of the age. Those who will not conform are openly called "bigots" or "homophobes" or sometimes worse.[5] There is an active campaign to push to the margins anyone who would treat homosexuality as sin.[6] The national mood is still changing on this issue. Emerging generations of Christians are going to face pressure like never before to abandon what the Bible teaches lest they face social marginalization. There is a conflict coming.

Defections from the Biblical View[7]

Some evangelicals have been weathering the storm, but others have opted for obfuscation or avoidance. In 2006 on *Christianity Today*'s leadership blog, Pastor Brian McLaren urged evangelical leaders to find a "pastoral response" to their parishioners on the issue of homosexuality. In short, he argued that the Bible is not clear on the moral status of homosexuality and that the ancient ethic of the Christian church offends moderns too much to be useful. He calls, therefore, upon evangelicals to stop talking about the issue. Here he is in his own words:

---

[5] On May 1, 2010, the *Washington Post*'s David Weigel wrote, "I can empathize with everyone I cover except for the anti-gay marriage bigots. In 20 years no one will admit they were part of that" (David Weigel, "Covering Same-sex Marriage," *Washington Post*, May 1, 2010, http://voices.washingtonpost.com/right-now/2010/05/covering_gay_marriage.html). See also Frank Rich, "The Bigots' Last Hurrah," *New York Tmes*, April 18, 2009, http://www.nytimes.com/2009/04/19/opinion/19Rich.html, accessed May 25, 2010.
[6] This warning from Girgis, Anderson, and George is already coming true: "As the conjugal view comes to be seen as irrational, people's freedom to express and live by it will be curbed. . . . If civil marriage is redefined, believing what virtually every human society once believed about marriage—that it is a male-female union—will be seen increasingly as a malicious prejudice, to be driven to the margins of culture." See Girgis, Anderson, and George, *What Is Marriage?*, 9.
[7] The remainder of the chapter is an extensive revision of Denny Burk, "Why Evangelicals Should Not Heed Brian McLaren: How the New Testament Requires Evangelicals to Render a Judgment on the Moral Status of Homosexuality," *Themelios* 35, no. 2 (2010): 212–26.

Frankly, many of us don't know what we should think about homosexuality. We've heard all sides but no position has yet won our confidence so that we can say "it seems good to the Holy Spirit and us. ". . . If we think that there may actually be a legitimate context for some homosexual relationships, we know that the biblical arguments are nuanced and multilayered, and the pastoral ramifications are staggeringly complex. We aren't sure if or where lines are to be drawn, nor do we know how to enforce with fairness whatever lines are drawn.

Perhaps we need a five-year moratorium on making pronouncements. In the meantime, we'll practice prayerful Christian dialogue, listening respectfully, disagreeing agreeably. When decisions need to be made, they'll be admittedly provisional. We'll keep our ears attuned to scholars in biblical studies, theology, ethics, psychology, genetics, sociology, and related fields. Then in five years, if we have clarity, we'll speak; if not, we'll set another five years for ongoing reflection.[8]

When Brian McLaren made this statement, it was only one year after *Time* magazine had selected him as one of 2005's twenty-five most influential evangelicals.[9] In recent years his influence has primarily been within the progressive wing of evangelicalism, but at the time of this statement he had a much wider hearing within the movement.

Nevertheless, McLaren broke his moratorium before the five years were up. With still a year remaining on his personal embargo, McLaren issued a definitive judgment on the moral status of homosexuality. In his 2010 book *A New Kind of Christianity*, McLaren redefines the Christian faith for a new day—a redefinition that calls on evangelicals to abandon what the Bible teaches about homosexuality. He pillories traditional beliefs as "fundasexuality," which he defines as a "reactive, combative brand of religious *fun-*

---

[8] Brian McLaren, "Brian McLaren on the Homosexual Question: Finding a Pastoral Response," *Out of Ur*, January 23, 2006, http://www.outofur.com/archives/2006/01/brian_mclaren_o.html.

[9] "The 25 Most Influential Evangelicals in America," *Time*, February 7, 2005, 45. The article in *Time* reports that when McLaren was asked to comment on gay marriage, he replied, "You know what, the thing that breaks my heart is that there's no way I can answer it without hurting someone on either side."

damentalism that preoccupies itself with *sexuality*. . . . It is a kind
of *heterophobia*: the fear of people who are different."[10] Traditional
evangelicals, he argues, need an enemy against which they can
coalesce in common cause: he says that no group can exist without
an enemy, and that is why conservative evangelicals have vilified
gay people. In his own words, "Gay, lesbian, bisexual, and trans-
gendered people are an ideal choice for this kind of scapegoating."[11]
For McLaren, traditionalist faith is less about theology than it is
about psychology. Evangelicals need someone to loathe, and homosexuals are the unfortunate target. What is clear in all of this is
that McLaren has come to a definitive judgment in spite of what
he said in 2006. Apparently, the moratorium was not really meant
for people who would endorse homosexuality, but for those who
would not.

McLaren is not the only one to have jumped the gun. In the
fall of 2008, Tony Jones, the former national coordinator of Emer-
gent Village, wrote:

> Gay persons are fully human persons and should be afforded all
> of the cultural and ecclesial benefits that I am. . . . I now believe
> that GLBTQ can live lives in accord with biblical Christianity (at
> least as much as any of us can!) and that their monogamy can and
> should be sanctioned and blessed by church and state.[12]

Jones's pronouncement and many others like it show how unten-
able McLaren's advice was from the outset. For those who care
about what the Bible teaches, it simply will not do to postpone
judgment on this question. We dare not shrug our shoulders at the
issue as if we do not know what the Bible teaches or as if what it
does teach is too divisive to state publicly. McLaren's devolution on
the issue raises questions about the Bible's meaning and authority.

---

[10] Brian McLaren, *A New Kind of Christianity: Ten Questions That Are Transforming the Faith* (New York: HarperOne, 2010), 174–75.
[11] Ibid., 175.
[12] Tony Jones, "How I Went from There to Here: Same Sex Marriage Blogalogue," *The New Christians*, November 2008, http://blog.beliefnet.com/tonyjones/2008/11/same-sex-marriage-blogalogue-h .html.

And he is not alone in challenging Christianity's unambiguous and universal witness on sexuality.

McLaren is but one voice among the many in the progressive wing of evangelicalism that are calling for traditionalists to either change their views or back down from the issue. Many in that wing agree with McLaren's claim that the Bible is not clear about the moral status of homosexuality and that Christians need not press this divisive issue since it drives away potential converts. Some of them question the authority of Scripture altogether. My aim in what follows is to interrogate these claims concerning homosexuality from a biblical perspective. (1) Is it right for evangelicals to be silent on the issue so that Christianity might appeal more widely to the culture? (2) How does the Bible function as a normative basis for our ethical judgments? (3) Is it true that the Bible is unclear about the moral status of homosexuality? We will begin with the first question.

Should Evangelicals Be Silent?

In January of 2012, evangelical pastor Louie Giglio was invited to offer the benediction at President Barack Obama's second inaugural ceremony. The move surprised many observers because the president had not been known for being popular among evangelicals. Nevertheless, the president's inaugural committee invited Giglio to be a part of the program. Within a day of the announcement, a gay activist website located the audio of a sermon that Giglio had preached nearly twenty years before. The sermon was titled "In Search of a Standard-Christian Response to Homosexuality," and in it Giglio offered a traditional message about the sinfulness of homosexuality, the certainty of judgment, and the sufficiency of Christ to save all those who believe in the gospel. At one point, Giglio quoted from 1 Corinthians 6:9–11, which says that the "effeminate" and "homosexuals" will not inherit the kingdom of God.[13] In short, it was a biblical message about homosexuality that

---

[13] Louie Giglio, "In Search of a Standard-Christian Response to Homosexuality," *Discipleship Library*, http://turret2.discipleshiplibrary.com/8169A.mp3, accessed January 10, 2013.

was consistent with what every branch of Christianity has taught about homosexuality for its entire two-thousand-year history.

After the sermon was discovered online, it was publicized by a number of homosexual rights groups opposed to Giglio's participation in the event. The backlash was so severe among the president's supporters that the White House decided something had to be done. The *New York Times* reported that the White House contacted the inaugural committee on a Wednesday night and informed them that the selection of Giglio was causing problems for the president. The White House instructed the committee to "fix it," and by the next morning Giglio was no longer on the program.[14]

After Giglio was effectively disinvited from the event, a spokesperson for the inaugural committee released this statement: "We were not aware of Pastor Giglio's past comments at the time of his selection and they don't reflect our desire to celebrate the strength and diversity of our country at this inaugural." Notice what this statement says. It effectively bars any person from participating who holds to what Christianity teaches about homosexuality. It makes one's opinion about homosexuality the litmus test for participation in public life. Those who do not toe the line for the normalization of homosexual conduct are deemed homophobic and bigoted. On this line of thinking, a president could no more invite a practicing Christian to pray than he could a member of the KKK. They are morally equivalent because they both hold views that are to be excluded from the public space.

What this whole imbroglio reveals is that every Christian pastor is eventually going to get smoked out on this issue. Every one

---

[14] Sheryl Gay Stolberg, "Minister Pulls Out of Inauguration after Outcry," *New York Times*, January 10, 2013, http://www.nytimes.com/2013/01/11/us/politics/minister-withdraws-from-inaugural-program-after-controversy-over-comments-on-gay-rights.html: "An official with Mr. Obama's Presidential Inaugural Committee said the committee, which operates separately from the White House, vetted Mr. Giglio. People familiar with internal discussions between administration and committee officials said the White House viewed the selection as a problem for Mr. Obama, and told the panel on Wednesday night to quickly fix it. By Thursday morning, Mr. Giglio said he had withdrawn." Within less than a day of its appearance, the above quotation was scrubbed from the *New York Times* website. The part about the White House telling the committee to "fix it" had been removed, and it did not appear in the version that was published in the print edition the following day. What you see above is the paragraph as it appeared on *nytimes.com* early in the afternoon of January 10, 2013.

will eventually have to take a stand on one side or the other. As American attitudes change about homosexuality, our political leaders will feel more emboldened to enforce litmus tests as they did with Giglio. This will likely lead to some measure of marginalization in the public square. And Christians must not go silent in the face of this challenge.

The controversy also revealed that Christians will not be able to avoid marginalization simply by advocating for causes that progressives otherwise approve of. Giglio was invited to participate because of his leadership in mobilizing students to help end human trafficking. But even his work in this area could not erase the stain of his Christian conviction about homosexuality. As Jonathan Capehart of the *Washington Post* commented: "[Giglio] got on the radar because of his work and leadership against human trafficking. . . . But whatever good works Giglio has done in that arena are marred by his anti-gay statements. . . . It is our right not to have an unrepentant bigot be given such a high honor on Inauguration Day."[15]

Can Christians be silent and not enter the fray on the issue of homosexuality? I think not. The wider culture is forcing the issue, and everyone will have to come forth to support one side or the other. There is no middle ground.

Biblical Authority and Sexual Ethics

In the face of a culture that is growing increasingly hostile to the church's two-thousand-year-old sexual ethic, it is no wonder that some evangelicals would elect to stay silent and not offend that culture. After all, we have to live in this culture, and things are a lot easier if we do not buck societal mores. Yet at the heart of this question is the issue of authority. Who or what determines when Christians should and should not speak? If the New Testament provides a normative, universally binding ethic, then one can hardly make the case that Christians can be silent about what

---

[15] Jonathan Capehart, "Louie Giglio Out from Inaugural: Good," *Washington Post*, January 10, 2013, http://www.washingtonpost.com/blogs/post-partisan/wp/2013/01/10/louie-giglio-out-from-inaugural-good/.

God's revelation says about human sexuality. This question—how the New Testament functions as a normative basis for ethics—is one of the central concerns of Christian ethics, and those participating in the discussion do not all agree with one another.

Consider, for instance, the methodological framework for New Testament ethics that Richard Hays put forth in his watershed book *The Moral Vision of the New Testament*.[16] Hays argues that New Testament ethics has a fourfold task: the descriptive, synthetic, hermeneutical, and pragmatic.[17] The descriptive task of New Testament ethics is primarily historical and exegetical—determining what the New Testament authors meant by what they wrote. The synthetic task is concerned with the canonical context of Scripture and the "possibility of coherence among the various witnesses."[18] The hermeneutical task aims to relate the New Testament's ethical content to our current situation, and the pragmatic task involves "embodying Scripture's imperatives in the life of the Christian community."[19] For Hays, the hermeneutical and pragmatic tasks must proceed from the assumption that the Bible functions as the authority over Christian faith and practice. He writes,

> The canonical Scriptures constitute the *norma normans* for the church's life, whereas every other source of moral guidance (whether church tradition, philosophical reasoning, scientific investigation, or claims about contemporary religious experience) must be understood as *norma normata*. Thus, normative Christian ethics is fundamentally a *hermeneutical* enterprise: it must begin and end in the interpretation and application of Scripture for the life of the community of faith.[20]

16 Richard B. Hays, *The Moral Vision of the New Testament: Community, Cross, New Creation, A Contemporary Introduction to New Testament Ethics* (New York: HarperOne, 1996).
17 Ibid., 3–7.
18 Ibid., 4.
19 Ibid., 7.
20 Ibid., 10. I find, however, that Hays inconsistently applies this principle. Later on in *Moral Vision*, Hays warns against forced harmonizations of the Scriptures that suppress the "tensions" that exist among the various writers of the New Testament: "For example, Romans 13 and Revelation 13 are not two complementary expressions of a single principle or a single New Testament understanding of the state; rather, they represent radically different assessments of the relation of the Christian community to the Roman Empire. . . . If these texts are allowed to have their say, they will force us either to choose between them or to reject the normative claims of both" (190). This exegesis shows a fundamental inconsistency in Hays's approach. How can the New Testament be

All of those writing in the area of New Testament ethics, however, do not share Hays's insistence on the authority of Scripture. In fact, many begin their program with an explicit repudiation of the Bible's ethical norms. For them, Scripture is not the *norma normans* of the church's life, because the Scripture can be normed by our own experiences and opinions. Take Luke Timothy Johnson, for instance, who writes:

> I have little patience with efforts to make Scripture say something other than what it says, through appeals to linguistic or cultural subtleties. The exegetical situation is straightforward: we know what the text says. But what are we to do with what the text says? . . .
>
> I think it important to state clearly that we do, in fact, reject the straightforward commands of Scripture, and appeal instead to another authority when we declare that same-sex unions can be holy and good. And what exactly is that authority? We appeal explicitly to the weight of our own experience and the experience thousands of others have witnessed to, which tells us that to claim our own sexual orientation is in fact to accept the way in which God has created us. By so doing, we explicitly reject as well the premises of the scriptural statements condemning homosexuality—namely, that it is a vice freely chosen, a symptom of human corruption, and disobedience to God's created order.[21]

I have at least one thing in common with Johnson. I too have little patience with those who do hermeneutical gymnastics with Scripture in order to obscure or eliminate the Bible's clear condemnations of homosexual behavior. But where we disagree pro-

---

the *norma normans* of the church's life when the church inevitably has to "reject" one or more of the Bible's teachings? This stance is totally incomprehensible to me. If the New Testament contradicts itself in some places (as Hays suggests is the case with Romans 13 and Revelation 13), then that undermines any claim to its authority.

[21] Luke Timothy Johnson and Eve Tushnet, "Homosexuality and the Church: Two Views," *Commonweal* (June 15, 2007): 15. On whether homosexuality is "freely chosen," Richard Hays argues, "Paul's condemnation of homosexual activity does not rest upon an assumption that it is freely chosen; indeed, it is precisely characteristic of Paul to regard 'sin' as a condition of human existence, a condition which robs us of free volition and drives us to disobedient actions which, though involuntary, are nonetheless culpable. . . . The gulf is wide between Paul's viewpoint and the modern habit of assigning culpability only for actions assumed to be under free control of the agent." Richard B. Hays, "Relations Natural and Unnatural: A Response to John Boswell's Exegesis of Romans 1," *Journal of Religious Ethics* 14 (1986): 209.

foundly is what we should do with the Scripture's teaching on this matter.

How does all of this relate to our previous question? Who or what determines when Christians should and should not speak to a given moral issue? Is it okay for Christians to stop discussing their opposition to homosexuality as McLaren originally suggested? If your approach to Scripture matches that of Johnson, then clearly the answer is yes. Scriptural teaching can be trumped by other considerations external to it. If your hermeneutical framework matches Hays's, then the answer is no. If Scripture is the norm that is not normed by any other norm, then we cannot set homosexuality aside as an issue of moral indifference. In other words, it is impossible to hold to biblical authority *and* follow McLaren's view. They are mutually exclusive. We cannot be silent on this. The revisionists are not silent, and faithful Christians dare not be either. The stakes are too high because Paul says that *homosexuals* and *effeminate* persons will not inherit the kingdom of God (1 Cor. 6:9). Would not evangelical silence on this issue be a death sentence for sinners who must repent?

Hays's hermeneutical framework has special relevance for evangelicals who wish to be faithful to Scripture but who face a culture that is increasingly hostile to scriptural mores. None of us works in a vacuum, and we are all conditioned by our experiences and context. Yet our experiences and context should never be turned into a pretext for distorting the interpretation of Scripture. As the song writer Rich Mullins said about orthodoxy in general, we might well say of the Bible in particular: "I did not make it. It is making me."

Is the Bible Unclear about Homosexuality?

Is it true that we cannot be sure what the Bible teaches about homosexuality? It is one thing to assert the Bible's authority. It is another thing to know what the authoritative Bible teaches. Unfortunately, there is no shortage of Bible interpreters who have taken a revisionist approach to biblical texts dealing with homosexuality. Tex Sample, for instance, declares that "the preponderance of scholarly opinion no longer supports" the church's traditional teaching on the moral status of homosexuality.[22] Sample suggests that the traditional reading has little basis in New Testament scholarship, but is that claim true? In the last several decades, there have been a number of scholars who have tried to revise or undermine traditional interpretations of the key biblical texts in the debate. We should note, however, that the revisionists often propose interpretations that are at odds with every interpretation of these texts prior to the middle of the twentieth century.[23] If one takes the long view, the "preponderance of scholarly opinion" hardly falls on the side of the revisionists.

Nevertheless, we cannot ignore the revisions that biblical scholars have indeed suggested concerning the moral status of homosexuality. The exegetical discussion has been voluminous and wide ranging for several decades with arguments for both the revisionist view[24] and the traditional view.[25] But the fact that

---

[22] Tex Sample, "Introduction: The Loyal Opposition," in *The Loyal Opposition: Struggling with the Church on Homosexuality*, ed. Tex Sample and Amy E. De Long (Nashville, TN: Abingdon, 2000), 20.

[23] This is Andreas J. Köstenberger's judgment on revisionist interpretations of Genesis 19 in Andreas J. Köstenberger and David W. Jones, *God, Marriage, and Family: Rebuilding the Biblical Foundation*, 2nd ed. (Wheaton, IL: Crossway, 2010), 205.

[24] A couple of early revisionist works that continue to exert significant influence in this discussion are Robin Scroggs, *The New Testament and Homosexuality: Contextual Background for Contemporary Debate* (Philadelphia: Fortress, 1983); and John Boswell, *Christianity, Social Tolerance, and Homosexuality: Gay People in Western Europe from the Beginning of the Christian Era to the Fourteenth Century* (Chicago: University of Chicago Press, 1980). Both of these works suggest new readings that still define the revisionist field today. Victor Paul Furnish (*The Moral Teaching of Paul: Selected Issues*, 2nd ed. [Nashville, TN: Abingdon, 1985]) is also an important early work claiming that Paul's views on homosexuality can no longer be considered normative. More recent works of note include David L. Balch, *Homosexuality, Science, and the "Plain Sense" of Scripture* (Grand Rapids, MI: Eerdmans, 2000). This volume includes essays from both sides of the issue and considers work from both scientific and exegetical scholarship. While these early revisionist approaches are still prominent in recent work, so are hermeneutical discussions that relativize the normative importance of biblical texts condemning homosexuality. See, for instance, David J. Lull, "Jesus, Paul, and Homosexuals," *Currents in Theology and Mission* 34, no. 3 (June 2007): 199–207. See also Dan O. Via's contribution to Dan O. Via and Robert A. J. Gagnon, eds., *Homosexuality and the Bible: Two Views* (Minneapolis, MN: Augsburg Fortress, 2003). On the hermeneutical question, Via argues that the Bible's strictures against homosexuality should not be taken at face value and that the Bible is not the ultimate norm for ethics (1–2). Another interesting revisionist work is Jack Rogers, *Jesus, the Bible, and Homosexuality: Explode the Myths, Heal the Church* (Louisville, KY: Westminster, 2006), which narrates his change of heart from a traditionalist to a revisionist perspective.

[25] The most important recent defenses of the traditional view are Robert A. J. Gagnon, *The Bible and Homosexual Practice: Texts and Hermeneutics* (Nashville, TN: Abingdon, 2001); and James B. DeYoung, *Homosexuality: Contemporary Claims Examined in Light of the Bible and Other Ancient Literature and Law* (Grand Rapids, MI: Kregel, 2000). These two books work through all of the relevant

the matter is contested does not necessarily mean that the New Testament itself is unclear (as we shall see in a moment). The three primary New Testament texts are Romans 1:26–27; 1 Corinthians 6:9–10; and 1 Timothy 1:9–10.[26] The 1 Corinthians and 1 Timothy texts comprise vice lists that include homosexuality among a host of other acts condemned by God. The most important of these three texts, however, is Romans 1:26–27.[27] For that reason, I will comment briefly on the interpretation of the first two and then focus most of our attention on the text from Romans.

1 Corinthians 6:9–10 and 1 Timothy 1:9–10

The literature on the interpretation of these verses is voluminous, and the exegesis is highly contested. Perhaps the most significant question is the proper interpretation of the word that is sometimes translated as "homosexual," *arsenokoitēs*. In 1 Corinthians 6:9, *arsenokoitēs* appears in a list with other sinners who will not inherit the kingdom of God. In 1 Timothy 1:10 *arsenokoitēs* also appears in a long list of sinners—in particular, those who live "contrary to sound teaching." In both texts, *arsenokoitēs* is condemned as sinful behavior. The debate over these verses is about what exactly *arsenokoitēs* means. The traditional interpretation says that it refers to those who practice homosexuality. Newer revisionist interpretations suggest that ordinary homosexual acts between consenting adults is not in view here. Rather, they suggest that *arsenokoitēs* involves pederasty or prostitution. Thus what Paul condemns here is not necessarily homosexual relations per se, but only exploitative homosexual conduct.[28] Thus Paul does not forbid loving homo-

---

biblical texts with great exegetical precision and care. A very helpful overview of the state of discussion among New Testament scholars through 1996 is Thomas R. Schreiner, "A New Testament Perspective on Homosexuality," *Themelios* 31, no. 3 (2006): 62–75. Richard Hays's chapter on homosexuality should not be overlooked (Hays, *The Moral Vision of the New Testament*), nor should Stanley J. Grenz's *Welcoming but Not Affirming: An Evangelical Response to Homosexuality* (Louisville, KY: Westminster, 1998).

[26] We might also add Jude 7 to this list as it appears to indicate that homosexual sin was at least part of the basis for God's judgment of Sodom and Gomorrah in Genesis 19.

[27] Schreiner, "A New Testament Perspective on Homosexuality," 65.

[28] Dale Martin argues that ἀρσενοκοῖται refers to exploitative sexual behavior and not to homosexual acts per se (Dale B. Martin, "Arsenokoitês and Malakos: Meaning and Consequences," in *Biblical Ethics and Homosexuality: Listening to Scripture*, ed. Robert L. Brawley [Westminster John

sexual relations between consenting adults in this text.[29] The 1984 edition of the NIV reflects the revisionist interpretation: "Neither the sexually immoral nor idolaters nor adulterers nor male prostitutes nor homosexual offenders . . . will inherit the kingdom of God" (1 Cor. 6:9–10). As we shall see, this revisionist interpretation is unlikely for a number of reasons.

In 1 Corinthians 6:9, *arsenokoitēs* is paired with a term that means "soft" or perhaps "effeminate" (*malakos*). The most widely held interpretation of these two terms together is that they simply denote the active and passive partners in a male homosexual encounter.[30] Thus, many scholars believe this text denounces male homosexual activity in general—a view that Paul held in common with Judaism and its Scriptures.[31] Paul characteristically follows the sexual ethic inscribed in the Old Testament. In 1 Corinthians 5:1, for instance, he follows the prohibition against incest from Leviticus 18:8. Likewise, in this text, Paul appears to be following the general prohibition against homosexuality also described in Leviticus 18. As commentators have noted, Paul appears to be the first author in all of Greek literature to use the term *arsenokoitēs*,[32] and it looks like his use of the word derives from the two terms used in Leviticus to describe homosexual acts in general—*arsenos koitēs* (see Lev. 18:22 and 20:13 in LXX).[33] As James De Young ar-

---

Knox, 1996], 119–23). Robin Scroggs argues that ἀρσενοκοῖται and μαλακοί refer not to homosexuality in general, nor even to pederasty in general, but to a specific form of pederasty that involved sex-slave dealers who peddle children for brothel houses (Scroggs, *The New Testament and Homosexuality*, 106–9, 118–21, 126). Such narrowing of the scope of μαλακοί, and ἀρσενοκοῖται has been compellingly refuted by Gagnon, *The Bible and Homosexual Practice*, 303–39. See also DeYoung, *Homosexuality*, 178–203; Schreiner, "A New Testament Perspective on Homosexuality," 70–71.

[29] Anthony Thiselton describes the competing interpretations this way: "The debate tends mainly to turn on whether the joint use of the two terms signifies *male prostitution* (Boswell; cf. Scroggs), or homosexual relations between the more 'passive' and more 'active' partner, *without specific reference* to pederasty (Scroggs) or to prostitution (Boswell)." Anthony C. Thiselton, *The First Epistle to the Corinthians*, New International Greek Testament Commentary (Grand Rapids, MI: Eerdmans, 2000), 449).

[30] The key terms in 1 Cor. 6:9 are μαλακοί, and ἀρσενοκοῖται, and the most widely held interpretation is the one found in BDAG: ἀρσενοκοῖται denotes the active partner in a male homosexual encounter, and μαλακοί, denotes the passive partner (BDAG, s.v. ἀρσενοκοίτης, 135; s.v. μαλακός, 613).

[31] E.g., Joseph A. Fitzmyer, *First Corinthians*, Anchor Yale Bible 32 (New Haven, CT: Yale University Press, 2008), 255–58; Richard B. Hays, *First Corinthians*, Interpretation (Louisville, KY: Westminster, 1997), 97.

[32] Thiselton, *First Epistle to the Corinthians*, 448: "This verse may well be the earliest occurrence of ἀρσενοκοῖτης [sic] as a compound adjectival form, and thus it has no lexicographical pre-history."

[33] So Hays, *First Corinthians*, 97: "Although the word *arsenokoitēs* appears nowhere in Greek literature prior to Paul's use of it, it is evidently a rendering into Greek of the standard rabbinic term for 'one who lies with a male [as with a woman]' (Lev. 18:22; 20:13)."

gues, "The evidence suggests that Paul coined the term, based on the juxtaposition of the two words *arsenos* and *koitēn* in the LXX of Leviticus 20:13 [and 18:22]."[34] Since the prohibition on homosexuality in Leviticus is a general one and not limited to exploitative acts, that strongly suggests that Paul's prohibition is a general one as well.

Paul's use of the term *arsenokoitēs* in 1 Corinthians informs our understanding of the term in 1 Timothy 1:10. In both cases, male homosexuality in general is in view, and in both cases it is portrayed as a sin.

Romans 1:26–27

John Boswell famously contested the traditional interpretation of Romans 1:26–27 in his 1980 book *Christianity, Social Tolerance, and Homosexuality*. He argues, "The New Testament takes no demonstrable position on homosexuality" as we know it.[35] He argues that Paul does not condemn all forms of homosexuality but only those acts that are committed by people who are "naturally" heterosexual. Boswell writes, "Paul did not discuss gay *persons* but only homosexual *acts* committed by heterosexual persons."[36] Thus, when Paul condemns what is *against nature*, he refers only to one's own private sexual orientation.

Robin Scroggs also renders Romans 1:27 irrelevant to the homosexual question by arguing that Paul only meant to condemn exploitive homosexual acts between men and boys—also known as *pederasty*.[37] Thus, since Paul condemns pederasty and not homosexual relations in general, this text (and 1 Cor. 6:9 and 1 Tim. 1:10) cannot be used to make an ethical judgment against what modern people mean by homosexuality. Gerald Sheppard relativizes what he calls the "homophobic"[38] interpretation of Romans 1:26–27 by

---

[34] DeYoung, *Homosexuality*, 195.
[35] Boswell, *Christianity, Social Tolerance, and Homosexuality*, 117.
[36] Ibid., 109.
[37] Scroggs, *New Testament and Homosexuality*, 126.
[38] Gerald T. Sheppard, "The Use of Scripture with the Christian Ethical Debate Concerning Same-Sex Oriented Persons," *Union Seminary Quarterly Review* 40 (1985): 18, 31.

arguing that "the Bible's own normative expression of intimate sexual love . . . *does* begin to suggest . . . some norms and rules in support of loving same-sex relationships."[39] In other words, the secondary matters of Scripture (like Paul's view of homosexuality) must give way to the primary emphases of biblical theology (like justification by faith).[40] In effect, therefore, Paul's manifest concern for justice trumps his hang-ups about homosexuality. Scholars such as Victor Paul Furnish and Margaret Davies make no pretense to honor the authority of Scripture as Sheppard does. Rather, their perspective resembles Luke Timothy Johnson's, mentioned above. They think that what we now know about homosexuality simply trumps Paul's condemnation of it.[41]

All of these proposals fail to convince.[42] Boswell fails because he misunderstands what Paul means by *nature*. For Paul, nature (φύσις word group) is not a reference to one's private sexual orientation. Nature refers to the creational purposes of God in the primeval event of making male and female.[43] To depart from nature is

---

[39] Ibid., 31.

[40] Ibid., 22.

[41] Furnish, *Moral Teaching of Paul: Selected Issues*, 79–80; Margaret Davies, "New Testament Ethics and Ours: Homosexuality and Sexuality in Romans 1:26–27," *Biblical Interpretation* 3 (1995): 318. Davies writes, "Pauline condemnation of homosexual practice is therefore to be understood as an anomalous emotional blindspot in an otherwise radical transformation of tradition" (318).

[42] In this summary and critique, I am following Schreiner, "A New Testament Perspective on Homosexuality," 65–71.

[43] The meaning of the φύσις word group in Rom. 1:26–27 has been fiercely contested—one side arguing that φύσις denotes *God's created order*, the other that it refers to the *personal qualities of an individual* (i.e., "orientation"). Boswell's watershed book famously argued that φύσις refers not to God's creational order, but to an individual's orientation: "'Nature' in Romans 1:26, then, should be understood as the personal nature of the pagans in question" (Boswell, *Christianity, Social Tolerance, and Homosexuality*, 111). Thus, according to Boswell, Paul was condemning individuals who had a heterosexual orientation but who went against "nature" to engage in homosexual acts. In Boswell's reading of Paul, not all homosexual acts are against "nature," thus defined. Boswell writes, "It cannot be inferred from this that Paul considered mere homoerotic attraction or practice morally reprehensible, since the passage strongly implies that he was not discussing persons who were by inclination gay and since he carefully observed, in regard to both the women and the men, that they changed or abandoned the 'natural' use to engage in homosexual activities" (112–13). Boswell's argument was roundly refuted by Hays, "Relations Natural and Unnatural: A Response to John Boswell's Exegesis of Romans 1." Hays shows that Boswell's exegesis is "seriously flawed" (184), anachronistic (200), and eisegetical (201). Hays writes, "His proposal falls apart completely *as exegesis of Paul* when we recognize that the whole conception of 'sexual orientation' is an anachronism when applied to this text. The idea that some individuals have an inherent disposition towards same-sex erotic attraction and are therefore constitutionally 'gay' is a modern idea of which there is no trace either in the NT or in any other Jewish or Christian writings in the ancient world" (200). "Paul identifies 'nature' with the created order" (194). Hays says that this meaning is so clear that "one is left wondering what an ancient writer could possibly have said to avoid being co-opted in the service of Boswell's hypothesis" (202). See also Hays, *Moral Vision of the New Testament*, 383–89. So also Markus Bockmuehl, *Jewish Law in Gentile Churches: Halakhah*

to depart from the heterosexual norm established in Genesis 1–2.[44] Scroggs's pederasty proposal fails because there is not one scintilla of evidence in the text that Paul is talking about relationships between men and boys. Paul speaks of "males in males" (ἄρσενες ἐν ἄρσεσιν) in Romans 1:27 (AT) without saying anything about young boys. Paul condemns same-sex relations between females in verse 26, but there is no evidence from antiquity that women and young girls are in view. Thus, in both verses 26 and 27, Paul is prohibiting same-sex relations in general. Sheppard, Furnish, and Davies fail because they manifestly undermine the authority of Scripture in their hermeneutical approach. Tom Schreiner correctly evaluates Sheppard, Furnish, and Davies: "This view at least has the virtue of honesty, but at the same time it removes itself from the realm of biblical and Christian ethics by surrendering to the tides of culture."[45] So, yes, it is true that the Bible's teaching on homosexuality is contested, but the recent revisions of the traditional view are seriously flawed. That an interpretation of a text might be contested is by no means grounds for concluding that we cannot know what that text means. N. T. Wright's comment to this effect is apt: "What we cannot do is to sideline this passage as irrelevant to Christian ethical discourse . . . or to pretend that it means something other than what it says."[46]

We should also note that revisionist interpretations have yet to win a consensus among commentators on Romans 1:26–27. The traditional understanding still holds in many if not most of the major critical commentaries.[47] For instance, Robert Jewett's 2007

and the Beginning of Christian Public Ethics (Edinburgh: T. & T. Clark, 2000), 130: "The context makes it plain that the appeal to 'nature' here (παρὰ φύσιν, v. 26) is in fact an appeal to the same created order which calls for the distinction between creature and creator."

[44] The New Testament elsewhere reaffirms this creational order: Matt. 19:5; Mark 10:7–8; 1 Cor. 6:16; Eph. 5:31.

[45] Schreiner, "A New Testament Perspective on Homosexuality," 68–69.

[46] N. T. Wright, "The Letter to the Romans," in *The New Interpreter's Bible*, vol. 10 (Nashville, TN: Abingdon, 2002), 435.

[47] E.g., C. E. B. Cranfield, *A Critical and Exegetical Commentary on The Epistle to the Romans*, vol. 1, International Critical Commentary (Edinburgh: T. & T. Clark, 1975), 127; James D. G. Dunn, *Romans 1–8*, Word Biblical Commentary (Dallas: Word Books, 1988), 64–66; Joseph A. Fitzmyer, *Romans: A New Translation with Introduction and Commentary*, Anchor Bible (New York: Doubleday, 1993), 275–76, 285–88; Robert Jewett, *Romans*, Hermeneia (Minneapolis, MN: Fortress, 2007), 172–81; Douglas J. Moo, *The Epistle to the Romans*, New International Commentary on the New Testament

Romans commentary for the Hermeneia series is a massive work of scholarship. After all the decades of homosexual-friendly interpretations, Jewett nevertheless holds the line on the traditional interpretation. In fact, he has gone further than anyone I have seen to show that Paul condemns homosexual behavior generally and not narrowly, with reference only to certain kinds of homosexual behavior. He does this in a rather idiosyncratic translation of verses 26–27:

> For this reason, God delivered them to the desires of their hearts for passions of dishonor, for their females exchanged the natural use for the unnatural, and likewise also the males, after they abandoned the natural use with females, were inflamed with their lust for one another, *males who work up their shameful member in other males*, and receive back for their deception the recompense that is *tightness in themselves*.[48]

Jewett's translation reveals an explicit depiction of homosexual acts, and Jewett argues that Paul sees them *all* as sinful. Jewett writes, "Paul simply follows . . . his Jewish cultural tradition by construing the entire realm of homosexual relations as evidence that divine wrath was active therein."[49] I am not citing Jewett as if his work is an unassailable authority on the interpretation of Romans. I am merely highlighting the fact that decades of revisionist interpretations have failed to gain a new consensus to replace the old one. Even this very recent major critical commentary emphatically enunciates the traditional view. Furthermore, Jewett comes to his conclusion without even one reference to the most important monograph defending the traditional view: Robert Gagnon's 2001 book *The Bible and Homosexual Practice: Texts and Hermeneutics*.[50]

(Grand Rapids, MI: Eerdmans, 1996), 113–17; Robert H. Mounce, *Romans*, New American Commentary (Nashville, TN: Broadman, 1995), 82–84; Thomas R. Schreiner, *Romans*, Baker Exegetical Commentary on the New Testament (Grand Rapids, MI: Baker, 1998); Ben Witherington III and Darlene Hyatt, *Paul's Letter to the Romans: A Socio-Rhetorical Commentary* (Grand Rapids, MI: Eerdmans, 2004), 69; Wright, "Letter to the Romans," 433–35.
[48] Jewett, *Romans*, 163 (italics mine).
[49] Ibid., 179.
[50] Gagnon, *The Bible and Homosexual Practice*. See also DeYoung, *Homosexuality*.

Once again, it is true that the Bible's teaching on homosexuality is contested, but the recent revisions of the traditional view are seriously flawed. Probably the most serious error of the revisionists is their failure to see that Paul simply reflects the heterosexual ideal that he inherited from Judaism. This fundamental flaw explains in large part why there is not yet a scholarly consensus reflected in major critical commentaries. The evidence still shows that Paul understood that the Old Testament prohibits homosexuality (Lev. 18:22; 20:13). He simply carries forward into the new covenant the sexual norm of his Jewish tradition.

Conclusion

It bears saying again that when Jesus and Paul set out new-covenant norms for marriage and sexuality, they do not appeal to polygamist kings such as David or Solomon or to polygamist patriarchs such as Abraham, Isaac, or Jacob. For all the importance these Old Testament figures have in the history of redemption, Jesus and Paul do not look to any of them as the paradigm for understanding marriage and sex. Instead, Jesus and Paul look back without exception to the pre-fall monogamous union of Adam and Eve in Genesis 2 as the norm of human sexuality and marriage. "For this cause a man shall leave his father and his mother and shall cling to his wife; and they shall become one flesh" (Gen. 2:24 AT; cf. Matt. 19:5; Mark 10:7–8; 1 Cor. 6:16; Eph. 5:31). The apostle Paul says that the great *mystery* of the Genesis 2 norm of marriage (one man and one woman in covenanted union) is that God intended it all along to be a shadow of a greater reality. From the garden of Eden forward, God intended marriage and the marriage act to enact a parable of another marriage: Christ's marriage to his church (Eph. 5:31–32). Homosexuality distorts that image—an image that God intends to redound to his glory.

Revisionists and progressives often present us with a false choice concerning the church's ministry to homosexuals. Christians can either walk the path of homophobia and hatred, or they can surrender their ancient beliefs to accommodate the normalization of homosexual practice.[51] But this is an unnecessary dilemma. There is another way. Christians and churches can love and minister to homosexuals while still holding fast to biblical norms for human sexuality. Because these dear people are likely already in our pews—some of them silently suffering and struggling among us—we must construct a framework to receive and minister to those who wish to be free from slavery to homosexual sin.

In 2003 John Piper drafted a statement for Bethlehem Baptist Church that provides such a framework. The statement, "Beliefs about Homosexual Behavior and Ministering to Homosexual Persons," outlines six points.[52] I commend this statement as a model starting point for any church wishing to reach homosexuals with the gospel:

1. We believe that heterosexuality is God's revealed will for humankind and that, since God is loving, a chaste and faithful expression of this orientation (whether in singleness or in marriage) is the ideal to which God calls all people.
2. We believe that a homosexual orientation is a result of the fall of humanity into a sinful condition that pervades every person. Whatever biological or familial roots of homosexuality may be discovered, we do not believe that these would sanction or excuse homosexual behavior, though they would deepen our compassion and patience for those who are struggling to be free from sexual temptations.
3. We believe there is hope for the person with a homosexual orientation and that Jesus Christ offers a healing alternative in which the power of sin is broken and the person is freed to know and experience his or her true identity in Christ and in the fellowship of his Church.

---

[51] Baptist historian Bill Leonard offers a similar false choice in his reflections on the decline of the Southern Baptist Convention. Leonard says that the SBC is at a fork in the road. In one direction are Mennonites, who separate themselves from the larger culture to ensure their own doctrinal purity, and in the other direction is greater popularity but a dilution of the doctrine (Jeffrey Weiss, "The Southern Baptist Convention Is Yesterday's News," *Politics Daily*, June 29, 2010, http://www.politicsdaily.com/2010/06/29/the-southern-baptist-convention-is-yesterdays-news/).
[52] John Piper, "Bethlehem's Position on Homosexuality," *Desiring God*, August 6, 2003, http://www.desiringgod.org/resource-library/taste-see-articles/bethlehems-position-on-homosexuality. Used by permission.

4. We believe that this freedom is attained through a process which includes recognizing homosexual behavior as sin, renouncing the practice of homosexual behavior, rediscovering healthy, non-erotic friendships with people of the same sex, embracing a moral sexual lifestyle, and in the age to come, rising from the dead with a new body free from every sinful impulse. This process parallels the similar process of sanctification needed in dealing with heterosexual temptations as well. We believe that this freedom comes through faith in Jesus Christ, by the power of his Spirit.

5. We believe that all persons have been created in the image of God and should be accorded human dignity. We believe therefore that hateful, fearful, unconcerned harassment of persons with a homosexual orientation should be repudiated. We believe that respect for persons with a homosexual orientation involves honest, reasoned, nonviolent sharing of facts concerning the immorality and liability of homosexual behavior. On the other hand, endorsing behavior which the Bible disapproves endangers persons and dishonors God.

6. We believe that Christian churches should reach out in love and truth to minister to people touched by homosexuality, and that those who contend Biblically against their own sexual temptation should be patiently assisted in their battle, not ostracized or disdained. However, the more prominent a leadership role or modeling role a person holds in a church or institution of the Conference, the higher will be the expectations for God's ideal of sexual obedience and wholeness. We affirm that both heterosexual and homosexual persons should find help in the church to engage in the Biblical battle against all improper sexual thoughts and behaviors.[53]

Piper's statement combines the Bible's countercultural teaching with a compassionate call for gospel ministry to homosexual sinners. Churches need to develop this kind of vision if they are to bring the gospel to bear upon every sinner in need of God's grace

---

[53] Piper says that the statement was drafted "with the help of Joe Hallet, who came out of the homosexual life by the power of Christ and lived faithfully with AIDS, and eventually with his wife, until his death in 1997" (ibid.).

in Christ. Where these kinds of principles define the church's ministry and mission, there is hope for even the most wayward of sinners. The hope of the gospel is for any sinner who will have it, and that includes homosexual sinners. That is why the apostle Paul was able to say to the homosexual sinners in Corinth, "But you were washed, but you were sanctified, but you were justified in the name of the Lord Jesus Christ and in the Spirit of our God" (1 Cor. 6:11). In 1 Timothy 1:9–10 Paul gives a list of some of the most repugnant sinners that one can find in the world: murderers, immoral men, homosexuals, kidnappers, liars, and perjurers. Among these, Paul names himself as the worst of the lot because he was a blasphemer, a persecutor, and a violent aggressor when God saved him (v. 13). In verse 14, Paul says that he found love when by the mercy of God he came to Christ. If God's love applies to Paul, the chief of sinners, it certainly applies to other sinners as well—including the homosexual sinners of verse 10. This is the message that God has given the church to proclaim, and it is the message that the world desperately needs to hear.

Your omnipotence is never far from us, even when we are far from you. Alternatively, I ought to have paid more vigilant heed to the voice from your clouds. . . . Had I paid careful attention to these sayings and "become a eunuch for the sake of the kingdom of heaven," I would have been happier finding fulfillment in your embraces.

—Augustine, *Confessions*

8

Glorify God with Your Singleness

Only in Matthew's gospel do we find Jesus's clearest and most extensive comments on singleness. It comes at the tail end of Jesus's teaching about divorce, in which the Lord offers a fairly restrictive view on divorce and remarriage.[1] Jesus's remarks provoke a stunned response from his disciples, who say: "If the relationship of the man with his wife is like this, it is better not to marry" (Matt. 19:10). In the minds of the disciples, if one must commit to the trials of marriage with such finality and permanence, then it would be easier simply to remain unmarried. The disciples probably did not mean to suggest that lifelong singleness was a serious option. In Jesus's day, it was unheard of that a man would choose to remain unmarried his entire life. A good Israelite saw it as his duty to have a family and children—to be fruitful and multiply.[2] Thus, the disciples' proposal was likely offered more as an instinctive response than as an actual possibility.[3]

It must have been stunning, therefore, when Jesus greeted their remark with affirmation rather than dismissal: "Not all men can accept this statement, but only those to whom it has been

---

[1] See the section in chap. 4 on divorce.
[2] John Nolland, *The Gospel of Matthew*, New International Greek Testament Commentary (Grand Rapids, MI: Eerdmans, 2005), 779.
[3] R. T. France, *The Gospel of Matthew*, New International Commentary on the New Testament (Grand Rapids, MI: Eerdmans, 2007), 722.

210 WHAT IS THE MEANING OF SEX?

given" (Matt. 19:11). There are some who think that the phrase "this statement" refers back to Jesus's prior teaching on divorce (vv. 3–9).[4] In context, it is more likely that "this statement" points to what the disciples had just spoken in the immediately preceding verse (v. 10).[5] Jesus means, therefore, to comment on the propriety of remaining unmarried. Jesus says that such a life is not something that just anyone can pursue. Singleness is only for those to whom it has been given. So Jesus does not view unmarried men with the disdain that his contemporaries probably would have had.[6] Instead, he views singleness as a gift from God.[7]

Singleness in the Teaching of Jesus

Jesus treats singleness as a calling—a vocation given to certain persons by the sovereign grant of God. Yet Jesus acknowledges that singleness does not come to each person in the same way, for the same duration of time, or even for the same reasons. To illustrate the point, Jesus expounds upon the condition of a certain class of persons known as eunuchs. In the most literal sense, a eunuch is someone who is physically incapable of procreation and thus who cannot marry. But, as I noted earlier, Jesus says that not all eunuchs come to this condition in the same way. First, "there are eunuchs who were born that way from their mother's womb" (v. 12a). This refers to people who are born with the physical inability to procreate. It may have included persons with disorders of sex development, as we discussed in chapter 6. Second, "there are eunuchs who were made eunuchs by men" (v. 12b). This is most likely a reference to the fact that in the ancient world, royal officials were sometimes castrated in order to ensure that they would pose no threat sexually to the king's harem.[8] Third, "there

---

[4] So Quentin Quesnell, "Made Themselves Eunuchs for the Kingdom of Heaven (Mt 19:12)," *Catholic Biblical Quarterly* 30, no. 3 (Jl 1968): 335–58.
[5] So France, *Gospel of Matthew*, 722–23; Craig L. Blomberg, *Matthew*, New American Commentary 22 (Nashville, TN: Broadman, 1992), 294; Nolland, *Gospel of Matthew*, 776–77.
[6] Nolland, *Gospel of Matthew*, 777ff.
[7] So William Loader, *Sexuality in the New Testament: Understanding the Key Texts* (Louisville, KY: Westminster, 2010), 108.
[8] France, *Gospel of Matthew*, 724–25; R. J. A. Sheriffs, "Eunuch," in *New Bible Dictionary*, ed. D. R. W. Wood et al., 3rd ed. (Downers Grove, IL: InterVarsity, 1996), 347.

are . . . eunuchs who made themselves eunuchs for the sake of the kingdom of heaven" (v. 12c). This final group should not be understood as those who have literally castrated themselves. It should be understood figuratively along the lines of some of the modern translations: "Those who choose to live like eunuchs" (NIV); "They have renounced marriage" (NAB); or "Some choose not to marry" (NLT).[9] The first two groups are those who are incapable of marriage. This final group comprises those who have voluntarily chosen celibacy and a life of singleness. The key difference that Jesus identifies among the three groups is that the final group has chosen their singleness, while the first two groups have not. Nevertheless, for all three groups, singleness comes to them by the sovereign grant of God.

For this reason, what Jesus says about singleness has important implications for all unmarried persons. Singles must recognize their unmarried state as a providential gift from God. For those who have been given the ability to set aside the desire for normal marital relations, their lives are to be leveraged for greater effectiveness for the kingdom of God. Single persons have opportunities that married persons do not have. Singleness frees people from the responsibilities of marriage and allows them greater flexibility with how they structure their time and invest emotional capital in others for the sake of the kingdom. Such service should be the aim and motivation of any Christian who chooses a life of celibacy. For those who have *not* chosen their singleness but who would otherwise like to be married, they need to recognize that God has called them to this season for a purpose. There is nothing wrong with their remaining open to and even actively pursuing marriage. In the meantime—for as long as God providentially allows the season of singleness to continue—trust in God's provision, chastity until marriage, and single-minded devotion to the kingdom should be the daily commitment of the Christian single.[10]

---

[9] France, *Gospel of Matthew*, 725.

[10] John Piper quotes at length from Margaret Clarkson's book *So You're Single!* She writes: "Through no fault or choice of my own, I am unable to express my sexuality in the beauty and intimacy of Christian marriage, as God intended when he created me a sexual being in his own image. To

Singleness in the Teaching of Paul

A Word for the Unmarried

In 1 Corinthians 7:7 Paul compares his own life as a single man to the experience of those who are married, and he says that—all things considered—he wishes that everyone could be like him. He writes, "Yet I wish that all men were even as I myself am. However, each man has his own gift from God, one in this manner, and another in that." Paul found the single life to be preferable to married life. He doesn't go into all his reasons for this preference in this one verse, but later in the chapter he elaborates at least two benefits to the single lifestyle.

The first benefit to being unmarried is the ability to avoid trouble. In 7:28 Paul warns, "But if you marry . . . such will have trouble in this life, and I am trying to spare you." Paul affirms what every married person already knows by experience: marriage is hard; it is not easy. When two sinners are put in close proximity to one another for an extended period of time, they will eventually have conflict. There will be unanticipated trials that exacerbate conflicts, and married persons must learn to run the gauntlet in order to hold their marriage together. It is sometimes difficult for singles to see this before marriage, and expectations for marital bliss can tend to be a little higher than reality would warrant. One preacher put it this way: "Guys, marriage is not going to be a twenty-four-hour-a-day sexual bonanza. Girls, marriage is not going to be one long meaningful conversation." Marriage offers great joys to those who choose to enter it, but it also brings great and abiding difficulties. Christian marriage requires two people willing to die to themselves daily. It

---

seek to do this outside of marriage is, by the clear teaching of Scripture, to sin against God and against my own nature. As a committed Christian, then, I have no alternative but to live a life of voluntary celibacy. I must be chaste not only in body, but in mind and spirit as well. Since I am now in my 60's I think that my experience of what this means is valid. I want to go on record as having proved that for those who are committed to do God's will, his commands are his enablings. . . . Why must I live my life alone? I do not know. But Jesus Christ is Lord of my life. I believe in the sovereignty of God, and I accept my singleness from his hand. He could have ordered my life otherwise, but he has not chosen to do so. As his child, I must trust his love and wisdom." See John Piper, "For Single Men and Women (and the Rest of Us)," in *Recovering Biblical Manhood and Womanhood: A Response to Evangelical Feminism* (Wheaton, IL: Crossway, 1991), xxv–xxvi.

is eminently difficult, and that is why Paul says, "I am trying to spare you."

The second benefit to being unmarried is the opportunity for undistracted devotion to the Lord. Paul says that unmarried persons are able to focus special attention on "the things of the Lord, how he may please the Lord" (v. 32). But those who are married are "concerned about the things of the world, how he may please his wife" (v. 33). Consequently, "his interests are divided" (v. 34). Paul does not aim to put a legalistic obligation of celibacy upon anyone, but he does wish to commend the single life as that which enables "undistracted devotion to the Lord" (v. 35).

Married persons have responsibilities—responsibilities to family that they cannot shirk. A husband has the responsibility to lead, to provide for, and to protect his wife. He cannot walk away from this responsibility for any reason. Likewise, a wife has the responsibility of being a helper to her husband (Gen. 2:18). She has a special responsibility to care for the household and to follow her husband's leadership (Titus 2:5). She cannot shirk this responsibility for any reason. Singleness affords the opportunity for people to be "undistracted" (1 Cor. 7:35) by these duties. It frees them to leverage their lives more completely for the sake of service to God's kingdom. This is the way Paul viewed the matter, and that is why he commends the single life to anyone who is able to accept it.

Paul has another crucial word about singleness in the second half of 1 Corinthians 7:7. He says it is not for everyone: "Yet I wish that all men were even as I myself am. However, each man has his own gift from God, one in this manner, and another in that." This means that even though Paul prefers singlehood, not everyone is called to be single. Each person has their own gift from God. Paul's counsel here seems to be an elaboration of Jesus's teaching recorded in Matthew 19:10–11. Paul seems to have known that Jesus taught that celibacy is a gift from God. But notice that it is not just singleness that Paul describes as a gift. Every Christian has his or her own gift from God, "one in this manner, and another in that." The married state is every bit as much a gift as the single state. Both of them issue from the sovereign grant of God to his people. Either status is a gift in Paul's view. A person can serve God faithfully, live fully, and mature with purpose in either situation.

A Word for the Once Married

The key to understanding 1 Corinthians 7:8–9 begins with understanding who it is that Paul is addressing. He says, "to the unmarried and to widows." The word *widows* is clear enough. A widow clearly refers to a woman who had once been married but whose husband had passed away. But who are these "unmarried" persons? Some people think he's referring to unmarried persons generally—anyone who is single. But this seems to be an unlikely interpretation. His general counsel to singles appears elsewhere in the chapter (vv. 7, 25ff.), and these two verses seem to be about a different group of people. Also, the word translated "unmarried" appears four times in the New Testament, and all four instances are in this chapter. In verse 11 and in verse 34, "unmarried" clearly refers to those who were formerly married. Because the Greek word for "widower" was very rare and because the term "unmarried" is paired with "widow" here, the "unmarried" in verse 8 most likely refers to widowers. Verses 8–9, therefore, are addressed to widows and widowers. So the question that Paul is addressing is what should people do whose spouses have passed away? Should they remarry or should they stay unmarried?

At this point, hardly anyone would be surprised to learn that Paul prefers widows and widowers to stay unmarried. He writes, "It is good for them if they remain even as I" (v. 8). In saying, "even as I," Paul seems to put himself in the very same category as the unmarried and the widow. I agree with those interpreters who suggest that Paul is giving us a hint that he, too, was once married but that his wife had passed away.[11] Paul was a Pharisee, and mar-

---

[11] So Richard B. Hays, *First Corinthians*, Interpretation (Louisville, KY: Westminster, 1997), 119; Gordon D. Fee, *The First Epistle to the Corinthians*, New International Commentary on the New Testament (Grand Rapids, MI: Eerdmans, 1987), 288n7.

riage was the norm for Pharisees.[12] It is very difficult to imagine, therefore, that a zealous Pharisee such as Paul would have been single (Gal. 1:14; Phil. 3:5; cf. Acts 22:3). So it is most likely the case that Paul was married and that he is addressing people in the same condition that he is in—single and no longer married. For Paul, the gift of celibacy consisted in "a genuine gift of freedom from sexual need."[13]

Paul acknowledges that not every widow or widower will be called to stay unmarried. He says that those who "do not have self-control" should pursue marriage, for "it is better to marry than to burn" (1 Cor. 7:9). There are at least two different interpretations of what this verse means. Some people think it means that it is better to marry than to burn with *lust*, while other people think it means that it is better to marry than to burn in *judgment* for not controlling one's sexual desires. Since Paul says the issue is "self-control," it seems that the first interpretation—"to burn with lust"—is the most likely one. Paul says that if you do not have "self-control"— meaning that you have an intense desire to enter into conjugal relations again with a spouse—then by all means you are free to pursue a situation in which you can fulfill that desire in a righteous way. In other words, you are free to pursue marriage. This is similar to the counsel Paul gave to older widows in 1 Timothy 5:3 who were called "widows indeed." These older widows had committed to stay unmarried, and their names were added to a list of women with special status in the congregation (1 Tim. 5:9–10). But Paul says to the younger widows that "when they feel sensual desires . . . they want to get married" (1 Tim. 5:11). So Paul says, "Therefore, I want younger widows to get married, bear children, keep house, and give the enemy no occasion for reproach" (1 Tim. 5:14). Paul wants these younger widows to get married because of their abiding desire for conjugal life. In both 1 Timothy 5 and in 1 Corinthians 7 Paul encourages such people to pursue marriage.

---

[12] Harvey McArthur, "Celibacy in Judaism at the Time of Christian Beginnings," *Andrews University Seminary Studies* 25, no. 2 (1987): 163–81.
[13] So Fee, *First Epistle to the Corinthians*, 287.

As a professor at a Christian college, I hear from time to time from students who struggle with the question of whether they should pursue marriage or a life of celibacy for the sake of the kingdom. I tell them that Paul's counsel in this text has implications not just for widows and widowers but also for singles in general. If one has a strong and abiding desire for conjugal life, that person should pursue marriage. There are other factors that determine whether a single will marry. Sometimes the door is closed even though a person might desire marriage. In any case, such persons who desire marriage are not in the wrong for pursuing it. In fact, Paul is saying that they probably should pursue it because it is better to marry than to burn.

Singleness and the Call to Chastity

Single Christians are not the only ones who must struggle to maintain sexual purity. Married persons are just as capable of sinning sexually as anyone else is. Nevertheless, there are some special challenges facing singles that are peculiar to our own historical moment and that make sexual purity especially difficult. Over the last generation, massive revisions to traditional sexual mores have changed the way that young people move into adulthood. Sociologists Mark Regnerus and Jeremy Uecker identify five elements that mark a young person's transition from adolescence to adulthood: (1) becoming economically independent, (2) moving out of parents' home, (3) completing one's education/commencing work, (4) marriage, and (5) children. Young people are moving through these markers at a much slower pace than they did two generations ago, and for some of them adulthood no longer includes all five of these elements. In 1960, 65 percent of men and 77 percent of women had reached all five of these markers by the time they were thirty. In the current day, only 31 percent of men and 46 percent of women reach these markers by age thirty.[14]

---

[14] Mark Regnerus and Jeremy Uecker, *Premarital Sex in America: How Young Americans Meet, Mate, and Think About Marrying* (New York: Oxford University Press, 2011), 5.

Premarital Sex

Those figures have important implications for Christians and the issue of premarital sex. A sizable percentage of young people today are delaying adulthood. In particular, they are delaying marriage and childbearing, but they are not delaying sex. As a result, demographers have observed a new life stage among modern people, called "prolonged adolescence" or "pre-adulthood,"[15] in which young people spend the better portion of their twenties delaying marriage while not delaying sexual activity. They move from partner to partner for nearly a decade before deciding to settle down, get married, and have children. Columnist David Brooks describes it this way:

> Now young people face a social frontier of their own. They hit puberty around 13 and many don't get married until they're past 30. That's two decades of coupling, uncoupling, hooking up, relationships and shopping around. This period isn't a transition anymore. It's a sprawling life stage, and nobody knows the rules.[16]

To the extent that Christian singles are caught up in these trends, they face pressing challenges. From a physiological perspective, they are delaying marriage through the period of their life in which they are most fertile and most ready to enjoy the gift of sex. This situation presents a conflict between burgeoning physical desires and the Christian ethic of sexual abstinence outside of marriage. Those who delay marriage through the decade of their twenties face temptations to find sexual release (premarital sexual activity, pornography, masturbation, etc.). Some singles answer the call to purity in the face of such challenges, but many others do not. So they begin a renegotiation of what is permissible sexually. The temptation is always there to suppress or revise biblical norms in order to accommodate the powerful twin influences of culture and fleshly desire.

---

[15] Mary Eberstadt, *Adam and Eve after the Pill: Paradoxes of the Sexual Revolution* (San Francisco: Ignatius, 2012), 17.

[16] David Brooks, "The New Lone Rangers," *New York Times*, July 10, 2007, sec. A21, http://www.nytimes.com/2007/07/10/opinion/10brooks.html.

Perhaps it is time for Christians to reevaluate just how much ground they have given to a cultural preference for delayed marriage. Early marriage is no silver bullet against the temptation to premarital sex, but not to consider it would be irresponsible in the face of the very real spiritual dangers of prolonged adolescence. Mark Regnerus argues that many evangelicals have made much ado about sex but have become slow and lackadaisical about marriage. Americans are marrying later—if at all—and having fewer children than previous generations. In 1970 the median age for first marriages was twenty-one for women and twenty-three for men. By 2009 that number had risen to twenty-six for women and twenty-eight for men. Evangelicals marry a little earlier than the larger populace, but not by much.[17] Regnerus writes,

> Evangelicals tend to marry slightly earlier than other Americans, but not by much. Many of them plan to marry in their mid-20s. Yet waiting for sex until then feels far too long to most of them. And I am suggesting that when people wait until their mid-to-late 20s to marry, it *is* unreasonable to expect them to refrain from sex. It's battling our Creator's reproductive designs. The data don't lie. Our sexual behavior patterns . . . give us away. Very few wait long for sex. Meanwhile, women's fertility is more or less fixed, yet Americans are increasingly ignoring it during their 20s, only to beg and pray to reclaim it in their 30s and 40s.[18]

I disagree that it is "unreasonable" to expect Christians to abstain from premarital sex. No Christian is exempt from the obligation to sexual purity. But Regnerus does have a point. Delaying marriage has consequences that many Christians must reckon with, and early marriage may be one of the ways we can encourage chastity in singles.

Sexual holiness means abstaining from all sexual activity outside of marriage. The biblical term for sex with someone else's spouse is *adultery*. The catchall term for any extramarital sexual

---

[17] Mark D. Regnerus, "The Case for Early Marriage," *Christianity Today* 53, no. 8, 2009, 23.
[18] Ibid., 23.

activity is *fornication* or *sexual immorality*.[19] Although the term *fornication* has fallen into disuse, I agree with Russell Moore that it
may be time to resurrect it. It is an antiquated term, but there is no
other one like it that describes both unlawful sexual activity and
the divine censure that goes along with it. Moore writes:

> Could it be that the loss of the words "fornicate" and "fornica-
> tion" is about something more than just updating our vocabulary
> to connect with the society around us? Could it be that we've
> lost something crucial about the grammar of the Christian faith?
> Moreover, could it be that, by using the language of "premarital
> sex," we've implicitly ceded the moral imagination to the sexual
> revolutionaries? . . . Part of what it means to recover a Christian
> vision of sexuality is to recover a lexicon worthy of the gravity
> of human sexuality.[20]

But beyond recovery of the word, we also need recovery of the
substance. A Christian sexual ethic means avoiding fornication,
no matter how long one remains single. Jesus said that fornication
was first and foremost a matter of the heart (Mark 7:21). The new
birth is therefore required to root out this particular sin (John
3:3, 5). But rooting it out must also issue forth in deeds, and in this
case *abstaining* from certain deeds. As the apostle Paul warned the
Corinthians, "Flee fornication!" (1 Cor. 6:18 AT).

The biblical testimony is clear. Premarital sexual activity is not
an option for the disciple of Jesus. But what about other kinds of
sexual activity that stop short of sexual intercourse? What about
those who might maintain "technical virginity" through a variety
of other activities as an alternative to actual intercourse?[21] The old
question that young singles seem to ask is, "How far is too far?"

---

[19] "Fornication" and "sexual immorality" are common translations of the Greek term πορνεία.
So Kyle Harper, "Porneia: The Making of a Christian Sexual Norm," *Journal of Biblical Literature* 131,
no. 2 (2012): 383.
[20] Russell D. Moore, "Sexual Iconoclasm," *Touchstone* 26, no. 1 (2013), http://www.touchstonemag
.com/archives/article.php?id=26-01-020-v.
[21] Mark Regnerus argues that even though some adolescence may maintain "technical virginity,"
it is not much motivated by a desire for sexual purity or for maintaining the status of "virginity."
See Mark Regnerus, *Forbidden Fruit: Sex and Religion in the Lives of American Teenagers* (New York:
Oxford University Press, 2007), 164, 167.

Other books on Christian sexual ethics consider a gamut of activities that unmarried couples might consider engaging in, and such books discuss the morality of each such as oral sex and petting.[22] I wonder if this level of detail is necessary.

I would suggest that all such activities should be evaluated by how they conform to what the Bible teaches about lust and about the purposes for sex. Jesus teaches that sexual immorality is a matter of the heart (Mark 7:21) and that lust is as sinful as committing the deed contemplated (Matt. 5:28). Perhaps certain activities are not explicitly forbidden by Scripture, but certainly lusting after someone who is not one's spouse is. We must insist, therefore, that any activity designed to arouse sexual climax with someone who is not one's spouse is sinful. In addition, the Scriptures teach that our accountability is to flee from sexual temptation (2 Tim. 2:22). Paul says to make no provision for the flesh with regard to its lusts (Rom. 13:14). That means that not only must Christians abstain from all forms of sexual activity; they must also flee from the situations in which they know they might be tempted to transgress. The question should not be, "How far can we go?" The question should be, "How far can we stay away?"

Finally, Christians are not merely interested in what is or what is not lawful. Christians must aim to achieve the purpose for which God created sex—the glory of God. That means that every expression of physical intimacy must be oriented toward marriage and whether such expressions achieve the unitive purposes of the marital act. Again, the question is not, "What is lawful?" but, "How can I glorify God?"

Solo Sex

Dennis Hollinger relates the following statistic in his book on sexual ethics: "90 percent of adolescent boys masturbate; the other 10 percent are liars."[23] Hollinger delivers this factoid tongue-in-

---

[22] E.g., Dennis P. Hollinger, *The Meaning of Sex: Christian Ethics and the Moral Life* (Grand Rapids, MI: Baker, 2009), 136–39.

[23] Ibid., 139.

cheek, but his point is well taken. This kind of activity is in fact ubiquitous among the male population, and not just among adolescents. Surveys indicate that over 60 percent of males ages eighteen to fifty-nine have masturbated in the last ninety days. Male solo sex rates are highest—at 95 percent—among men ages twenty-five to thirty-nine who are single and dating.[24] Surveys also indicate that a sizeable percentage of women participate in solo sexual activity. Over half of women ages eighteen to forty-nine report having masturbated in the last ninety days. The highest rates—at 94 percent—are among women ages twenty-five to twenty-nine who are single and dating.[25] Unmarried persons are not the only ones facing this temptation. The same surveys show that married persons are struggling with it too. This issue is too common to be ignored and can hardly be avoided in articulating a faithful Christian sexual ethic.

Christians have disagreed with one another in their moral assessment of solo sex. Opinions fall into three basic categories: (1) total acceptance, (2) total rejection, and (3) modified acceptance with qualifications.[26] Lewis Smedes comes close to the "total acceptance" position when he says, "It is not morally wrong," and when he counsels Christian parents to help their child "see and accept masturbation as part of his growth as a human being."[27] Daniel Heimbach advances the "total rejection" view, arguing that solitary sex "opposes every positive moral characteristic revealed to be essential in God's design for sex."[28] Dennis Hollinger aligns

---

[24] Michael Reece et al., "Sexual Behaviors, Relationships, and Perceived Health among Adult Men in the United States: Results from a National Probability Sample," *Journal of Sexual Medicine* 7, suppl 5 (2010): 293.

[25] Debby Herbenick et al., "Sexual Behaviors, Relationships, and Perceived Health Status among Adult Women in the United States: Results from a National Probability Sample," *Journal of Sexual Medicine* 7, suppl 5 (2010): 280, 281.

[26] Hollinger, *Meaning of Sex*, 140.

[27] Lewis B. Smedes, *Sex for Christians: The Limits and Liberties of Sexual Living*, rev. ed. (Grand Rapids, MI: Eerdmans, 1994), 140. Smedes's approach is far too therapeutic, in my view, and not enough concerned with the application of God's truth to this moral question. He writes, "Christian moral response will not bother too much with the theoretical question of whether masturbation as such is an evil" (ibid., 142).

[28] Daniel R. Heimbach, *True Sexual Morality: Recovering Biblical Standards for a Culture in Crisis* (Wheaton, IL: Crossway, 2004), 223. Michael Lawrence also advocates the "total rejection" view and offers some very helpful practical wisdom concerning married men who masturbate, in Mark

himself with the "qualified acceptance" view, arguing that "if one is able to use it to release built-up sexual tension without the lust, it is less morally problematic."[29]

As some are reluctant to offer a definitive answer to the question, others are quick to point out that the Bible does not forbid masturbation per se.[30] Sometimes interpreters will point to Onan's evil deed to condemn masturbation (Gen. 38:6–10). The story of Onan, however, has nothing to do with solo sex but with Onan's failure to fulfill his levirate duty to his brother's widow (cf. Deut. 25:5). Even without the Onan story, the Bible does in fact offer us ample help in addressing the issue. And even though the Bible never mentions masturbation per se, it has a great deal to say about lust and God's purpose for sex.

It is Jesus himself who warns that "everyone who looks at a woman with lust for her has already committed adultery with her in his heart" (Matt. 5:28). As noted above, Jesus insists that sexual immorality and adultery proceed from the heart (Mark 7:21). For Jesus, sexual sin has every bit as much to do with the mind as it does with the body. Lustful thoughts toward a person who is not one's spouse are sinful, and this cannot be ignored with respect to the ethics of solo sex. We are doubtful (contra Hollinger) that solo sex can be separated from lustful thoughts. In fact, solo sex seems to be an inducement toward such thoughts, and may for some people be a segue to pornography. We are called to have clean hands *and* a pure heart (Ps. 24:4). Is it really possible to have a pure heart while masturbating? Jesus requires his disciples to take radical measures to avoid the sin of lust—even to the point of cutting off hands and gouging out eyes (Matt. 5:29–30). Also, the solitary nature of the act runs crosswise with the purposes for sex outlined so far in this book. Obviously, the act is not directed

---

Dever et al., "Sex and the Single Man," in *Sex and the Supremacy of Christ*, ed. John Piper and Justin Taylor (Wheaton, IL: Crossway, 2005), 140–41.

[29] Hollinger, *Meaning of Sex*, 141.

[30] Mark Driscoll and Grace Driscoll, *Real Marriage: The Truth about Sex, Friendship, and Life Together* (Nashville, TN: Thomas Nelson, 2012), 183: "The Bible does not forbid masturbation and in fact may on one occasion report it positively between a husband and a wife." The Driscolls go on to elaborate other considerations that might make it sinful in certain situations.

toward procreation, nor to the consummation of marriage, nor to an expression of love for another person. Fulfilling the purposes of sex requires the participation of more than one person. They require directing one's love and affection toward one's spouse. It is clear, then, that solo sex falls short of the divine purposes for sex. Thus it falls short of the glory of God.[31]

Pornography

The ubiquity of online pornography has caused Christian counselor Heath Lambert to declare that "Pornography is the defining sexual sin of our day."[32] For anyone paying attention to the issue, it would be very difficult to argue with this judgment. Because of easy access through the Internet, a large percentage of males and females have becomes users and sometimes addicts of sexually explicit material. The statistics are staggering. Pornography is the most searched-for topic on the Internet with sixty-eight million pornographic hits per day.[33] According to one set of statistics, forty million American adults regularly visit Internet pornography sites; 20 percent of men admit to accessing pornography at work; and 53 percent of men identified with the "Promise Keepers" movement say they have viewed pornography in the last week. Seventy-two percent of visitors to pornographic websites are men, and 28 percent are women; 9.4 million American women have accessed pornography in the last month, and 13 percent of women report accessing it at work. The average age that children first see Internet pornography is eleven years old; 90 percent of eight- to sixteen-year-olds report having viewed online pornography; 80 percent of fifteen- to seventeen-year-olds say they have had multiple hard-

---

[31] Matthew Lee Anderson, *Earthen Vessels: Why Our Bodies Matter to Our Faith* (Minneapolis, MN: Bethany, 2011), 135: "While I remain skeptical that masturbation as a regular practice can be separated from looking at pornography or creating mental fantasies based on real women or men (the equivalent of lusting), the practice treats the body as an instrument for personal pleasure and gratification. Human sexuality is inherently social, and masturbation is not. In that sense, it represents a failure to fulfill the nature of Christian sexuality as God designed it."
[32] Heath Lambert, "The Problem of Pornography: Why It's Wrong and How to Help," *Journal for Biblical Manhood and Womanhood* 17, no. 2 (2012): 11.
[33] Hollinger, *Meaning of Sex*, 141.

core exposures to online pornography.[34] This onslaught of private perversion has led Lambert to conclude:

> In Christian circles adultery and homosexuality often capture more headlines, but I am persuaded that in terms of sheer numbers they cannot hold a candle to the devastation of pornography. Last year I counseled six people struggling with homosexuality and around eighteen caught in adultery and fornication. I don't know exactly how many I helped who were locked in pornography, but the number is in the dozens. As bad as that number sounds those people are not the ones I am concerned about. . . . The people who concern me are the ones that did not seek out me or anyone else. These people pose the deeper problem. They are the ones who are hiding in the dark while destroying their marriages, ministries, and Christian witness under the radar.[35]

Our ethical evaluation of pornography is fairly straightforward.[36] The production and use of pornography constitutes a grave violation of sexual holiness. Its use by anyone (married or single) contradicts everything that the Bible teaches about God's purposes for sex. There are at least five reasons for this judgment.[37]

First, pornography degrades women as well as every other participant in the production of pornographic material. Our ethical evaluation of pornography is not merely about how the material affects the user. It must start with the observation that the pictures on the pages or the Internet screen are real people performing sexually immoral acts. These people—who are made in the image of

---

[34] Jerry Ropelato, "Internet Pornography Statistics," *TopTenREVIEWS*, accessed January 10, 2013, http://internet-filter-review.toptenreviews.com/internet-pornography-statistics.html.

[35] Lambert, "The Problem of Pornography."

[36] Defining pornography has been notoriously controversial. Even the IVP dictionary on Christian ethics flounders in an attempt to define pornography. See J. H. Court, "Pornography," in *New Dictionary of Christian Ethics and Pastoral Theology*, ed. David J. Atkinson et al. (Downers Grove, IL: InterVarsity, 1995), 675–76. The Catechism of the Catholic Church may have as good a definition as any: "Pornography consists in removing real or simulated sexual acts from the intimacy of the partners, in order to display them deliberately to third parties. It offends against chastity because it perverts the conjugal act, the intimate giving of spouses to each other. It does grave injury to the dignity of its participants (actors, vendors, the public), since each one becomes an object of base pleasure and illicit profit for others. It immerses all who are involved in the illusion of a fantasy world. It is a grave offense. Civil authorities should prevent the production and distribution of pornographic materials." See Catechism of the Catholic Church §2354.

[37] These following five reasons follow Hollinger, *Meaning of Sex*, 142–43.

almighty God—are made into sexual objects for other people's enjoyment. This enjoyment consists in illicit sexual desires stoked by someone else's shame before God. It is unloving and hateful to become complicit in another person's debasement, much less to derive sexual pleasure from it. Yet that is exactly what happens every time someone accesses pornographic material. For Christians, love for our neighbor should provoke a different response (Mark 12:31). As Russell Moore rightly asks, "Where is the compassion for the cruelly named 'porn stars'—many of whom spend their hours [off] the screen in a heroin-induced, self-loathing depression?"[38] Christians have an obligation to oppose pornography out of love for those who are most directly debased by it.

Second, pornography creates lust, and lust is a sin. The Bible says that to be given over to lust is the very judgment of God (Rom. 1:24). Paul says that those who walk in the lusts of the flesh are "children of wrath" and are "indulging the desires of the flesh and of the mind" (Eph. 2:3). Paul also forbids believers from living in "lustful passion, like the Gentiles who do not know God" (1 Thess. 4:5). Lust characterizes the world in its rebellion against God: "For all that is in the world, the lust of the flesh and the lust of the eyes and the boastful pride of life, is not from the Father, but is from the world" (1 John 2:16). Pornography incites sinners to lust and to direct one's sexual attention away from the marital bond. It is therefore a grave sin and completely out of step with God's purposes for sex.

Third, pornography introduces perversions into people's intimate lives. Mark Regnerus reports a growing expectation among emerging-adult male users of pornography that they should experience with their partner what they view in online pornography. These men are increasingly requesting their female partners to mimic the behaviors that appear in pornography.[39] These expectations are sometimes carried over into marriage and cause great

---

[38] Russell D. Moore, "Jesus and the Hooters Girl," *Moore to the Point* (blog), May 10, 2005, http://www.russellmoore.com/2005/05/10/jesus-and-the-hooters-girl/.
[39] Regnerus and Uecker, *Premarital Sex in America*, 94–95.

difficulty between spouses.[40] It perverts the mind and prevents husbands from loving and serving their wives as Christ loved the church (Eph. 5:25).

Fourth, pornography can be addictive. Hollinger writes, "The more one is exposed, the more one needs pornographic stimulation the next time to get the same high as before."[41] William M. Struthers is a biopsychologist who has studied the neurochemical processes that influence addictive behavior. In his book *Wired for Intimacy*, he argues convincingly that pornography hijacks the proper functioning of men's brains and has a long-lasting effect on their thoughts and lives.[42] This kind of addictive behavior is a direct violation of Christ's lordship. As Paul wrote to the men sinning sexually in Corinth, "I will not be mastered by anything" (1 Cor. 6:12). This means that Paul was determined not to be controlled by anything or anyone but Christ alone. Pornography is dangerous because those who have been "mastered" by it can no longer be disciples of Christ (Matt. 6:24).

Fifth, pornography makes marital intimacy more difficult to enjoy. Indeed, some pornography users find themselves preferring virtual sex over sex with a real person. As a result, some men report decreased sexual appetite, as the presence of a real person is not as stimulating to them as the perversions they view on the Internet.[43] Pornography destroys the joys of marital sex, and that is just one more reason it stands contrary to God's purposes for the gift of sex (Prov. 5:18).

Conclusion

Jesus and Paul both commend by example and by teaching the nobility of the single life. To those who have the gift of celibacy,

[40] Driscoll and Driscoll, *Real Marriage*, 149: "Porn also degrades women and encourages men to do so. Seeking to emulate what they or their husbands view in porn compels women to push their bodies beyond God's created design. There is nothing loving, beautiful, cherishing, or honoring of women presented in porn."
[41] Hollinger, *Meaning of Sex*, 142.
[42] William M. Struthers, *Wired for Intimacy: How Pornography Hijacks the Male Brain* (Downers Grove, IL: InterVarsity, 2009), 11.
[43] Regnerus and Uecker, *Premarital Sex in America*, 98.

it allows them to leverage their lives more fully for the sake of the kingdom. Singles who have an abiding desire for the joys of conjugal life should pursue marriage. Even though the culture increasingly favors delaying marriage well into the late twenties, Christians who wish to marry should probably consider early marriage as a means to chastity and adulthood. Nevertheless, for as long as God allows a person to remain single, that person must remain sexually pure. That means abstaining from all sexual activity outside of marriage, including solo sex and the use of pornography. "For this is the will of God, your sanctification; that is, that you abstain from sexual immorality" (1 Thess. 4:3).

For the weapons of our warfare are not of the flesh,
but divinely powerful for the destruction of fortresses.
We are destroying speculations and every lofty thing
raised up against the knowledge of God, and we are taking every thought captive to the obedience of Christ.

—2 Corinthians 10:4–5

And do not be conformed to this world, but be transformed by
the renewing of your mind, so that you may prove what the
will of God is, that which is good and acceptable and perfect.

—Romans 12:2

Conclusion

Contemporary Western culture confronts Christians with a world-view in conflict with the Bible's teaching about human sexuality. This worldview has implications for almost every aspect of our lives, and Christians can hardly declare these matters outside the purview of their gospel concern.

A Sexually Confused Culture[1]

In the midst of a sexually confused culture, Christians are needed more than ever to embody a gospel-shaped counterculture. Christians should be in the world, not of the world, for the sake of the world on questions of gender and sexuality. Living in the world requires us to be like the men of Issachar, who understood the times and knew what the people of God were to do (1 Chron. 12:32). It is the church, after all, that is the pillar and foundation of the truth (1 Tim. 3:15). It is the church that God has appointed to make disciples of the nations (Matt. 28:19–20). And it is the church that must look into the face of a world that is destitute of biblical wisdom and see the sexually confused culture for what it is so that a gospel counterculture might flourish in it. But in order to do that, we must understand what the Scriptures claim over and against the spirit of the age. Whether it be the normalization of homosexuality or open antagonism toward the nuclear family,

---

[1] This chapter is a revision of Denny Burk, "Gender Confusion and a Gospel-Shaped Counter-Culture" in *Don't Call It a Comeback: The Old Faith for a New Day*, ed. Kevin DeYoung (Wheaton, IL: Crossway, 2011), 191–200. It is also an expansion of an editorial written in 2009 for *The Journal of Biblical Manhood and Womanhood*. See Denny Burk, "Editorial: A Collision of Worldviews and the Complementarian Response," *JBMW* 14.1 (2009): 2–5.

there are countless ways in which modern people express confusion about sex and gender. In this concluding chapter, we will take a look at three myths that prevail in our sexually confused culture, and then we will contrast them with principles derived from the foregoing study.

Myth 1: Gender Is Something You Learn, Not Something You Are

What does it mean to say that gender is something you learn, not something you are? It means that the idea of *male and female* is not a description of humanity as God has created it. Nor does *male and female* designate a universal, innate distinction among humans. Rather, the terms *male and female* comprise a set of stereotypes that we absorb from our culture. For many people, gender is nothing more than a social construct. Except for obvious biological differences, all other social distinctions between male and female are purely conventional. If there are any psychological distinctions between male and female, they are learned, and they can and need to be unlearned so that there can be a total equality between the sexes. This worldview is so entrenched in today's culture that one can hardly suggest that there might be innate differences between male and female without being dismissed as a sexist and a bigot.

The former president of Harvard University learned this fact the hard way after a speech he gave in 2005 to a group of scientists.[2] In this speech President Lawrence Summers tried to account for the fact that there is a "shortage of elite female scientists." He attributed the shortage in part to what may be "innate" differences between men and women. In the speech, he shared an anecdote about his daughter to illustrate the point. In an effort at "gender-neutral parenting," he once set before his daughter two toy trucks. In almost no time at all, his daughter began referring to one of the trucks as "daddy truck" and the other as "baby truck." The event led him to ponder whether there was any truth to the notion that

---

[2] Michael Dobbs, "Harvard Chief's Comments on Women Assailed" *Washington Post*, January 19, 2005, A02.

certain neurological inclinations might be connected to gender. For his daughter, at least, her playtime activity matched a feminine stereotype that she had not learned from him. In fact, he was conscientiously working against such stereotypes.

A firestorm of controversy ensued after Summers's remarks. One female biology professor from MIT who attended the speech said, "I felt I was going to be sick. My heart was pounding and my breath was shallow. I was extremely upset." Then she got up and walked out of the event. After that speech, Summers was impugned as a sexist and was reprimanded by the faculty of Harvard. He was on the outs with the faculty from then on and eventually had to resign. Summers found that there is a steep price to pay in our culture for suggesting that gender stereotypes may be more than mere human convention.

Myth 2: Sex Is for Pleasure, Not for God

We might call this the Sheryl Crow philosophy on sexuality—if it makes you happy, it can't be that bad. This worldview affirms any and all attempts to get sexual pleasure so long as such attempts do not harm others. If it feels good and you're not hurting anyone, then how could it possibly be wrong? The encroachment of this worldview explains to some extent why only about 74 percent of evangelical "Christian" teenagers say that they believe in abstaining from sex before marriage,[3] and why about 36 percent of white evangelical Protestants make their "sexual début" shortly after turning sixteen.[4] This libertine worldview has had its influence on Christian mores with devastating effect.

This point of view also accounts for the normalization of homosexuality in the wider culture. If the goal of sex is pleasure, and if gender is merely something we learn, not something we are, then same-sex attraction is okay (so long as it's between consenting

---

[3] Margaret Talbot, "Red Sex, Blue Sex: Why Do So Many Evangelical Teen-agers Become Pregnant?," *New Yorker*, November 3, 2008, http://www.newyorker.com/reporting/2008/11/03/081103 fa_fact_talbot?printable=true.

[4] Mark Regnurus, *Forbidden Fruit: Sex and Religion in the Lives of American Teenagers* (New York: Oxford University Press, 2007), 123, 127.

adults, and you don't hurt anybody). And that leads us to the third feature of the secular mind-set.

Myth 3: Marriage Is Cultural, Not Universal

The secular mindset says that marriage is something that comes to us from human culture, not from God. It has a human origin, not a divine one. With God out of the picture, humans are free to make marriage into whatever they want. This final piece accounts for much of the confusion and conflict surrounding the "culture war" on the issue of marriage in our society. Not only is this worldview evident in skyrocketing divorce rates and in legal outrages such as "no fault" divorce; it also undergirds the current push in our country for states to recognize same-sex marriage. If gender is something you learn and not something you are, and if sex is for pleasure and not for God, then same-sex relationships should not be treated any differently from heterosexual relationships. Once a society divorces *maleness and femaleness* and their respective sexualities from their Creator's design, there is no moral basis for privileging heterosexual unions over any other kind of union (homosexual or otherwise). The heterosexual norm of the Scriptures is regarded merely as a social convention forced on the masses to limit who can have sex with whom—a convention that must be cast off in a just society. Already in some sectors of our society, to privilege the heterosexual ideal of Scripture over homosexual sin is to engage in bigotry and hatred.

A Gospel-Shaped Worldview

A gospel-shaped worldview must *proclaim* and *embody* the gospel of Jesus Christ in such a way that God's design for gender, sex, and marriage is clear and compelling. That will require both a countercultural *message* from churches and countercultural *living* among individuals and families in those churches. Let me briefly outline three counterpoints to the aforementioned worldview that must be at the core of evangelical witness to our friends and neighbors.

Truth 1: Gender Is Something You Are before You Learn Anything

The distinctions between *male and female* find their origin in God's good creation, not in what we learn from culture. That is not to say that people do not absorb ideas about gender from the culture, some of which are quite unhelpful. But that fact should not be used to suppress the truth that in the beginning God differentiated humankind as male and female as a part of his original creation work. Nor should it obscure the fact that God unambiguously called this differentiation "good" (Gen 1:27, 31). The union of the first man and the first woman was the most healthy, wholesome, and satisfying union that has ever existed, and it involved a man leading his wife, and a wife following the leadership of her husband (Genesis 2; 1 Cor. 11:3; Eph. 5:21–33). And though no other marriage will reach this perfection this side of glory, every Christian must strive with integrity toward this ideal. And they need to do so even when it grates against the ingrained mores of the wider culture.

Truth 2: Sex Is for God before There Is Any Lasting Pleasure

God is not a cosmic killjoy when it comes to sex. God intends for his creatures to enjoy this great gift for his sake. But when people treat pleasure as the *goal* of sex, not only do they end up in immorality, but they also end up with less pleasure. The only way to maximize the pleasure that God intends for our sexuality is to live in light of the truth that our bodies are not for immorality but for the Lord.

As we saw in chapter 1, Paul once confronted a group of philandering whoremongers in the Corinthian church (1 Cor. 6:15). Paul explained to them that the Holy Spirit dwells within the believer's body and thus makes the physical body of utmost importance in the present age. Because the Holy Spirit resides within the temple of the believer's body, the believer has no ultimate claim to ownership over his body, "for you were bought at a price" (v. 20 AT). In this way, Paul reminds us that we do not own ourselves.

God owns us because he bought us at the cost of his Son and because God's Spirit dwells in us as a guarantee of final redemption. As Paul argued elsewhere, the presence of the indwelling Spirit is the ground of our hope that God will resurrect our physical bodies from the grave (Rom. 8:11).

Thus what we do with our bodies vis-à-vis sex matters to God. That is why Paul concludes 1 Corinthians 6 with an emphatic imperative: "Therefore, glorify God with your body" (1 Cor. 6:20 AT). Again, when Paul speaks of glorifying God with the body, he specifically has in mind how the body is used sexually. We might even paraphrase Paul to be saying in effect, "Glorify God with your sex." This means that the covenanted union of marriage is the most pleasurable and the most God-glorifying context in which to enjoy our sexuality. The Christian sexual ethic does not call people away from joy but toward it.

Truth 3: Marriage Is Universal, Not Cultural

The Bible teaches that marriage was designed and created by God, not by human culture. In fact, it is interesting to see how the New Testament proves this fact in light of the Old Testament. We have seen that when Jesus and Paul set out new-covenant marital norms, they do not appeal to polygamist kings such as David or Solomon or to polygamist patriarchs such as Abraham, Isaac, or Jacob. For all the importance these Old Testament figures have in the history of redemption, Jesus and Paul do not look to any of them as the paradigm for understanding marriage. Instead, Jesus and Paul look back without exception to the pre-fall monogamous union of Adam and Eve in Genesis 2 as the norm for human sexuality and marriage. "For this cause a man shall leave his father and his mother and shall cling to his wife; and they shall become one flesh" (Gen. 2:24 AT; see also Matt. 19:5; Mark 10:7–8; 1 Cor. 6:16; Eph. 5:31).

The apostle Paul says that the great "mystery" of the Genesis 2 norm for marriage (one man and one woman in covenanted union) is that God intended it all along to be a shadow of a greater reality. From the garden of Eden forward, God intended marriage to be an enacted parable of another marriage: Christ's marriage to his church (Eph. 5:31–32). Thus, marriage is not defined by the culture but by the gospel itself. Jesus loves his bride exclusively and self-sacrificially; and Jesus's bride is to respect and submit to her husband. In this way, marriage is meant to be a portrayal of a gospel archetype that is rooted in the eternal purposes of God. The gospel that shapes this archetype is also the hope for humanity and the context in which human happiness reaches its fullest potential. Here is the innermost meaning of marriage, and faithful Christians will engage the culture with proclamation and living that bears out this truth.

Conclusion

At the end of the day, the inhabitants of our sexually confused culture are not the main problem. They are but a symptom of a larger system that is set against Christ and his purposes in the world (1 John 2:15–17). And what our friends and neighbors need more than anything is for Christians and their churches to set forth a faithful counter witness on these issues. The messages coming from the culture are clear. Ours should be even more so.

Bibliography

Alcorn, Randy. *Does the Birth Control Pill Cause Abortions?* 8th ed. Sandy, OR: Eternal Perspective Ministries, 2007.

Anderson, Matthew Lee. *Earthen Vessels: Why Our Bodies Matter to Our Faith.* Minneapolis, MN: Bethany House, 2011.

Ash, Christopher. *Marriage: Sex in the Service of God.* Vancouver, British Columbia: Regent College Publishing, 2003.

Augustin. "On the Good of Marriage." In *Augustin: On the Holy Trinity, Doctrinal Treatises, Moral Treatises,* edited by Philip Schaff, 395–413. Nicene and Post-Nicene Fathers 3. Peabody, MA: Hendrickson, 2004.

———. "On Marriage and Concupiscence." In *Augustin: Anti-Pelagian Writings,* edited by Philip Schaff, 257–80. Nicene and Post-Nicene Fathers 5. Peabody, MA: Hendrickson, 2004.

———. "On Original Sin." In *Augustin: Anti-Pelagian Writings,* edited by Philip Schaff, 237–55. Nicene and Post-Nicene Fathers 5. Peabody, MA: Hendrickson, 2004.

Balch, David L. *Homosexuality, Science, and the "Plain Sense" of Scripture.* Grand Rapids, MI: Eerdmans, 2000.

Barrett, C. K. *The First Epistle to the Corinthians.* Black's New Testament Commentary. Peabody, MA: Hendrickson, 1968.

Barth, Markus. *Ephesians: Translation and Commentary on Chapters 4–6.* Anchor Bible. Garden City, NY: Doubleday, 1974.

Batey, Richard. "The MIA SARX Union of Christ and the Church." *New Testament Studies* 13 (n.d.): 270–81.

Belluck, Pam. "No Abortion Role Seen for Morning-After Pill." *New York Times,* June 6, 2012.

Birth Control Guide. FDA Office of Women's Health, 2012. http://www.fda.gov /downloads/ForConsumers/ByAudience/ForWomen/FreePublications /UCM282014.pdf.

Block, Daniel L. *The Book of Ezekiel, Chapters 1–24.* New International Commentary on the Old Testament. Grand Rapids, MI: Eerdmans, 1997.

Blomberg, Craig L. *Matthew.* New American Commentary 22. Nashville, TN: Broadman, 1992.

————. *1 Corinthians.* NIV Application Commentary. Grand Rapids, MI: Zondervan, 1994.

————. "Marriage, Divorce, Remarriage, and Celibacy: An Exegesis of Matthew 19:3–12." *Trinity Journal* 11, no. 2 (1990): 161–96.

Bockmuehl, Markus. *Jewish Law in Gentile Churches: Halakhah and the Beginning of Christian Public Ethics.* Edinburgh: T. & T. Clark, 2000.

Boice, James Montgomery. *The Sermon on the Mount: Matthew 5–7.* Grand Rapids, MI: Baker, 1972.

Boswell, John. *Christianity, Social Tolerance, and Homosexuality: Gay People in Western Europe from the Beginning of the Christian Era to the Fourteenth Century.* Chicago: University of Chicago Press, 1980.

Brawley, Robert L., ed. *Character Ethics and the New Testament: Moral Dimensions of Scripture.* Louisville, KY: Westminster, 2007.

Brooks, David. "The New Lone Rangers." *New York Times,* July 10, 2007, sec. A21. http://www.nytimes.com/2007/07/10/opinion/10brooks.html.

Brown, C. A. "Teleology." In *New Dictionary of Christian Ethics and Pastoral Theology,* edited by David J. Atkinson, David F. Field, Arthur Holmes, and Oliver O'Donovan, 835. Downers Grove, IL: InterVarsity, 1995.

Bruce, F. F. *1 and 2 Corinthians.* New Century Bible Commentary. Grand Rapids, MI: Eerdmans, 1971.

Burk, Denny. "Christ's Functional Subordination in Philippians 2:6: A Grammatical Note with Trinitarian Implications." In *The New Evangelical Subordinationism? Perpectives on the Equality of God the Father and God the Son,* edited by Dennis W. Jowers and H. Wayne House, 82–107. Eugene, OR: Pickwick, 2012.

————. "Discerning Corinthian Slogans through Paul's Use of the Diatribe in 1 Corinthians 6.12–20." *Bulletin for Biblical Research* 18, no. 1 (2008): 99–121.

———. "Real Marriage: The Truth about Sex, Friendship, and Life Together [Review]." *The Southern Baptist Journal of Theology* 16, no. 1 (2012): 72–79.

———. "Why Evangelicals Should Not Heed Brian McLaren: How the New Testament Requires Evangelicals to Render a Judgment on the Moral Status of Homosexuality." *Themelios* 35, no. 2 (2010): 212–26.

Burridge, Richard A. *Imitating Jesus: An Inclusive Approach to New Testament Ethics*. Grand Rapids, MI: Eerdmans, 2007.

Bussmann, Hadumod. *Routledge Dictionary of Language and Linguistics*. Translated by Gregory Trauth and Kerstin Kazzazi. London: Routledge, 1996.

Butler, Judith. *Gender Trouble*. New York: Routledge, 1990.

Calvin, John. *Commentaries on the First Book of Moses Called Genesis*. Translated by John King. Vol. 1. Calvin's Commentaries. Reprint, Grand Rapids, MI: Baker, 1996.

Campolo, Tony. *Red Letter Christians: A Citizen's Guide to Faith and Politics*. Ventura, CA: Regal, 2008.

Capehart, Jonathan. "Louie Giglio Out from Inaugural: Good." *Washington Post*, January 10, 2013. http://www.washingtonpost.com/blogs/post-partisan/wp/2013/01/10/louie-giglio-out-from-inaugural-good/.

Catholic Church. *Catechism of the Catholic Church: Revised in Accordance with the Official Latin Text Promulgated by Pope John Paul II*. 2nd ed. Washington, DC: Libreria Editrice Vaticana, 2000.

Ciampa, Roy E., and Brian S. Rosner. *The First Letter to the Corinthians*. Pillar New Testament Commentary. Grand Rapids, MI: Eerdmans, 2010.

Clines, David J. A. "What Does Eve Do to Help? and Other Irredeemably Androcentric Orientations in Genesis 1–3." In *What Does Eve Do To Help? And Other Readerly Questions to the Old Testament*. Sheffield, UK: Sheffield Academic Press, 1990.

Coffey Tousley, Nikki, and Brad J. Kallenberg. "Virtue Ethics." In *Dictionary of Scripture and Ethics*, edited by Joel B. Green, 814–19. Grand Rapids, MI: Baker, 2011.

Conybeare, W. J., and J. S. Howson. *The Life and Epistles of St. Paul*. Grand Rapids, MI: Eerdmans, 1949.

Coogan, Michael. *God and Sex: What the Bible Really Says*. New York: Twelve, 2010.

Cornwall, Susannah. *Sex and Uncertainty in the Body of Christ: Intersex Conditions and Christian Theology*. Gender, Theology and Spirituality. London and Oakville, CT: Equinox, 2010.

Court, J. H. "Pornography." In *New Dictionary of Christian Ethics and Pastoral Theology*, edited by David J. Atkinson, David F. Field, Arthur Holmes, and Oliver O'Donavan, 675–77. Downers Grove, IL: InterVarsity, 1995.

Cranfield, C. E. B. *A Critical and Exegetical Commentary on The Epistle to the Romans*. Vol. 1. International Critical Commentary. Edinburgh: T. & T. Clark, 1975.

Cross, F. L., and E. A. Livingstone, eds. "Matrimony." *Oxford Dictionary of the Christian Church*. New York: Oxford University Press, 1997.

————. "Prohibited Degrees." *Oxford Dictionary of the Christian Church*. New York: Oxford University Press, 2005.

Crystal, David. *A Dictionary of Language*. 2nd ed. Chicago: University of Chicago Press, 2001.

Cutrer, William, and Sandra Glahn. *Sexual Intimacy in Marriage*. Grand Rapids, MI: Kregel, 1998.

Davies, Margaret. "New Testament Ethics and Ours: Homosexuality and Sexuality in Romans 1:26–27." *Biblical Interpretation* 3 (1995): 315–31.

Davis, John Jefferson. *Evangelical Ethics: Issues Facing the Church Today*. 3rd ed. Phillipsburg, NJ: P&R, 2004.

Davis, Muller. "Fault or No Fault? Rethinking Divorce Laws." *Christian Century* 119, no. 12 (2002): 28–31.

DeCook, Joseph L., et al. "Birth Control Pills: Contraceptive or Abortifacient," January 1998. https://www.cuw.edu/departments/institutes/bioethics/assets/BirthControlfile.pdf.

Deming, Will. "The Unity of 1 Corinthians 5–6." *Journal of Biblical Literature* 115 (1996): 289–312.

Dever, Mark, Michael Lawrence, Matt Schmucker, and Scott Croft. "Sex and the Single Man." In *Sex and the Supremacy of Christ*, edited by John Piper and Justin Taylor, 133–50. Wheaton, IL: Crossway, 2005.

DeYoung, James B. *Homosexuality: Contemporary Claims Examined in Light of the Bible and Other Ancient Literature and Law*. Grand Rapids, MI: Kregel, 2000.

Dillow, Linda, and Lorraine Pintus. *Intimate Issues: 21 Questions Christian Women Ask about Sex*. Colorado Springs, CO: WaterBrook, 1999.

Dodd, Brian J. "Paul's Paradigmatic 'I' and 1 Corinthians 6.12." *Journal for the Study of the New Testament* 59 (1995): 39–58.

Driscoll, Mark, and Grace Driscoll. *Real Marriage: The Truth about Sex, Friendship, and Life Together*. Nashville, TN: Thomas Nelson, 2012.

Dunn, James D. G. *Romans 1–8*. Word Biblical Commentary. Dallas: Word, 1988.

Eberstadt, Mary. *Adam and Eve after the Pill: Paradoxes of the Sexual Revolution*. San Francisco: Ignatius, 2012.

Erickson, Millard J. *Who's Tampering with the Trinity? An Assessment of the Subordination Debate*. Grand Rapids, MI: Kregel, 2009.

Evans, Rachel Held. *A Year of Biblical Womanhood: How a Liberated Woman Found Herself Sitting on Her Roof, Covering Her Head, and Calling Her Husband "Master."* Nashville, TN: Thomas Nelson, 2012.

Fanning, Buist M. "Approaches to Verbal Aspect." In *Biblical Greek Language and Linguistics*, edited by Stanley E. Porter and D. A. Carson. Sheffield, UK: JSOT Press, 1993.

Fee, Gordon D. *The First Epistle to the Corinthians*. New International Commentary on the New Testament. Grand Rapids, MI: Eerdmans, 1987.

Feinberg, John S., and Paul D. Feinberg. *Ethics for a Brave New World*. 2nd ed. Wheaton, IL: Crossway, 2010.

Fisk, Bruce. "PORNEUEIN as Body Violation: The Unique Nature of Sexual Sin in 1 Corinthians 6:18." *New Testament Studies* 42, no. 4 (1996): 540–58.

Fitzmyer, Joseph A. *First Corinthians*. The Anchor Yale Bible 32. New Haven, CT: Yale University Press, 2008.

———. *Romans: A New Translation with Introduction and Commentary*. Anchor Bible. New York: Doubleday, 1993.

Frame, John R. *The Doctrine of the Christian Life*. Phillipsburg, NJ: P&R, 2008.

France, R. T. *The Gospel of Matthew*. New International Commentary on the New Testament. Grand Rapids, MI: Eerdmans, 2007.

Fretheim, Terence E. "The Book of Genesis." In *The New Interpreter's Bible*, 1:319–674. Nashville, TN: Abingdon, 1994.

Furnish, Victor Paul. *The Moral Teaching of Paul: Selected Issues.* 2nd ed. Nashville, TN: Abingdon, 1985.

Gagnon, Robert A. J. *The Bible and Homosexual Practice: Texts and Hermeneutics.* Nashville, TN: Abingdon, 2001.

Gallagher, Maggie, and Barbara Dafoe Whitehead. "End No-Fault Divorce." *First Things* 75 (1997): 24–30.

Garland, David E. *1 Corinthians.* Baker Exegetical Commentary on the New Testament. Grand Rapids, MI: Baker, 2003.

Gault, Brian P. "A 'Do Not Disturb' Sign? Reexamining the Adjuration Refrain in Song of Songs." *Journal for the Study of the Old Testament* 36, no. 1 (2011): 93–104.

———. "An Admonition Against 'Rousing Love': The Meaning of the Enigmatic Refrain in Song of Songs." *Bulletin for Biblical Research* 20, no. 2 (2010): 161–84.

Giglio, Louie. "In Search of a Standard-Christian Response to Homosexuality." *Discipleship Library.* Accessed January 10, 2013. http://turret2 .discipleshiplibrary.com/8169A.mp3.

Girgis, Sherif, Robert P. George, and Ryan T. Anderson. "What Is Marriage?" *Harvard Journal of Law and Public Policy* 34 (2010): 245–87.

Girgis, Sherif, Ryan T. Anderson, and Robert P. George. *What Is Marriage? Man and Woman: A Defense.* New York: Encounter Books, 2012.

Grenz, Stanley J. *Sexual Ethics: An Evangelical Perspective.* Louisville, KY: Westminster, 1997.

———. *Welcoming but Not Affirming: An Evangelical Response to Homosexuality.* Louisville, KY: Westminster, 1998.

Groothuis, Rebecca Merrill, and Ronald W. Pierce. "Introduction." In *Discovering Biblical Equality: Complementarity without Hierarchy*, edited by Ronald W. Pierce, Rebecca Merrill Groothuis, and Gordon D. Fee 13–19. Downers Grove, IL: InterVarsity, 2004.

Grudem, Wayne. *Evangelical Feminism and Biblical Truth: An Analysis of More Than 100 Disputed Questions.* Wheaton, IL: Crossway, 2004.

———. *Systematic Theology: An Introduction to Biblical Doctrine.* Grand Rapids, MI: Zondervan, 1994.

Gundry, Robert H. *Sōma in Biblical Theology with Emphasis on Pauline Anthropology.* Cambridge, UK: Cambridge University Press, 1976.

Haddad, Mimi, and Alvera Mickelsen. "Helping the Church Understand Biblical Equality." In *Discovering Biblical Equality: Complementarity without Hierarchy*, edited by Ronald W. Pierce, Rebecca Merrill Groothuis, and Gordon D. Fee 481–93. Downers Grove, IL: InterVarsity, 2004.

Haddorff, David W. "Can Character Ethics Have Moral Rules and Principles? Christian Doctrine and Comprehensive Moral Theory." *Horizons* 23, no. 1 (1996): 48–71.

Hafemann, Scott J. "Corinthians, Letters to The." In *Dictionary of Paul and His Letters*, edited by Gerald F. Hawthorne, Ralph P. Martin, and Daniel G. Reid, 164–79. Downers Grove, IL: InterVarsity, 1993.

Hamilton, James M., Jr.. *God's Glory in Salvation through Judgment: A Biblical Theology*. Wheaton, IL: Crossway, 2010.

Hamilton, Victor P. *The Book of Genesis, Chapters 1–17*. New International Commentary on the Old Testament. Grand Rapids, MI: Eerdmans, 1990.

Harper, Kyle. "Porneia: The Making of a Christian Sexual Norm." *Journal of Biblical Literature* 131, no. 2 (2012): 363–83.

Hauerwas, Stanley. *The Peaceable Kingdom: A Primer in Christian Ethics*. Notre Dame, IN: University of Notre Dame Press, 1983.

Hays, Richard B. *First Corinthians*. Interpretation. Louisville, KY: Westminster, 1997.

———. *The Moral Vision of the New Testament: Community, Cross, New Creation, A Contemporary Introduction to New Testament Ethics*. New York: HarperOne, 1996.

———. "Relations Natural and Unnatural: A Response to John Boswell's Exegesis of Romans 1." *Journal of Religious Ethics* 14 (1986): 184–215.

Heimbach, Daniel R. *True Sexual Morality: Recovering Biblical Standards for a Culture in Crisis*. Wheaton, IL: Crossway, 2004.

Herbenick, Debby, et al. "Sexual Behaviors, Relationships, and Perceived Health Status among Adult Women in the United States: Results from a National Probability Sample." *Journal of Sexual Medicine* 7, suppl 5 (2010): 277–90.

Hess, Richard S. "Equality with and without Innocence: Genesis 1–3." In *Discovering Biblical Equality: Complementarity without Hierarchy*, edited by Ronald W. Pierce, Rebecca Merrill Groothuis, and Gordon D. Fee, 79–95. Downers Grove, IL: InterVarsity, 2004.

Heth, William A. "Divorce, but No Remarriage." In *Divorce and Remarriage: Four Christian Views*, edited by H. Wayne House, 73–129. Downers Grove, IL: InterVarsity, 1990.

———. "Jesus on Divorce: How My Mind Has Changed." *Southern Baptist Journal of Theology* 6, no. 1 (2002): 4–29.

Hirsch, E. D., Jr. *Validity in Interpretation*. New Haven, CT: Yale University Press, 1967.

Hirshman, Linda. *Victory: The Triumphant Gay Revolution: How a Despised Minority Pushed Back, Beat Death, Found Love, and Changed America for Everyone*. New York: HarperCollins, 2012.

Hollinger, Dennis P. *The Meaning of Sex: Christian Ethics and the Moral Life*. Grand Rapids, MI: Baker, 2009.

Horton, Michael. *The Christian Faith: A Systematic Theology for Pilgrims on the Way*. Grand Rapids, MI: Zondervan, 2011.

Hugenberger, Gordon P. *Marriage as a Covenant: Biblical Law and Ethics as Developed from Malachi*. Grand Rapids, MI: Baker, 1994.

Instone-Brewer, David. *Divorce and Remarriage in the Bible: The Social and Literary Context*. Grand Rapids, MI: Eerdmans, 2002.

Jewett, Robert. *Romans*. Hermeneia. Minneapolis, MN: Fortress, 2007.

John Paul II. *Man and Woman He Created Them: A Theology of the Body*. Translated by Michael Waldstein. Boston: Pauline Books and Media, 2006.

Johnson, Luke Timothy, and Eve Tushnet. "Homosexuality and the Church: Two Views." *Commonweal* (June 15, 2007).

Johnston, J. William. *The Use of PAS in the New Testament*. Studies in Biblical Greek 11. New York: Peter Lang, 2004.

Jones, Tony. "How I Went from There to Here: Same Sex Marriage Blogalogue." *The New Christians*, November 2008. http://blog.beliefnet.com /tonyjones/2008/11/same-sex-marriage-blogalogue-h.html.

Kant, Immanuel. *The Fundamental Principles of the Metaphysics of Ethics*. Translated by Otto Manthey-Zorn. New York: Appleton-Century-Crofts, 1938.

Karkazis, Katrina. *Fixing Sex: Intersex, Medical Authority, and Lived Experience*. Durham, NC:: Duke University Press, 2008.

Kimball, Cynthia Neal. "Nature, Culture and Gender Complementarity." In *Discovering Biblical Equality: Complementarity Without Hierarchy*, edited by Ronald W. Pierce and Rebecca Merrill Groothuis, 464–80. Downers Grove, IL: InterVarsity, 2004.

Kiuci, Nobuyoshi. *Leviticus*. Apollos Old Testament Commentary 3. Downers Grove, IL: InterVarsity, 2007.

Klein, Rick. "Obama: 'I Think Same-Sex Couples Should Be Able to Get Married.'" *ABC News*, May 9, 2012. http://abcnews.go.com/blogs/politics/2012/05/obama-comes-out-i-think-same-sex-couples-should-be-able-to-get-married/.

Köstenberger, Andreas J., and David W. Jones. *God, Marriage, and Family: Rebuilding the Biblical Foundation*. 2nd ed. Wheaton, IL: Crossway, 2010.

Kreeft, Peter. *Everything You Ever Wanted To Know about Heaven—But Never Dreamed of Asking*. San Francisco: Ignatius, 1990.

Lambert, Heath. "The Problem of Pornography: Why It's Wrong and How to Help." *Journal for Biblical Manhood and Womanhood* 17, no. 2 (2012): 11–16.

Larimore, Walter L., and Joseph B. Stanford. "Postfertilization Effects of Oral Contraceptives and Their Relationship to Informed Consent." *Archives of Family Medicine* 9, no. 2 (2000): 126–33.

Lawton, Kim A. "'No Fault' Divorce Under Assault : Lawmakers Hope to Make the Road to Divorce Court More Difficult." *Christianity Today* 40, no. 4 (1996): 84–87.

Levey, Samson H. *The Text and I: Writings of Samson H. Levey*. Edited by Stanley F. Chyet. South Florida Studies in the History of Judaism 166. Atlanta, GA: Scholars Press, 1998.

Lewis, Jeffrey D., and Dennis M. Sullivan. "Abortifacient Potential of Emergency Contraceptives." *Ethics and Medicine* 28, no. 3 (2012): 113–20.

Loader, William. *Sexuality in the New Testament: Understanding the Key Texts*. Louisville, KY: Westminster, 2010.

Lull, David J. "Jesus, Paul, and Homosexuals." *Currents in Theology and Mission* 34, no. 3 (June 2007): 199–207.

Marchal, Joseph A. "Bodies Bound for Circumcision and Baptism: An Intersex Critique and the Interpretation of Galatians." *Theology and Sexuality* 16, no. 2 (2010): 163–82.

Martin, Dale B. "Arsenokoitês and Malakos: Meaning and Consequences." In *Biblical Ethics and Homosexuality: Listening to Scripture*, edited by Robert L. Brawley, 117–36. Louisville, KY: Westminster John Knox, 1996.

Mathews, Kenneth A. *Genesis 1–11:26*. Vol. 1a. New American Commentary. Nashville, TN: Broadman, 1996.

Mayo Clinic Staff. "Morning-after Pill: Why It's Done." *Mayo Clinic*, May 25, 2012. http://www.mayoclinic.com/health/morning-after-pill/MY01190/Dsection=why-its-done.

McArthur, Harvey. "Celibacy in Judaism at the Time of Christian Beginnings." *Andrews University Seminary Studies* 25, no. 2 (1987): 163–81.

McLaren, Brian. *A New Kind of Christianity: Ten Questions That Are Transforming the Faith*. New York: HarperOne, 2010.

———. "Brian McLaren on the Homosexual Question: Finding a Pastoral Response." *Out of Ur*, January 23, 2006. http://www.outofur.com/archives/2006/01/brian_mclaren_o.html.

Meilaender, Gilbert C., Jr. "Sexuality." In *New Dictionary of Christian Ethics and Pastoral Theology*, edited by David J. Atkinson, David F. Field, Arthur Holmes, and Oliver O'Donavan, 71–78. Downers Grove, IL: IVP Academic, 1995.

Milgrom, Jacob. *Leviticus 17–22: A New Translation with Introduction and Commentary*. Anchor Bible. New York: Doubleday, 2000.

Mohler, R. Albert, Jr. "Can Christians Use Birth Control?" *Journal for Biblical Manhood and Womanhood* 18.1 (2013): 7–9.

Moo, Douglas J. *The Epistle to the Romans*. New International Commentary on the New Testament. Grand Rapids, MI: Eerdmans, 1996.

———. "What Does It Mean Not to Teach or Have Authority over Men?" In *Recovering Biblical Manhood and Womanhood: A Response to Evangelical Feminism*, edited by John Piper and Wayne Grudem, 179–93. Wheaton, IL: Crossway, 1991.

Moore, Russell D. "Jesus and the Hooters Girl." *Moore to the Point*, May 10, 2005. http://www.russellmoore.com/2005/05/10/jesus-and-the-hooters-girl/.

———. "Sexual Iconoclasm." *Touchstone* 26, no. 1 (2013). http://www.touchstonemag.com/archives/article.php?id=26-01-020-v.

———. "Southern Baptist Sexual Revolutionaries: Cultural Accommodation, Spiritual Conflict and the Baptist Vision of the Family." *Southwestern Journal of Theology* 49, no. 1 (2006): 3–29.

Mounce, Robert H. *Romans*. New American Commentary. Nashville, TN: Broadman, 1995.

Murphy-O'Connor, Jerome. *1 Corinthians*. New Testament Message 10. Wilmington, DE: Michael Glazier, 1979.

———. "Corinthian Slogans in 1 Cor 6:12–20." *Catholic Biblical Quarterly* 40, no. 3 (1978): 391–96.

Murray, John. *Principles of Conduct: Aspects of Biblical Ethics*. Grand Rapids, MI: Eerdmans, 1957.

Nelson, M. T. "Deontology." In *New Dictionary of Christian Ethics and Pastoral Theology*, edited by David J. Atkinson, David F. Field, Arthur Holmes, and Oliver O'Donovan, 297. Downers Grove, IL: InterVarsity, 1995.

Nolland, John. *The Gospel of Matthew*. New International Greek Testament Commentary. Grand Rapids, MI: Eerdmans, 2005.

O'Brien, P. T. "Mystery." In *Dictionary of Paul and His Letters*, edited by Gerald F. Hawthorne, Ralph P. Martin, and Daniel G. Reid, 621–23. Downers Grove, IL: InterVarsity, 1993.

O'Donovan, Oliver. *Resurrection and Moral Order: An Outline for Evangelical Ethics*. 2nd ed. Grand Rapids, MI: Eerdmans, 1994.

Oremus, Will. "Wait, Was Jesus a Homophobe? What about All the Other People in Galilee?" *Slate* (April 9, 2012). http://www.slate.com/articles /news_and_politics/explainer/2012/04/was_jesus_a_homophobe _how_jews_and_early_christians_felt_about_homosexuality_.html.

Ortlund, Raymond C., Jr. "Male-Female Equality and Male Headship: Genesis 1–3." In *Recovering Biblical Manhood and Womanhood: A Response to Evangelical Feminism*, edited by John Piper and Wayne Grudem, 95–112. Wheaton, IL: Crossway, 1991.

Padgett, Alan G. *As Christ Submits to the Church: A Biblical Understanding of Leadership and Mutual Submission*. Grand Rapids, MI: Baker, 2011.

Paeth, Scott. "Teleological Theories of Ethics." In *Dictionary of Scripture and Ethics*, edited by Joel B. Green, 766–69. Grand Rapids, MI: Baker, 2011.

Paris, Jenell Williams. *The End of Sexual Identity: Why Sex Is Too Important to Define Who We Are*. Downers Grove, IL: InterVarsity, 2011.

Paul VI (pope). *Humanae Vitae: Encyclical Letter of His Holiness Pope Paul VI on the Regulation of Births*. Translated by Marc Calegari. San Francisco: Ignatius, 1998.

Payne, Philip B. *Man and Woman, One in Christ: An Exegetical and Theological Study of Paul's Letters*. Grand Rapids, MI: Zondervan, 2009.

Pierce, Ronald W, Rebecca Merrill Groothuis, and Gordon D. Fee, eds. *Discovering Biblical Equality: Complementarity without Hierarchy*. Downers Grove, IL: InterVarsity, 2004.

Piper, John. "Bethlehem's Position on Homosexuality." *Desiring God*, August 6, 2003. http://www.desiringgod.org/resource-library/taste-see -articles/bethlehems-position-on-homosexuality.

———. "Clarifying Words on Wife Abuse," December 19, 2012. http://www .desiringgod.org/blog/posts/clarifying-words-on-wife-abuse.

———. "For Single Men and Women (and the Rest of Us)." In *Recovering Biblical Manhood and Womanhood: A Response to Evangelical Feminism*, edited by John Piper and Wayne Grudem, xvii–xxviii. Wheaton, IL: Crossway, 1991.

———. *This Momentary Marriage: A Parable of Permanence*. Wheaton, IL: Crossway, 2009.

———. "A Vision of Biblical Complementarity." In *Recovering Biblical Manhood and Womanhood: A Response to Evangelical Feminism*, edited by John Piper and Wayne Grudem, 31–59. Wheaton, IL: Crossway, 1991.

———. *What Jesus Demands from the World*. Wheaton, IL: Crossway, 2006.

Porter, Stanley E. *Idioms of the Greek New Testament*. 2nd ed. Biblical Languages: Greek 2. Sheffield, UK: Sheffield Academic Press, 1994.

Quesnell, Quentin. "Made Themselves Eunuchs for the Kingdom of Heaven (Mt 19:12)." *Catholic Biblical Quarterly* 30, no. 3 (1968): 335–58.

Rattray, Susan. "Marriage Rules, Kinship Terms, and Family Structure in the Bible." In *Society of Biblical Literature 1987 Seminar Papers*, edited by Kent Harold Richards, 537–44. Atlanta: Scholars Press, 1987.

Reece, Michael et al. "Sexual Behaviors, Relationships, and Perceived Health among Adult Men in the United States: Results from a National Probability Sample." *Journal of Sexual Medicine* 7, suppl 5 (2010): 291–304.

Regnerus, Mark D. "The Case for Early Marriage." *Christianity Today* 53, no. 8 (2009): 22–28.

———. *Forbidden Fruit: Sex and Religion in the Lives of American Teenagers*. New York: Oxford University Press, 2007.

Regnerus, Mark, and Jeremy Uecker. *Premarital Sex in America: How Young Americans Meet, Mate, and Think about Marrying*. New York: Oxford University Press, 2011.

Rich, Frank. "The Bigots' Last Hurrah." *New York Times*, April 18, 2009. Accessed May 25, 2010. http://www.nytimes.com/2009/04/19/opinion/19Rich.html.

Rogers, Jack. *Jesus, the Bible, and Homosexuality: Explode the Myths, Heal the Church*. Louisville, KY: Westminster, 2006.

Ropelato, Jerry. "Internet Pornography Statistics." *TopTenREVIEWS*. Accessed January 10, 2013. http://internet-filter-review.toptenreviews.com/internet-pornography-statistics.html.

Saad, Lydia. "U.S. Acceptance of Gay/Lesbian Relations Is the New Normal." *Gallup*, May 14, 2012. http://www.gallup.com/poll/154634/Acceptance-Gay-Lesbian-Relations-New-Normal.aspx.

Sample, Tex. "Introduction: The Loyal Opposition." In *The Loyal Opposition: Struggling with the Church on Homosexuality*, edited by Tex Sample and Amy E. De Long, 15–23. Nashville, TN: Abingdon, 2000.

Schneider, Laurel C. "Homosexuality, Queer Theory, and Christian Theology." *Religious Studies Review* 26, no. 1 (2000): 3–12.

Schreiner, Thomas R. "An Interpretation of 1 Timothy 2:9–15: A Dialogue with Scholarship." In *Women in the Church: An Analysis and Application of 1 Timothy 2:9–15*, edited by Andreas J. Köstenberger and Thomas Schreiner, 85–120. 2nd ed. Grand Rapids, MI: Baker, 2005.

———. "A New Testament Perspective on Homosexuality." *Themelios* 31, no. 3 (2006): 62–75.

———. *Romans*. Baker Exegetical Commentary on the New Testament. Grand Rapids, MI: Baker, 1998.

———. "Women in Ministry: Another Complementarian Perspective." In *Two Views on Women in Ministry*, edited by James R. Beck, 263–322. Revised ed. Counterpoints. Grand Rapids, MI: Zondervan, 2005.

Scroggs, Robin. *The New Testament and Homosexuality: Contextual Background for Contemporary Debate*. Philadelphia: Fortress, 1983.

Shapley, Harlow. *Of Stars and Men: The Human Response to an Expanding Universe*. Boston: Beacon, 1958.

Sheppard, Gerald T. "The Use of Scripture with the Christian Ethical Debate concerning Same-Sex Oriented Persons." *Union Seminary Quarterly Review* 40 (1985): 13–35.

Sheriffs, R. J. A. "Eunuch." In *New Bible Dictionary*, edited by D. R. W. Wood, I. H. Marshall, A. R. Millard, J. I. Packer, and D. J. Wiseman, 347. 3rd ed. Downers Grove, IL: InterVarsity, 1996.

Smedes, Lewis B. *Sex for Christians: The Limits and Liberties of Sexual Living.* Revised ed. Grand Rapids, MI: Eerdmans, 1994.

Smith, Jay E. "The Roots of a 'Libertine' Slogan in 1 Corinthians 6:18." *Journal of Theological Studies* 59, no. 1 (2008): 63–95.

Stein, Robert H. "Is It Lawful for a Man to Divorce His Wife?" *Journal of the Evangelical Theological Society* 22, no. 2 (1979): 115–21.

Stolberg, Sheryl Gay. "Minister Pulls Out of Inauguration after Outcry." *New York Times*, January 10, 2013. http://www.nytimes.com/2013/0 1/11/us/politics/minister-withdraws-from-inaugural-program-after -controversy-over-comments-on-gay-rights.html.

Struthers, William M. *Wired for Intimacy: How Pornography Hijacks the Male Brain.* Downers Grove, IL: InterVarsity, 2009.

Sullivan, Dennis M. "The Oral Contraceptive as Abortifacient: An Analysis of the Evidence." *Perspectives on Science and Christian Faith* 58, no. 3 (2006): 189–95.

Thielman, Frank. *Ephesians.* Baker Exegetical Commentary on the New Testament. Grand Rapids, MI: Baker Academic, 2010.

Thiselton, Anthony C. *The First Epistle to the Corinthians.* New International Greek Testament Commentary. Grand Rapids, MI: Eerdmans, 2000.

Time. "The 25 Most Influential Evangelicals in America." February 7, 2005.

Trussell, James, and Beth Jordan. "Mechanism of Action of Emergency Contraceptive Pills." *Contraception* 74 (2006): 87–89.

Trussell, James, and Elizabeth G. Raymond. "Emergency Contraception: A Last Chance to Prevent Unintended Pregnancy." *Emergency Contraception Website*, September 2012. http://ec.princeton.edu/questions/ec -review.pdf.

Van der Horst, Pieter Willem. *The Sentences of Pseudo-Phocylides: With Introduction and Commentary.* Studia in Veteris Testamenti Pseudepigrapha 4. Leiden: Brill, 1978.

Vanhoozer, Kevin J. *Is There a Meaning in This Text?: The Bible, the Reader, and the Morality of Literary Knowledge.* Grand Rapids, MI: Zondervan, 1998.

The Vatican Today. "Pope: Address to the Roman Curia." December 21, 2012. http://www.news.va/en/news/pope-address-to-the-roman-curia.

Via, Dan O., and Robert A. J. Gagnon, eds. *Homosexuality and the Bible: Two Views.* Minneapolis, MN: Augsburg Fortress, 2003.

Wallace, Daniel B. *Greek Grammar Beyond the Basics: An Exegetical Syntax of the New Testament.* Grand Rapids, MI: Zondervan, 1996.

Walton, John H. *Genesis.* NIV Application Commentary. Grand Rapids, MI: Zondervan, 2001.

Ware, Bruce A. *Father, Son, and Holy Spirit: Relationships, Roles, and Relevance.* Wheaton, IL: Crossway, 2005.

Webb, William J. *Slaves, Women, and Homosexuals: Exploring the Hermeneutics of Cultural Analysis.* Downers Grove, IL: InterVarsity, 2001.

Weigel, David. "Covering Same-Sex Marriage." *The Washington Post,* May 1, 2010. http://voices.washingtonpost.com/right-now/2010/05/covering _gay_marriage.html.

Weiss, Jeffrey. "The Southern Baptist Convention Is Yesterday's News." *Politics Daily,* June 29, 2010. http://www.politicsdaily.com/2010/06/29 /the-southern-baptist-convention-is-yesterdays-news/.

Wenham, Gordon J. *The Book of Leviticus.* New International Commentary on the Old Testament. Grand Rapids, MI: Eerdmans, 1979.

———. *Genesis 1–15.* Word Biblical Commentary. Waco, TX: Word Books, 1987.

Wenham, Gordon J., and William A. Heth. *Jesus and Divorce.* London: Hodder and Stoughton, 1984.

White, John. *Eros Defiled: The Christian and Sexual Sin.* Downers Grove, IL: InterVarsity, 1977.

Wilcox, W. Bradford. "Conservative Protestants and the Family: Resisting, Engaging, or Accommodating Modernity?" In *A Public Faith: Evangelicals and Civic Engagement,* edited by Michael Cromartie, 51–67. Lanham, MD: Rowan and Littlefield, 2003.

———. *Soft Patriarchs, New Men: How Christianity Shapes Fathers and Husbands.* Chicago: University of Chicago Press, 2004.

Williamson, P. R. "Covenant." In *New Dictionary of Biblical Theology,* edited by T. Desmond Alexander and Brian S. Rosner, 419–29. Downers Grove, IL: InterVarsity, 2000.

Witherington, Ben, III. *Conflict and Community in Corinth: A Socio-Rhetorical Commentary on 1 and 2 Corinthians*. Grand Rapids, MI: Eerdmans, 1995.

———. *The Indelible Image: The Theological and Ethical Thought World of the New Testament, Vol. 1: The Individual Witnesses*. Downers Grove, IL: IVP Academic, 2009.

———. *The Indelible Image: The Theological and Ethical Thought World of the New Testament, Volume 2: The Collective Witness*. Downers Grove, IL: IVP Academic, 2010.

Witherington, Ben, III, and Darlene Hyatt. *Paul's Letter to the Romans: A Socio-Rhetorical Commentary*. Grand Rapids, MI: Eerdmans, 2004.

Wrede, William. *Paul*. Translated by Edward Lummis. London: Philip Green, 1907.

Wright, Bradley R. E. *Christians Are Hate-Filled Hypocrites . . . and Other Lies You've Been Told: A Sociologist Shatters Myths from the Secular and Christian Media*. Bloomington, MN: Bethany House, 2010.

Wright, N. T. "The Letter to the Romans." In *New Interpreter's Bible*, 10:393–770. Nashville, TN: Abingdon, 2002.

———. *What Saint Paul Really Said: Was Paul of Tarsus the Real Founder of Christianity?* Grand Rapids, MI: Eerdmans, 1997.

Yep, Gust A., Karen E. Lovaas, and John P. Elia. "Introduction: Queering Communication: Starting the Conversation." In *Queer Theory and Communication: From Disciplining Queers to Queering the Discipline(s)*, edited by Gust A. Yep, Karen E. Lovaas, and John P. Elia, 1–10. Binghamton, NY: Harrington Park, 2003.

General Index

Scripture Index

CPSIA information can be obtained
at www.ICGtesting.com
Printed in the USA
BVHW032005050822
643800BV00004B/9